Edited by Marlene Brant Castellano,
Lynne Davis, and Louise Lahache

Aboriginal Education:
Fulfilling the Promise

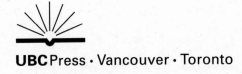

UBC Press · Vancouver · Toronto

Printed in Canada on acid-free paper ∞

"Aboriginal Education: Fulfilling the Promise" includes revised and adapted
versions of selected research papers and recommendations of the Royal
Commission on Aboriginal Peoples.

Reproduced and adapted with the permission of the Minister of Public Works and
Government Services, 2000.

Canadian Cataloguing in Publication Data

Main entry under title:
Aboriginal education

Includes bibliographical references and index.
ISBN 0-7748-0782-2 (bound); ISBN 0-7748-0783-0 (pbk.)

1. Native peoples – Education – Canada. 2. Canada. Royal Commission on
Aboriginal Peoples. I. Castellano, Marlene Brant, 1935- II. Davis, Lynne. III.
Lahache, Louise, 1953-

E96.2.A25 2000	371.829'97071	C00-910441-0

UBC Press acknowledges the financial support of the Government of Canada
through the Book Publishing Industry Development Program (BPIDP) for our
publishing activities.

Canada

We also gratefully acknowledge the support of the Canada Council for the Arts for
our publishing program, as well as the support of the British Columbia Arts Council.

All royalties from this volume will be contributed to the Aboriginal Peoples'
Television Network to support educational programming.

Set in Stone by Brenda and Neil West, BN Typographics West
Printed and bound in Canada by Friesens
Copy-editor: Joanne Richardson Proofreader: Deborah Kerr

UBC Press
University of British Columbia
2029 West Mall
Vancouver, BC V6T 1Z2
(604) 822-5959
www.ubcpress.ubc.ca

Contents

Foreword

Marie Battiste

The summer of 1990 – where were you? Think Oka and it may jog your memory.

That summer I was painting and wallpapering my daughter's bedroom with a friend, listening to the radio, and intermittently running downstairs to watch television as the confrontation between the Mohawk community at Kanesatake and the Canadian government unfolded. The events shocked my complacent senses, awakened my inner civil rights fires, and recalled for me the years of Martin Luther King, the American Indian Movement, and Wounded Knee. At the time, they gave new meaning to my awareness of being an Indian and part of a marginalized minority, clearly delineating my loyalties. And in 1990, the events at Oka once again put me on full alert for what might happen next.

For the Canadian people, Oka had a dramatic and chilling effect. The barricades and staring confrontations captured by the media portrayed the problem in visual form, but not the complexity and history behind them. Some months later Prime Minister Brian Mulroney established the Royal Commission on Aboriginal Peoples (RCAP) to unravel those complexities. Its task – which took five years to complete – was to review everything from the origins and structures of Aboriginal governments and the nature of claims settlements to the social, economic, educational, and cultural concerns of Aboriginal peoples. The commissioners crossed the country, visiting hundreds of Aboriginal communities, gathering the stories, testimonies, and documents from Aboriginal people, and then called on researchers to address those issues and concerns from their experience and perspectives.

The RCAP report, which spans five volumes, 3,500 pages, and makes 440 recommendations, described how every aspect of Aboriginal life had been trampled on. The challenge for the commissioners was to take the stories and histories, consider the impact of abusive policies and practices, and then translate them into coherent and comprehensible prose that would capture the essence of Aboriginal peoples' experiences, their anguish and pain, and their dreams and expectations. As well, they would need to offer some hope in their analyses and recommendations for future government action.

The education section had to explain how education had been implicated in this pain and anguish, how Aboriginal languages had been eroded by the government's assimilationist policies, what factors contributed to the diminished effect of the current policy on First Nations control of education, and what successes have nevertheless flowed from policy reform.

The magnitude of the problems experienced by Aboriginal peoples cannot be encompassed by a policy document, even one as wide-ranging as the RCAP report. The big questions confronting Aboriginal peoples themselves still have to be addressed. As Thomas Berry observed in David Suzuki's *The Sacred Balance*, "It's all a question of story. We are in trouble just now because we do not have a good story. We are in between stories. The old story, the account of how we fit into it, is no longer effective. Yet we have not learned the new story."

Aboriginal people need a new story. The old story – of how our lives have been – is now known, and Canadians can now perceive its demoralizing effects on Aboriginal people. But Aboriginal people recognize that we are in between stories. We do not trust the old story of government paternalism, and we are trying to get a clearer picture of our new story. Ultimately, this new story is about empowering Aboriginal worldviews, languages, knowledge, cultures, and most important, Aboriginal peoples and communities.

In this book, Professor Emerita Marlene Brant Castellano (former Research Director for the Royal Commission on Aboriginal Peoples), Lynne Davis, and Louise Lahache offer their selection of the research papers that helped inspire the accounts and analysis underpinning the education recommendations in the RCAP report. Anyone who has read the chapter on education in Volume 3 of the report (*Gathering Strength*) will recognize the stories of how Aboriginal peoples are using education to make concrete changes in their lives. In particular, there are examples of Aboriginal practices, systems, designs, and strategies, together with the obstacles and challenges brought about by a lack of financial and institutional resources. There is also evidence of the pervasive Eurocentric ideology that continues to obstruct the efforts being made in Aboriginal curriculum development, language maintenance and restoration, and infrastructure development.

Aboriginal Education: Fulfilling the Promise presents the findings of both Aboriginal and non-Aboriginal researchers in case studies, literature reviews, interpretations, and analyses. The collection focuses particularly on empowering models of education that seek to address the needs and dreams of Aboriginal peoples. It also offers analyses of remaining obstacles.

This book makes a valuable contribution to Aboriginal education by offering fresh insights and examples of projects that stretch our imagination as well as celebrate some milestones reached in three decades of striving for First Nations control of First Nations education. The collection offers models and educational options that place Aboriginal culture, knowledge, and values at the core of learning systems and designs that are based on the experience of practitioners and researchers working in Aboriginal communities, provincial school systems, and post-secondary institutions. Educators are challenged to unravel stereotypical assumptions and theories entangled in cognitive imperialism – the persisting ideologies from our colonial past that remain part of our educational systems.

The old story is one of destruction and pain, while the emerging one is that of the ongoing vitality of Aboriginal people, from whose experience we can learn. Aboriginal people believe that education is an integral means of helping the new story unfold, and it can happen only when their fully actualized selves are accepted and recognized as the foundation for their future. But we are not whole yet, having been diminished by our past, and we do not know who will articulate that future, that new story. Aboriginal government? Aboriginal politicians? Elders? Educators? The responsibility ultimately rests with Aboriginal people themselves in a continuing journey of collaboration and negotiation, healing and rebuilding, creating and experimenting, and visioning and celebrating.

Marie Battiste
University of Saskatchewan
Saskatoon

Acknowledgments

As editors, we are indebted to many people whose generosity of spirit helped to make this volume possible.

We express gratitude to the authors who accommodated our revision requests with great patience and careful consideration. We received moral and material support from a number of individuals and organizations: the National Association of Indian Friendship Centres, the Odawa Friendship Centre, Mary Brodhead, Andy Siggner, Emily Faries, Georges Erasmus, and René Dussault all contributed to our efforts. Frank Polson graciously allowed us to reproduce his painting, *Family Spirituality*, on the cover. A grant from Heritage Canada provided much needed financial support that allowed us to meet the practical expenses of communicating, meeting, and developing the manuscript over geographical distances.

We are grateful to Marie Battiste for agreeing to write the foreword to this volume, linking it to the legacy of her own work and that of her colleagues who share the vision of education rooted in Aboriginal wisdom. Our work with the Royal Commission on Aboriginal Peoples made an enormous contribution to our learning. We thank the commissioners for the opportunity to share in that historic process.

UBC Press editor Jean Wilson was supportive from the outset and showed great determination in bringing this volume to press. We thank her and former editor Laura Macleod for their valued advice.

We express our deep appreciation to Vincent Castellano, Cameron Brown, and Gordon Polson, who have offered unfailing personal support during the long journey bringing the volume together. The younger members of our families have been a special inspiration. Their voices remind us that the experiences contained in these pages offer urgent lessons from which all must learn if we are to create education systems that promote growth, learning, and a more hopeful future for Aboriginal peoples. This is, after all, the reason that we began our work on *Aboriginal Education: Fulfilling the Promise*.

Introduction

Marlene Brant Castellano, Lynne Davis, and
Louise Lahache

> Despite the painful experiences Aboriginal people carry with
> them from formal education systems, they still see education as
> the hope for the future and they are determined to see education
> fulfill its promise.
>
> – Royal Commission on Aboriginal Peoples (1996, 3:434)

Aboriginal peoples[1] have an unquenchable hope in the promise of education: they believe that it will instruct them in ways to live long and well on Mother Earth and that it will instill in them the wisdom and the capacity to carry their responsibilities in the circle of all life. This hope is rooted in a fundamentally spiritual understanding of the universe and has been repeatedly frustrated in encounters with colonial society. As we begin a new century and a new millennium, as the discourse between Aboriginal and non-Aboriginal leaders and governments turns to treaty making as a way of resolving centuries-old disputes about land, as the relationship between Aboriginal and non-Aboriginal peoples is undergoing renewal in negotiations concerning self-government, the hope of devising strategies and systems to fulfill the promise of education takes on new vitality.

Education is at the heart of the struggle of Aboriginal peoples to regain control over their lives as communities and nations.[2] This collection of articles, based on research and dialogue generated by the Royal Commission on Aboriginal Peoples (RCAP), documents the uneven progress towards transforming the contemporary experience of education from one of assimilation to one of self-expression and self-determination.

Until very recently, the concepts of education embedded in the languages and cultures of Aboriginal peoples of Canada have been little known or appreciated by professional educators. Oral cultures, perceived through the lens of social Darwinism, were considered to be "pre-literate," not yet having reached the level of development that gives rise to writing. Languages rich in metaphor were considered to be "concrete" and not suited to the expression of complex or abstract ideas. Education extended by colonial society was designed to lift Aboriginal peoples from their savage state and introduce them to the benefits of civilization. The error of these ethnocentric views and the invasions of Aboriginal societies that they supported have been successfully challenged only in the present generation.

In the political arena and in Canadian courts of law Aboriginal peoples and organizations have asserted that they were nations when Europeans first arrived on this continent; they were nations and recognized as such when they made treaties with the newcomers; and they continue to be nations, despite the assumptions implicit in laws imposed on them without their consent. A fundamental responsibility of nations is the education of their citizens, preparing them to take their place as members of the community and the world at large. Therefore, Aboriginal nations place control of education at the core of their agenda, which is to restore their authority to govern themselves and their capacity for self-reliance.

While Aboriginal leaders struggled to define a legitimate place for their nations in the Canadian federation, Aboriginal educators were searching for answers to the question: "What is Aboriginal about Aboriginal education?" In their communities and classrooms, in emerging Aboriginal institutions, in conferences, and in journals and books, they carried on a dialogue with Elders, parents, and colleagues, seeking to articulate the ideals, the content, and the process of Aboriginal education.

Aboriginal peoples have long known that their philosophies and approaches to education are distinct. In attempts at intercultural dialogue they have affirmed their intention to retain that distinctiveness. For example, following the signing of a treaty in 1744 the Iroquoian chief and orator Red Jacket is recorded as saying:

> We are convinced that you mean to do us Good by your Proposal [to educate our young men]; and we thank you heartily. But you, who are wise, must know that different Nations have different Conceptions of things and you will therefore not take it amiss if our ideas of this kind of Education happen not to be the same as yours ... We are ... not the less oblig'd by your kind Offer, tho' we decline accepting it; and to show our grateful Sense of it, if the Gentlemen of Virginia will send us a Dozen of their Sons, we will take Care of their Education, instruct them in all we know, and make Men of them. (Drake 1834, 27)

In the 1980s, the new feature of intercultural dialogue was the readiness on the part of mainstream policy makers and institutions to acknowledge that Aboriginal concepts of education were valid for Aboriginal peoples. And a few isolated voices were beginning to articulate an awareness that Aboriginal approaches might have value for a broader constituency. To a limited extent, the climate of negotiation that was taking hold in the political sphere was also taking hold in the educational sphere. Adding impetus to the demand for change was the continuing failure of provincial and federal schooling to alter the social and economic disadvantages suffered by the majority of Aboriginal people in Canada – disadvantages not suffered by non-Aboriginal people.

Aboriginal educators have assumed a leading role in interpreting Aboriginal philosophies of education. Their formulations are featured in *Aboriginal Education in Canada: The Circle Unfolds* (Battiste and Barman 1995), which brings together in one volume statements of philosophy and reports of experience by Aboriginal and non-Aboriginal educators from diverse nations and different regions across Canada. Prominent in these articles is the conception of education as a lifelong holistic experience rooted in particular cultures and geographies.

The Medicine Wheel, a teaching device that originated among the First Nations of the Plains, has gained broad acceptance as a means of maintaining awareness of the interrelatedness of all life while we deepen our understanding by focusing on segments of the whole. The vertical and horizontal axes of the Medicine Wheel reach out in the four directions to include all peoples and cultures and draw attention to the harmony that can be achieved when divergent elements are brought into balance within the circle of life. Applied to education, the Medicine Wheel illustrates the necessity of attending to the physical, emotional, intellectual, and spiritual dimensions of learning and personal development (Figure 1).

Efforts to incorporate Aboriginal approaches to education into formal schooling began to gain acceptance in the 1970s. A number of these approaches were documented in *Indian Education in Canada,* Volume 2, *The Challenge* (Barman, Hébert, and McCaskill 1987). A decade later innovations had matured to the point where they provided persuasive evidence of the effectiveness of Aboriginal leadership and control. The *Report of the Royal Commission on Aboriginal Peoples* (RCAP 1996, 3:433-584) is rich with case examples and statistics that point to recent achievements. Two important publications in this period set out the goals and direction of change: the position paper *Indian Control of Indian Education* (National Indian Brotherhood 1972) and the subsequent comprehensive survey and analysis *Tradition and Education: Towards a Vision of Our Future* (Assembly of First Nations 1988).

Over the past twenty-five years there have been many positive developments in the administration, content, and methods of Aboriginal education. It is now common for First Nations and Inuit communities to manage their local schools. Aboriginal school boards have been established under land claims settlements and/or self-government agreements. Specially designed teacher education programs have increased the numbers of Aboriginal teachers in schools. Métis and Aboriginal people living off reserve, who constitute a major portion of the population in some northern regions, have assumed an influential place in regional school boards. Curriculum

Figure 1

Dimensions of Aboriginal education

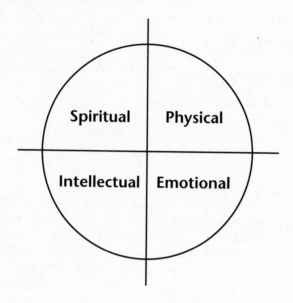

in Aboriginal schools and some provincial districts has been revised to reflect Aboriginal cultures more accurately.

Nevertheless, the promise of an education that delivers the skills to survive in a post-industrial global economy while affirming the ethical and spiritual foundations of Aboriginal cultures is far from being fulfilled. An analysis of census data from 1981 and 1996 shows that, while the proportion of Aboriginal people who have left school without high school graduation has declined, the proportion who go on to complete a college diploma or university degree has increased only marginally. In the same period educational levels in the general population have been rising, responding to the demands of a technology-based economy and widening the gap between Aboriginal and non-Aboriginal college and/or university graduates. It is clear that, without a major improvement in the effectiveness of education, the relative disadvantage of Aboriginal people could worsen.

RCAP notes that, where Aboriginal people have assumed control of the education of their children, youth, and adults, the results with regard to program completion, personal satisfaction, and successful preparation for employment or continuing education are much improved. Still, these initiatives struggle at the margins of education systems that operate under provincial and territorial jurisdiction and that continue to deliver curriculum that has a strong assimilationist bent.

In its recommendations on education, RCAP endorses Aboriginal control of Aboriginal education in the form of institutions mandated by Aboriginal governments, designated schools managed by Aboriginal authorities within provincial and territorial jurisdictions, and greater accountability on the part of integrated institutions serving Aboriginal students. Some RCAP recommendations are directed towards adapting mainstream educational institutions so that they give appropriate recognition to the Aboriginal presence in Canadian life and foster a respectful, reciprocal relationship between Aboriginal and non-Aboriginal peoples.

The chapters in this volume present the core content of selected research reports and round table papers on education commissioned by RCAP and revised and updated by the original authors.[3] Two new articles set out the rationale for an Aboriginal university and describe RCAP's electronic information legacy. The chapters are complemented by brief commentaries, which introduce each thematic section, and a concluding essay by the editors of the volume. Together, the articles provide context and in-depth analyses for those considering successes to this date and significant challenges that still confront practitioners and policy makers in Aboriginal education.

Introducing the collection is a chapter on the evolution of policy in Aboriginal education. Frances Abele, Carolyn Dittburner, and Katherine Graham draw on their major historical study, *Public Policy and Aboriginal Peoples, 1965-1992*, to demonstrate how changes in the discourse on education have reflected the halting progress towards effective communication, and the establishment of a relationship of mutuality, between Aboriginal peoples and Canadian governments in the larger sphere of Aboriginal affairs. They conclude that participants in the dialogue on Aboriginal policy have interpreted key words such as "control" and "consultation" in different ways, breeding frustration among participants and resulting in the failure to achieve meaningful dialogue (the prerequisite for achieving consensus). The absence of a process to sustain discussion on complex and controversial issues and the power differential between Aboriginal and government actors have resulted in further impediments to achieving a common vision on education policy.

Three chapters in Part 2 focus on efforts to conserve Aboriginal languages and bring Aboriginal voices into communications media. Generations of assimilative schooling have systematically undermined the vitality of Aboriginal languages; the images of Aboriginal people conveyed in school texts and popular media have distorted the self-concept of Aboriginal people themselves and contributed to negative stereotypes in the general population. Two chapters on language emphasize respectively the necessity of public policy to support community efforts at language renewal and the need to devise appropriate pedagogies for language transmission.

The chapter on communications details strategies to make a place for authentic Aboriginal expression in public communications media.

Five chapters in Part 3 discuss approaches and innovations in pedagogy. Case studies of educational reform focus on the Mohawk community of Akwesasne, the Kativik School Board in northern Quebec, and the Vancouver School District. The conclusion drawn from each of the community case studies is that Aboriginal initiatives are creative and productive but that they struggle for resources in a competitive environment and remain fragile and localized. A chapter newly written for this volume describes the educational applications of the CD-ROM *For Seven Generations: An Information Legacy of the Royal Commission on Aboriginal Peoples*. It illustrates the potential of new technologies to give a voice to Aboriginal people in educational activities. The section concludes with a review of research on Aboriginal learning styles and a call to refocus research on understanding the dynamic practices of learning and teaching to be found in Aboriginal communities.

Four chapters in Part 4 turn their attention to post-secondary education, the area in which gains in establishing Aboriginal control and introducing Aboriginal knowledge have been slowest. Institutional developments are examined in case studies of Gabriel Dumont Institute in Saskatchewan and the First Nations House of Learning at the University of British Columbia. The challenge of creating space for Aboriginal knowledge in higher education is taken up in the argument for establishing an Aboriginal Peoples' International University, building on institutional strengths that already exist in such places as the Saskatchewan Indian Federated College. A report on extensive experimentation with distance education returns to the theme of technology and education, underlining the necessity of supporting innovation with affirmative policy and strategic planning.

The collection's conclusion situates efforts to transform Aboriginal education within the context of ongoing negotiations between peoples with widely disparate power bases. The challenges are great but no greater than the responsibilities articulated by an Iroquois Elder speaking to the members of RCAP:

In our language we call ourselves Ongwehonwe. Some people say it means real people ... It says that we are the ones that are living on the earth today, right at this time. We are the ones that are carrying the responsibility of our nations, of our spirituality, of our relationship to the Creator, on our shoulders. We have the mandate to carry that today, at this moment in time.

Our languages, our spirituality and everything that we are was given to us and was carried before us by our ancestors, our grandparents who have passed on. When they couldn't carry it any longer and they went to join the spirit world, they handed it to us and they said: "Now you are the real ones. You have to carry it." Now they are in the spirit world. They are our past.

Now we have a responsibility to carry that because we hear seven generations in the future. They are our future. They are the ones that are not yet born. (Charlie Patton in RCAP 1997)

Aboriginal wisdom places the present generation at the fulcrum of history, looking back seven generations to where we have come from, looking forward seven generations to the children not yet born.

The promise of education will be fulfilled. Aboriginal people know that the will to learn is inseparable from the will to live. The hope that Aboriginal ways of knowing and learning will be restored to dignity has stayed alive, sometimes like a dampened fire, through difficult years. Aboriginal people are working to renew the vitality of their cultures, putting their minds together to discern the lessons to be learned from Elders' teachings and the world around them, from the insights of other cultures and their own spiritual resources. This book is offered as the authors' contribution to the work of "the real people" – those who carry the responsibility of seeing that the continuing promise of education is fulfilled in this generation.

Notes

1 In this collection the term "Aboriginal" refers to First Nations, Inuit, and Métis persons and collectivities. Authors in various sections may use any of the foregoing terms as well as "Indian" or Native," depending on the context and the usage current in their regions or work environments. Where experience in a particular territory is under discussion, the nation name (e.g., Sto:lo or Mohawk) is usually preferred.

2 For a review of historical developments since 1969, see Dianne Longboat, "First Nations Control of Education: The Path to Our Survival as Nations," in *Indian Education in Canada*, vol. 2, *The Challenge*, ed. Jean Barman, Yvonne Hébert, and Don McCaskill (Vancouver: UBC Press, 1987).

3 Original research reports on which a number of the chapters in this volume are based appear in *For Seven Generations: An Information Legacy of the Royal Commission on Aboriginal Peoples*, CD-ROM (Ottawa: Libraxus, 1997). RCAP commissioned three major studies of residential schools, which are not represented in this collection. See Roland Chrisjohn and Sherri L. Young, *The Circle Game: Shadows and Substance in the Indian Residential School Experience in Canada* (Penticton, BC: Theytus, 1997); John S. Milloy, *A National Crime: The Canadian Government and the Residential School System 1879 to 1986* (Winnipeg: University of Manitoba Press, 1999); and Denise G. Réaume and Patrick Macklem, "Education for Subordination: Redressing the Adverse Effects of Residential Schooling," in *For Seven Generations: An Information Legacy of the Royal Commission on Aboriginal Peoples*, CD-ROM (Ottawa: Libraxus, 1997). The full text of the original research reports by Chrisjohn and Young, and Milloy also appear on the CD-ROM.

References

Assembly of First Nations. 1988. *Tradition and Education: Towards a Vision of Our Future*. Ottawa: Assembly of First Nations/National Indian Brotherhood.

Barman Jean, Yvonne Hébert, and Don McCaskill, eds. 1987. *Indian Education in Canada*. Vol. 2: *The Challenge*. Vancouver: UBC Press.

Battiste, Marie, and Jean Barman, eds. 1995. *First Nations Education in Canada: The Circle Unfolds*. Vancouver: UBC Press.

Chrisjohn, Roland, and Sherri L. Young. 1997. *The Circle Game: Shadows and Substance in the Residential School Experience in Canada*. Penticton, BC: Theytus. The original research report on which the book is based is available on the CD-ROM *For Seven Generations: An Information Legacy of the Royal Commission on Aboriginal Peoples*. 1997. Ottawa: Libraxus.

Drake, Samuel G. 1834. *Biography and History of the Indians of North America*, Third Edition, Book 1. Boston: O.L. Perkins and Hillard, Gray and Company.

Graham, Katherine, Carolyn Dittburner, and Frances Abele. 1996. *Public Policy and Aboriginal Peoples, 1965-1992*. Vols. 1-4. Ottawa: Canada Communications Group.

Milloy, John S. 1999. *A National Crime: The Canadian Government and the Residential School System 1879 to 1986*. Winnipeg: University of Manitoba Press. The original research report on which the book is based is available under the title "Suffer the Little Children" on the CD-ROM *For Seven Generations: An Information Legacy of the Royal Commission on Aboriginal Peoples*. 1997. Ottawa: Libraxus.

National Indian Brotherhood. 1972. *Indian Control of Indian Education*. Ottawa: National Indian Brotherhood.

Réaume, Denise G., and Patrick Macklem. 1997. *Education for Subordination: Redressing the Adverse Effects of Residential Schooling*. In *For Seven Generations: An Information Legacy of the Royal Commission on Aboriginal Peoples* (CD-ROM). Ottawa: Libraxus.

Royal Commission on Aboriginal Peoples (RCAP). 1996. *Report of the Royal Commission on Aboriginal Peoples*. Vol. 3: *Gathering Strength*. Ottawa: Canada Communication Group.

–. 1997. Testimony at RCAP public hearings: Charlie Patton, Mohawk Trail Longhouse. Akwesasne, 6 May 1993. In *For Seven Generations: An Information Legacy of the Royal Commission on Aboriginal Peoples* (CD-ROM). Ottawa: Libraxus.

Part 1
A Journey through History:
Pursuing the Promise

1
Towards a Shared Understanding in the Policy Discussion about Aboriginal Education

Frances Abele, Carolyn Dittburner, Katherine A. Graham

> To deny the past and to refuse to recognize its implications is to
> distort the present; to distort the present is to take risks with the
> future that are blatantly irresponsible.
>
> – Indian Tribes of Manitoba (1971, ii)

Schools and schooling have been at the heart of the relations between the Indigenous nations of Canada and settlers for centuries. Public policy in the field of education expresses, usually quite directly, the changes in the relationship between Aboriginal and non-Aboriginal peoples. This chapter examines the course of public discussion concerning education policy, as it relates to Aboriginal peoples, from 1965 to 1992. It focuses on the extent to which the documentary policy record reveals progress towards mutual understanding between Aboriginal and non-Aboriginal perspectives concerning the context of education in Aboriginal life and the role of education policy in supporting constructive relations between Aboriginal peoples and Canadian society. In short, we are interested in the extent to which there has been effective public policy dialogue.

This chapter is based on *Soliloquy and Dialogue: Overview of Major Trends in Public Policy relating to Aboriginal Peoples* (Graham, Dittburner, and Abele 1996), which was conducted for the Royal Commission on Aboriginal Peoples (RCAP). This review examines official public policy discourse in a range of policy fields (including education), beginning with the release of H.B. Hawthorn's influential research and policy study, *Survey of the Contemporary Indians of Canada* (Canada 1966, 1967) and ending in 1992, with the launch of RCAP's work.

Soliloquy and Dialogue contains a number of definitions and methodological features that should be noted before we look at the specific case of education. In it we use an inclusive and behavioural definition of "policy": policy is what any government decides to do or not to do. Based on this definition, a policy is not necessarily formally articulated as "policy" (although often it is). For the purposes of our research, "discourse" refers to the published texts of key documents on Aboriginal education, which we consider very simply in terms of *who* was involved in policy discussions, *how* policy discussions occurred, and *what* was said about key issues in the domain of Aboriginal affairs.

Reliance upon the documentary record has clear limitations. Frequently policy documents embody compromises that may conceal quite diverse perspectives: the route travelled in the production of a document can be as informative about social realities as its final form. We have not studied the process through which documents were produced and, for practical purposes, have taken each as a finished artefact. From this position, we can comment upon what was said but not upon what happened or upon whether what was said was true. On the other hand, paying attention to what was being said and how it "officially" changed over time reveals a good deal about the ways in which problems were identified and how this could change. We can see, above all, whether the discussion has potential to move from a *dialogue de sourds* to one in which there is growing mutual understanding.

The discussion that follows identifies three distinct phases in the policy discourse related to education: (1) the period from the release of the Hawthorn Report until 1982, the year of constitutional patriation; (2) the period from 1982 until 1988, the year the Assembly of First Nations blueprint for education, *Tradition and Education: Towards a Vision of Our Future* (Assembly of First Nations 1988), was released; and (3) 1988 until 1992, just after the establishment of RCAP. As we treat each period, it should become evident that prevailing paradigms concerning, for example, the construction of society and/or individual versus collective action influenced the discourse concerning Aboriginal education. We will also see, from both Aboriginal and broader Canadian perspectives, the importance of specific events in shaping education policy.

1967 to 1982: After Hawthorn
The 1960s and early 1970s were marked by a number of seminal Canadian events. The country celebrated its centennial, which was accompanied by a sense of maturity and vitality. Canada now had a distinctive flag, and the centennial year coincided with the twentieth anniversary of a fundamental change in Canada's citizenship regime: Canadians were no longer British subjects; they were Canadians. In 1971, fuelled largely by the negative reaction of ethnic groups to the work of the Royal Commission on Bilingualism and Biculturalism, the Government of Canada formally adopted a policy of multiculturalism within a bilingual framework. This move was an important precursor to other important developments, such as the establishment of human rights commissions at the provincial and federal levels and the creation of the Canadian Charter of Rights and Freedoms.

Since 1971, the Canadian political framework has been characterized by a notion of equality, which insists that "all individuals receive equal treatment and equal protection under the law, while respecting and valuing ... diversity" (Canada, House of Commons, 1988). The impact of multiculturalism on the development of the discourse on Aboriginal education is rarely explicitly recognized in the public record. Nonetheless, one should bear in mind that there are important parallels between ideas and events that occurred in the respective spheres of multiculturalism and Aboriginal education.

This period was also characterized by political activism and change, both internationally and domestically. Aboriginal issues gained prominence internationally with the rise of Aboriginal political organizations in many parts of the world, including Canada. This was the time when we saw the formation of major Indian, Inuit, and Métis political organizations. As we shall demonstrate, the intellectual leadership of Aboriginal organizations in the field of education policy is particularly striking, given that in some other policy areas, such as justice, non-Aboriginal participants have frequently set the terms of debate.[1]

While the Hawthorn Report began to raise public awareness of the situation of Aboriginal peoples in Canada, the 1969 *Statement of the Government of Canada on Indian Policy*, known as the White Paper (Canada 1969), initiated a controversy concerning the relationship between the federal government and Indian peoples. The federal government's White Paper proposed, among other things, to have the provinces assume responsibility for Indians as for any other citizens. Prior to the release of the White Paper, the federal government had been promoting a policy of integration in the field of Indian education. It had initiated comprehensive capital and tuition agreements with provincial governments without the involvement of Indian First Nations or Indian parents. Therefore, Indian First Nations saw the White Paper as the final step in the federal government's desire to transfer jurisdiction over Indian education (among other things) to provincial governments.

In the aftermath of the release of the White Paper, the Indian Association of Alberta's *Red Paper* (Indian Chiefs of Alberta, *Citizens Plus*, 1970) dealt extensively with the issue of Indian education. Following the *Red Paper*'s publication, the Indian Association of Alberta, in conjunction with the National Indian Brotherhood, entered into a series of discussions with the federal Cabinet, pressing for an extensive review of federal approaches to Indian education. While this process was under way, the Department of Indian Affairs continued to reject Indian requests for improvements to on-reserve schools, in part because of its financial commitments to provincially operated schools located in towns near the reserves.

Symbolic of the temper of the times, in September 1970, Blue Quills School in St. Paul, Alberta, became the first school in Canada to be completely administered by Indian people. The Department of Indian Affairs had decided to close Blue Quills without consulting the affected communities. These communities responded by conducting a long and bitter school strike and by occupying Blue Quills School until their concerns were addressed. The debate and political struggles that attended these events are but one sign that Aboriginal peoples were now explicitly questioning the existing educational system. Around the same time, two Indian political organizations, the Manitoba Indian Brotherhood and the National Indian Brotherhood, issued seminal reports that emphasized the importance of education and redefined such concepts as "control" and "integration" (Indian Tribes of Manitoba, *Wahbung Our Tomorrows* 1971; National Indian Brotherhood, *Indian Control of Indian Education* 1972).

During this period of time, the documents of the Aboriginal organizations saw the issue of education primarily as one involving the federal government and Indian governments. Responsibility for education was seen as being under local Aboriginal control and as being funded by the federal government. Preference for this bilateral approach to education is seen, for example, in the recommendations made in *Indian Control of Indian Education*. These call for the establishment of a task force made up solely of Indian and federal government representatives, with no role for the provinces.

This is not, however, to suggest that provincial governments were absent from the policy discourse during this period. An important provincial preoccupation concerned the challenge of dealing with issues related to the heterogeneity of Aboriginal peoples. The provincial documents are the only ones to deal with "Native" education and to show some signs of struggling with the question of commonality versus diversity. The *Summary Report of the Task Force on the Educational Needs of the Native Peoples of Ontario* grouped the concerns of all Native peoples together. It found that "certain concerns are common to all Native peoples of Ontario, regardless of their status as Treaty, Métis or Non-Status Indians, or their location" (Ontario Task Force on the Educational Needs of Native Peoples 1976, Abstract). One important implication of this statement is that the needs of Métis and non-status Indians are not isolated from those of treaty Indians. *Native Education in the Province of Alberta*, on the other hand, explicitly recognizes the special needs of different groups of Native peoples, particularly the Métis, in its recommendations for the improvement of Native education:

The educational needs of Native peoples vary according to their tribal background, geographic location, and legal status. Recognition of these differences is particularly important for the welfare of Alberta's Métis population. The Métis are not protected by legal rights; except for the few who live on colonies, they do not have land provided for them; their lack of cultural identity and community cohesiveness leaves them in a state of socio-cultural disintegration. *Since Métis receive no special considerations by the Federal Government, the interests of Métis people should be of particular concern to the Government of Alberta.* (Alberta Task Force on Intercultural Education 1972, 159. Emphasis in original)

As stated earlier, this was the period during which Aboriginal organizations in Canada mobilized, influenced by the galvanizing effect of the 1969 White Paper and a general trend of political activism. This is also the period during which governments began to respond to pressures for citizen engagement and social change. One element of government response was the rise, at least rhetorically, of public consultation as part of policy making. The discussions with Indian leaders in 1968 about the future of the Indian Act were a manifestation of these developments (Weaver 1993). Not surprisingly, then, the documents from this period reflect a preoccupation with the legitimacy of Aboriginal advocates as representatives of their constituency as well as with the need for consultation. *Indian Control of Indian Education*, for instance, is based on the positions of the territorial and provincial associations that comprise the National Indian Brotherhood, which were then accepted in principle by the National Indian Brotherhood's general assembly. The Brotherhood considered its report to be representative of the views of Indian people: "The National Indian Brotherhood is confident that it expresses the will of the people it represents when it adopts a policy based on two fundamental principles of education in a democratic country: parental responsibility and local control" (National Indian Brotherhood 1972, 30-1).

In *Native Education in the Province of Alberta*, a chapter entitled "What Do the Native People Want: A Survey" is based on papers and submissions by Native organizations: "The Task Force assumed that the views of the Native organizations are representative of the feelings of Native peoples and that the recommendations offered by them to government agencies are concurrent with the wishes of the majority of the Indian people" (Alberta Task Force on Intercultural Education 1972, 98). This statement can be taken as a reflection of the government's general acceptance of the ability of Native organizations to communicate the wishes of the people they represent.

Consistent with the rise of consultative models of policy making, many other documents from this period reveal a preoccupation with public consultation, especially consultation with Aboriginal people. Examples include the 1971 report of the federal Standing Committee on Indian Affairs and

Northern Development concerning the status of Indian and "Eskimo" education in Canada (the Watson Report) and the *Summary Report of the Task Force on the Educational Needs of Native Peoples of Ontario* (Ontario Task Force on the Educational Needs of Native Peoples 1976). The latter document, for example, reports extraordinary efforts to have Native interests represented at all stages of the consultation process and to ensure that the voices of Native peoples themselves are heard.

Despite this emerging trend of consultation, there were few references to establishing permanent institutions for consultation or co-management in the field of education policy. The only efforts to establish a formal structure for information gathering and discussion were seen in the Ontario Task Force on the Educational Needs of Native Peoples and the Alberta Task Force on Intercultural Education, whose first report dealt exclusively with the education of Aboriginal people in Alberta. Ironically, the Alberta task force lacked representativeness, as it was comprised solely of provincial government officials. The tripartite nature of the Ontario task force stands out as one case of institutionalized collaboration. As the term "task force" implies, however, its mandate was temporary. Nonetheless, it suggests the basis for a model that would become more popular in later periods.

Finally, the period between 1967 and 1982 witnessed a major change in how issues of education were understood and expressed. There was a move from thinking of education as a means for assimilation to thinking of it as a means for the revitalization of Indian cultures and economies. Many of the documents reviewed establish a link between education and cultural preservation (and promotion), especially those written by Aboriginals. In *Indian Control of Indian Education*, for instance, the National Indian Brotherhood's statement of values centres around the issues of culture: "We want education to provide the setting in which our children can develop the fundamental attitudes and values which have an honoured place in Indian tradition and culture. We want the behaviour of our children to be shaped by those values which are most esteemed in our culture. It is important that Indian children have a chance to develop a value system which is compatible with Indian culture" (National Indian Brotherhood 1972, 2).

This link between education and culture was reflected in a holistic view of education – a view particularly prominent within the documents of Aboriginal organizations. *Wahbung Our Tomorrows*, for example, attacks residential schools for their "disregard for the essential feature of education that is a total experience. Unrecognized were questions pertaining to Indian language, Indian culture, Indian life and customs, and the participation of the Indian parent in the shaping of education" (Indian Tribes of Manitoba 1971, 106). Education was viewed broadly, and it included adult education, substance and drug abuse education, pre-school, vocational education, and cultural events.

Although, as noted earlier, permanent consultative or co-management institutions were not a distinguishing feature of this period, the concepts of partnership, cooperation, and joint responsibility were introduced into the policy discourse. Documents published by all policy participants, including provincial governments, Aboriginal organizations, and the federal government, acknowledge the need to establish harmonious relations between Aboriginal peoples/governments and the broader community/non-Aboriginal governments. *Native Education in the Province of Alberta*, for instance, recommends joint responsibility between Native and non-Native communities: "Natives and Whites should join forces in cooperatively designing programs to fulfill the educational wants and needs of Alberta's Native peoples. Neither group should attempt to operate independently; nor should either group abdicate its responsibilities. The joint action should be carried forward with an eye to the future and avoid reference to past hostilities" (Alberta Task Force on Intercultural Education 1972, 159).

Similarly, *Indian Control of Indian Education* speaks of the need for Indian parents to seek "participation and partnership with the Federal Government, whose legal responsibility for Indian education is set by the treaties and the Indian Act" (National Indian Brotherhood 1972, 3); and the Watson Report recommends that the government establish "full consultation and partnership with the Indian and Eskimo people of Canada" (Canada, Standing Committee on Indian Affairs and Northern Development, 1971, 27).

The principles of parental responsibility and local control were also prominent in the documents released by Aboriginal organizations. In this case, the discourse was centred on the need to transfer decision-making authority over education to the local or community level in order to give parents and communities greater control over the education of their children. These principles were repeatedly supported, and a broad consensus emerged at this early stage of the discourse: it was agreed that greater control for communities and parents would make Indian education more effective.

A key development, which informs later policy discourse, is that, in an announcement that occurred less than two months after the publication of *Indian Control of Indian Education*, the idea of parental and local control was accepted by the federal government as the basis of its new policy on Indian education. As this policy was to be operationalized, however, the problem, at both the federal and provincial levels, became how to define "control." For example, while the *Summary Report of the Task Force on the Educational Needs of the Native Peoples of Ontario* defines "control" in terms of "input," Aboriginal documents define it as the total or partial transfer of jurisdiction over education to the local community level. For instance, *Indian Control of Indian Education* and *Wahbung Our Tomorrows* explain Indian control largely in terms of the local control enjoyed by school boards: "Until now, decisions on the education of Indian children have been made by anyone and everyone, except Indian parents. This must stop. Band Councils should be given total or partial authority for education on reserves, depending on local circumstances, and always with provisions for eventual complete autonomy, analogous to that of a provincial school board vis-à-vis a provincial Department of Education" (National Indian Brotherhood 1972, 27).

In summary, the period following the Hawthorn Report is extremely significant. We see the first signs of the federal government moving away from an assimilationist paradigm. Perhaps the political nadir of the concept of assimilation, at least during this period, was concomitant with the 1969 White Paper. In the field of education, assimilationist thought was, by this period, firmly entrenched in the establishment and operation of residential schools. The essential changes that occurred during this period are marked by the fact that the discussion of Aboriginal education engaged all three main parties: Aboriginal (mainly Indian) organizations, provincial governments, and the federal government. All parties to the discussion appeared to move towards acceptance of the idea that cooperation and "partnership" were important, although discussion concerning the institutional means of achieving this was rudimentary at best. Debates about assimilation gave way to debates about how to revitalize Aboriginally controlled education. This was reflected in the widely discussed themes of parental responsibility and local control – although there were certainly varying ideas about the meaning of local control.

1982 to 1988: A Change in Participants, a Change in Focus
This period is marked by two major events. In 1982, after an arduous period of federal-provincial negotiation and the intervention of Aboriginal peoples in the process, Canada patriated its Constitution and, in the process, introduced the Canadian Charter of Rights and Freedoms. A crucial victory for Aboriginal peoples was the inclusion of Section 35 of the Constitution Act, which states: "The existing aboriginal and treaty rights of the aboriginal peoples of Canada are hereby recognized and affirmed" (Section 35[1]). Recognition of Indian, Inuit, and Métis as Aboriginal peoples is specified. A formal plan for three first ministers' conferences on constitutional Aboriginal matters was agreed upon during the pre-patriation negotiations. This "FMC process" occurred between 1983 and 1987. The discussions between first ministers and the national Aboriginal leaders focused increasingly on Aboriginal self-government, but they failed to achieve agreement on explicitly entrenching the right of self-government in the Constitution Act.

Nonetheless, during this time there was a watershed with regard to the recognition of Aboriginal self-government. In 1983, the report of a special parliamentary committee on Indian self-government, commonly known as the Penner Report, was released. It recommended the constitutionally entrenched recognition of the right of Indian self-government and developed a model of self-government that recognized Aboriginal authority in the key areas of education and child care (among others) (Graham, Dittburner, and Abele 1996, 156-7).

Looking specifically at developments in the field of education, the years between 1976, when the *Summary Report of the Task Force on the Educational Needs of the Native Peoples of Ontario* was published, and 1983 are notable for their relative absence of documents. This might be partly explained by a preoccupation with the process leading up to the proclamation of the Constitution. This gap, however, might be considered the calm before the storm, for between 1984 and 1987, thirteen significant reports on Aboriginal education were published.

Provincial and territorial governments dominated the discourse of this period. They published a number of reports, some of which exclusively addressed the concerns of Aboriginal peoples, some of which addressed their concerns within the context of multiculturalism and education in general. Only one document discussed in *Soliloquy and Dialogue* – "Education Proposal by the Ontario Métis and Non-Status Indian Association" (Ontario Métis and Non-Status Indian Association 1985) – was published by an Aboriginal organization. It is noteworthy that Aboriginal organizations participated in the development of many of the provincial documents. This may be a legacy of the politics of constitutional patriation. Patriation engaged provinces and Aboriginal organizations in matters outside their traditional orbit, drew them into intense interaction, and changed some conceptions regarding the role of governments in the provision of services.

There were at least two other influences stimulating provincial/territorial activity. First, interest in the teaching of languages other than English and French as well as in the teaching of courses on non-dominant cultures (born out of the federal government's 1971 multiculturalism policy) was given new life with the proclamation of the Charter of Rights and Freedoms and the equality provisions of Section 15 (which came into effect in 1985). Second, there was a growing number of Aboriginal children in urban schools and a growing recognition of social problems among the urban Aboriginal population, particularly in the Prairies.

The Prairie provinces produced a multitude of documents during the 1980s. Saskatchewan, in particular, emerged as a forerunner in tackling issues of Indian (legally registered) and Native (all others of Native origin) education. The years 1984 and 1985 saw a proliferation of documents on this subject from the Government of Saskatchewan, and also in Alberta. Particularly evident in Saskatchewan is the extent to which the reports build on their predecessors. Later reports from Saskatchewan, such as *Education Equity* (Saskatchewan Human Rights Commission 1985), build on the findings of previous reports. *Education Equity* reviews and updates the recommendations found in several documents, previously published in the province and elsewhere, that deal with issues of education equity and Native education. Interestingly enough, no documents in *Soliloquy and Dialogue* were produced by the Manitoba government. Policy discourse on Aboriginal education in Manitoba remained dominated by documents from the Manitoba Indian Brotherhood (which had been published in the previous period).

It is interesting to examine the lexicon of provincial government documents from this period in light of the specific identification of Indians, Inuit, and Métis as the Aboriginal peoples of Canada in the Constitution Act, 1982. The 1970s' focus on "Indian" education shifted in the 1980s to a focus on "Native" education, the term used in many provincial government documents of this period. Most of these documents make little distinction between the situations of the Indian, Métis, and non-status peoples. Certain provincial government reports, however, such as *Reaching Out: Report of the Indian and Métis Education Consultations* (Saskatchewan, Department of Education, 1985), refer to "Indian and Métis" rather than to "Native" consultations. Similarly, *Education Equity: A Report on Native Indian Education in Saskatchewan* (Saskatchewan Human Rights Commission 1985) was, despite its title, billed as a report on "Indian/Métis" education in Saskatchewan. This distinction between "Native" and "Indian and Métis" may reflect a greater formal recognition, at least on the part of the Government of Saskatchewan, of the diversity of Aboriginal peoples. This stands in sharp contrast to the reports from the Alberta government, for instance, which make no effort to subdivide the category of "Native" peoples and, instead, contend that there is a large degree of consensus among Native peoples. The report *Native Education in Alberta: Alberta Native People's Views on Native Education*, for instance, claims to present "a consensus of the perspectives held by Native people of Alberta on ways to ensure that Native students have opportunities to obtain the high quality education enjoyed by all Alberta students" (Alberta, Ministry of Education, 1985). Other provincial and territorial government reports (e.g., those of the Yukon, British Columbia, and New Brunswick governments) focus on "Indian" and, in the case of British Columbia, on "First Nations" education. This largely reflects the composition of the Aboriginal population in those jurisdictions as well as, perhaps, the nature of prevailing provincial government policy and attitudes.

The interplay of consultation and institution building as themes in the discourse on education continues to be important. One salutary development during this period is greater emphasis on the institutionalization of Aboriginal-government relations for the purpose of dealing with issues of education.

Heavy emphasis on extensive consultations is evident throughout the documents of this period. It is important to note, however, that many of the consultative processes used in the preparation of the documents were conducted by provincial government officials. Thus, while efforts were made to base the reports on the view of the Aboriginal persons, communities, and organizations consulted, these views were incorporated into the various reports by government officials. Some reports, such as *Learning: Tradition and Change* (Northwest Territories Special Committee on Education 1982) and *Kwiya: Towards a New Partnership in Education* (Yukon Joint Commission on Indian Education and Training 1987), the latter being chaired by a representative from the Council for Yukon Indians, rely heavily on direct excerpts from the consultations. Within this period, the only document that goes to great length to ensure a large degree of representativeness is the report of the Native Curriculum Review Committee, *A Five-Year Action Plan for Native Curriculum Development* (Saskatchewan, Department of Education, Native Curriculum Review Committee 1984), which consisted of representatives of a variety of programs and organizations involved in the field of Native education in Saskatchewan.

A Five-Year Action Plan is also noteworthy for its support for more institutionalized processes for interaction and discussion. It recommends that the Native Curriculum Review Committee be made a permanent structure and that formal links be made between it and the provincial government through membership on the provincial policy committee. Another attempt to institutionalize the process can be found in *Native Education in Alberta's Schools: Alberta Native People's Views on Native Education,* which recommends that "four regional Native education councils should be established. A provincial Native education coordinating committee comprised of the chairman of each regional Aboriginal educational council, Ministerial appointees, and Alberta Education should be formed" (Alberta, Ministry of Education, 1985). Additionally, *Kwiya* calls for the establishment of an Indian education commission to represent the interests of Indian people: "The Government of Yukon, in the past, has not responded to suggestions for reform in support of Indian education concerns. There is a need for the Government to demonstrate leadership by initiating new policy directions. These changes must be accompanied by a demonstrated willingness to work with the Indian community. The Commission has recommended the establishment of an Indian Education Commission to fulfill this immediate requirement" (Yukon Joint Commission on Indian Education and Training 1987, 38).

In addition to calling for more institutionalized structures to aid in interaction, many of the documents in this period call for special remedial programs to deal with the unique needs of Native students. This is in keeping with the focus on special programs, initiated during this period, to deal with students from other cultures.

There is a continued focus on communication, on the involvement and participation of parents and communities, and on community-parental control of the system. "Control," however, continues to be an ambiguous concept. *Learning: Tradition and Change* (Northwest Territories Special Committee on Education 1982) defines control in terms of devolution of authority to division boards. This may be a product of the demographics of the Northwest Territories; that is, local control could more easily be exercised in a manner that ensures Aboriginal control when the majority of the territorial population is Aboriginal. We also continue to see considerable emphasis placed on notions of "partnership." There is, however, no reference to the transfer of full control over education to Aboriginal peoples and their governments in the documents of this period. This is consistent with the state of Aboriginal self-government on the broader stage.

Finally, the increasing frequency of references to human rights and human dignity during this period is worth noting. This emphasis is seen clearly, for example, in the *Five-Year Action Plan*, whose discussion of curriculum is based on the principle that "Native people must be presented as human beings having human societies" (Saskatchewan, Department of Education, Native Curriculum Review Committee, 1984, 2). This preoccupation is also evident in the different conceptions of equality and of rights. While *Education Equity: A Report on Native Indian Education in Saskatchewan* spoke of the need for "equal benefit," defined as equal opportunity plus examination of results (Saskatchewan Human Rights Commission 1985, 1), other documents spoke of equality of opportunity versus equality of access (Yukon Joint Commission on Indian Education and Training 1987, 13-4) and of the tension between equality, access, and affordability (British Columbia Royal Commission on Education 1988).

In summary, in this period we see the emergence of provincial and territorial governments as prominent participants in the discourse on Aboriginal education, with many making efforts to incorporate the views of Aboriginal residents. There is relatively little documentary expression of an independent Aboriginal voice. At the same time, the processes for discussion and interaction became more regularized, and there were increasing calls to establish institutions to deal with issues of Aboriginal education in the context of Canadian society. Issues of greater Aboriginal involvement and control, communication and partnership, continued to be important, and there was a greater focus on issues of human dignity and rights. In the greater policy context, there is also an interplay (involving both mutual reinforcement and some confusion) between efforts to advance "multicultural" education and the goals of Aboriginal education. There were, in short, a great many contrary forces and trends during this period.

1988 to 1992: Tradition and Education and Its Aftermath

Both the struggles and advances of Aboriginal peoples since the Hawthorn Report provide the main context for the final phase of our review. Recall that, in 1972, in response to assimilationist pressures (including the powerful effect of the residential school policy), the National Indian Brotherhood advanced arguments for extending to Indians those educational rights taken for granted by other Canadians; namely, local control and responsibility (National Indian Brotherhood 1972). This seminal document, supported by the endorsement of the concept of self-government contained in the Penner Report (Canada 1983), provided a pathway towards a major turning point in the evolution of policy discourse on education. This was marked by the 1988 publication of *Tradition and Education: Towards a Vision of the Future* by the Assembly of First Nations (the successor organization to the National Indian Brotherhood).

Tradition and Education is the culmination of a four-year study and represents the most comprehensive report on Aboriginal education in our document collection. Although *Tradition and Education* advances the arguments presented in *Indian Control of Indian Education*, it does so in a way that reflects a clear shift from thinking about control in terms of authority and devolution to thinking about education in terms of self-government: "Education is one of the most important issues in the struggle for self-government and must contribute towards the objective of self-government. First Nations' governments have the right to exercise their authority in all areas of First Nation education. Until First Nations' education institutions are recognized and controlled by First Nations' governments, no real First Nations' education exists. The essential principles are that each First Nation government should make its own decisions and arguments and apply its own values and standards rather than having them imposed from outside" (Assembly of First Nations 1988, 1: 47).

Tradition and Education, consistent with the Assembly of First Nations' constitutional position, demands a constitutional amendment, or, at the very least, the introduction of federal legislation that explicitly recognizes the inherent right of First Nations to self-government, including control over education. This legislation would "recognize the right of First Nations to exercise jurisdiction over their education and mandate federal, provincial, and territorial governments to vacate the field of First Nations education. No delegation of authority over education to First Nations

governments is acceptable as a substitute for aboriginal First Nations jurisdiction which is recognized and affirmed in the Constitution of Canada"
(Assembly of First Nations 1988, 3: 27).

Tradition and Education is based upon a national review of First Nations
education. Information was gathered through a community survey program, a secondary research program, and a committee of inquiry. The
national review also includes a review of First Nations schools, a policy
development program, and a legislative development program. These
illustrate the variety of methods employed to reinforce the validity of the
information collected: "The National Review of First Nations Education
has fulfilled its mandate of gathering enough data on the four areas of
jurisdiction, quality, management and resourcing of First Nations education to articulate a clear philosophy of First Nations education that can
[drive] the change necessary to put into practice First Nations aims and
objectives" (Assembly of First Nations 1988, 3: 28).

Changes in thinking about education centred around the concept of self-
government. The discourse on Aboriginal education no longer emphasizes
local control over education or community-based change but, rather, looks
to constitutional amendment as the best means of recognizing the inherent right of self-government and, hence, as the best way to achieve First
Nations control over education. *Tradition and Education* forges a vital and
inextricable link between education and self-government. These changes
in thinking are reflected in such phrases as "sovereignty of First Nations";
"the end of paternalism"; a "failed federal system"; and, of course, the
"inherent Aboriginal right to self-government." The use of the term "First
Nations" itself reflects a change in thinking with respect to the relationship between Aboriginal and non-Aboriginal peoples and governments.

The importance of *Tradition and Education* to the discourse on education
was recognized by the Department of Indian Affairs and Northern Development (DIAND), which asked James MacPherson of Osgoode Hall Law
School to review the document. His review, *MacPherson Report on Tradition
and Education: Towards a Vision of Our Future*, was submitted in September
1991. The three-year gap between the publication of the documents is not
explained in the MacPherson Report, despite its praise for DIAND's timely
response: "DIAND should also be complimented, first for providing substantial financial resources to support the research, consultations and publication of *Tradition and Education*, and secondly, for signaling that it wants
to give serious and timely attention to *Tradition and Education*" (MacPherson 1991, 41).

The MacPherson Report's interpretation of the recent history of Indian
education and of the future under self-governing arrangements stands in
sharp contrast to that presented by the Assembly of First Nations in *Tradition and Education*. While *Tradition and Education* cites the ineffective

implementation of the federal government's 1972-3 policy of Indian control of Indian education as a major reason for the poor quality of Indian education in Canada today, the MacPherson Report is considerably less scathing:

> Since 1973 federal policy with respect to Indian education has, in theory, been driven by adherence to the goals and principles of *Indian Control of Indian Education*. Moreover, in practice there can be no doubt that major and useful steps consistent with this document have been taken. If one compared the 1991 and 1973 pictures in the field of Indian education, one would have to conclude, in fairness, that both parental responsibility for, and local control of, Indian education are much more prevalent today than in 1973. So in that sense there is an element of "success" about post-1973 developments. It is both logical and fair, in my view, to conclude that at least some of that success flows from the education policies put in place and pursued by the federal Government in recent years. (MacPherson 1991, 3)

The two documents also diverge on the issue of self-government. While the MacPherson Report seems to accept the fundamental tenet of *Tradition and Education*, which is that Indian jurisdiction over Indian education must be achieved in the context of self-government, there are some aspects of its discussion of self-government that reflect a different understanding. MacPherson entirely avoids the term "inherent right," even when summarizing the major themes and specific proposals of the Assembly of First Nations (AFN) document. Furthermore, he compares what he calls Native self-government to self-governing professions, defining self-government as "native jurisdiction and control over and responsibility for the matters which affect the lives of Canadian natives."

> Native self-government should not be a scary concept for Canadian governments. If governments for decades have permitted, by legislation, professions like lawyers and doctors to be "self-governing," and have allowed them real independence in the governance and operation of their affairs, and if conservative American administrations in the 1970s and 1980s have not choked on at least the theory of self-government for American Indians, then it should not be much of a leap of imagination for Canadian governments to accept, and genuinely implement, the concept of Native self-government in Canada. We should not allow our preoccupation with the place of Quebec in Canada or our political and legal thinking rooted in the concept and definition of federalism, to lead us to the facile, but wrong, conclusion that self-government means independence or self-determination. Self-government does not mean these things. What

it means is native jurisdiction and control over and responsibility for the matters which affect the lives of Canadian natives. (MacPherson 1991, 42)

This interpretation contrasts with that presented in *Tradition and Education*. The AFN asserts not only that the inherent right includes the right to exercise local self-determination, but that Aboriginal-federal government relations must be conducted on a nation-to-nation basis:

The recognition and reflection of the inherent right to be and to remain distinct First Nations and to exercise local self-determination over local education programs through self-government is at the heart of this Declaration of First Nations Jurisdiction Over Education. (Assembly of First Nations 1988, 38)

First Nations have an inherent aboriginal right to self-government. First Nations' inherent aboriginal rights of self-government and treaties are the basis for government-to-government relationships between First Nations and the Government of Canada. Within Canada, First Nations are an order of government apart from the federal government and the governments of the provinces and territories. (Assembly of First Nations 1988, 1)

One effect of the release of *Tradition and Education*, with its framing of education issues within the context of self-government, and the competing paradigm offered by MacPherson's review was to move the policy debate back into the national arena. This shift was also likely influenced by Aboriginal concerns about the federal government's intention to limit access to funding for post-secondary education just as more and more Aboriginal students were trying to enter universities and colleges. It is certainly the case that, from the late 1980s onward, the federal government once again emerged as a prominent participant in the public policy discourse concerning Aboriginal education, harkening back to Hawthorn and the period immediately following release of his report.

Among Aboriginal organizations, only the AFN became heavily involved in documenting issues of education, language, and literacy. In this period, the AFN becomes the legitimate "voice" for First Nations regional, provincial, and territorial organizations. No similar Canada-wide document was produced by Inuit, Métis, or non-status Indians, but there was work being conducted by many Aboriginal organizations and groups at the community level.

The ways in which participants interacted in the policy discourse also changed between the pre-1988 and post-1988 periods. Consider the process of consultation. When the Standing Parliamentary Committee on Aboriginal Affairs prepared *Review of the Post-Secondary Student Assistance*

Program of the Department of Indian Affairs and Northern Development, it was besieged by Aboriginal communities who insisted that the process of consultation used by the federal government in developing its policy was so inadequate that a moratorium on the policy changes that resulted from it was essential (Canada, Standing Committee on Aboriginal Affairs, 1989). The report of this standing committee and other documents of this period, such as *Breaking Barriers: Report of the Task Force on Access for Black and Native People* (Dalhousie University Task Force on Access for Black and Native People 1989), place continued emphasis on the value of consultation, but with increasing demands for the definition of what constitutes sincere and meaningful consultation.

This period was characterized by attempts to define and reform the policy-making process. A common thread that weaves through this period is a sense of frustration over lack of progress and a trend towards providing increasingly precise definitions in order to promote a quickened pace of development. The growing frustration over the lack of progress during this period led to several incidents. Both *Review of the Post-Secondary Student Assistance Program of the Department of Indian Affairs and Northern Development* and *Breaking Barriers*, for instance, were spurred by disturbing incidents. Several protests by Aboriginal people over restrictions on post-secondary funding occurred in the run up to the 1989-90 academic year, including a well publicized hunger strike. In Nova Scotia, there had been a series of racially based conflicts in the education system (Canada, Standing Committee on Aboriginal Affairs 1989, 25; Dalhousie University Task Force on Access for Black and Native People 1989, viii).

If we look beyond the sphere of Aboriginal education, then we can see a number of factors that may have exacerbated this frustration, including the failure of the constitutional conferences and the exclusion of provisions for self-government from the Meech Lake Accord. An economic recession and reduced public spending no doubt also contributed to the lack of fundamental change and fuelled frustration. But we must also look to problems in the discourse on Aboriginal education, including the ambiguity of ideas presented and the lack of understanding and genuine communication between different participants. In response to the culmination of these frustrations, the reports of this period begin to evince greater precision and greater detail in the hope of generating change. The tendency for documents to attempt to pin down what constitutes meaningful consultation and to clearly define strategies for implementing their recommendations suggests that Aboriginal people perceived government action to be evasive.

This emphasis on greater precision and clearer definitions was also evident in some of the ideas that emerged during this period. Documents of the late 1980s and early 1990s offer increasingly specific recommendations.

The document that launches this period of our review, *Tradition and Education* (Assembly of First Nations 1988), proposes a detailed, five-stage implementation strategy. Government reports also offer implementation strategies. For example, *Report of the Provincial Advisory Committee on Post-Secondary Education for Native Learners* (British Columbia 1990) recommends providing appropriate staff and database requirements as well as a tripartite committee in order to implement its recommendations. Also, in the same report, the use of priority recommendations illustrates the committee's concern that many of its recommendations may not be implemented.

We also see changes in the scope of the issues addressed. Issues of post-secondary education become prominent in the document collection; this may be a by-product of the growing recognition of the interrelatedness of self-government, economic self-sufficiency, and higher educational achievement, which is evident in such documents as the *Report of the Provincial Advisory Committee on Post-Secondary Education for Native Learners* (British Columbia Provincial Advisory Committee on Post-Secondary Education for Native Learners 1990). This may also be a reflection of the impact of *Tradition and Education* (Assembly of First Nations 1988) on how education is conceptualized within the context of the inherent right to self-government.

Several documents, such as *Partners in Action: Action Plan of the Indian and Métis Education Advisory Committee* (Saskatchewan Indian and Métis Education Advisory Committee 1991) and *Literacy for Métis and Non-Status Indian Peoples: A National Strategy by the Gabriel Dumont Institute of Native Studies and Applied Research* (Gabriel Dumont Institute 1991), emphasize the diversity of Aboriginal peoples and, in the case of *Report of the Provincial Advisory Committee on Post-Secondary Education for Native Learners* (British Columbia Provincial Advisory Committee on Post-Secondary Education for Native Learners 1990), the diversity among British Columbia First Nations. There is also, in many cases, a clinging to language that embraces commonality, perhaps in order to strengthen the force of arguments addressing the situation of Aboriginal education, but more likely to simplify the process of discussion and consultation for non-Aboriginal governments. Perhaps the most noteworthy example of this approach is *Breaking Barriers: Report of the Task Force on Access for Black and Native People* (Dalhousie University Task Force on Access for Black and Native People 1989). Arguably, this is the most evident link of the interplay between Aboriginal issues and the construction of Canada as a multicultural/multiracial society.

In summary, we can think of the last phase of our review as revealing important touchstones for the work of RCAP. At the level of high policy and politics, the link between education and self-government emerged. It

is reasonable to suggest that this was the first illumination of this fundamental connection for non-Aboriginal participants in the discourse and,
perhaps, for some Aboriginal people as well. This period also reveals an
increasing preoccupation with the "nitty gritty" of when and how education reforms should be undertaken, along with a redefinition of the roles
of Aboriginal and Canadian governments. The foundation of parental
and community responsibility, first articulated in *Indian Control of Indian
Education* (National Indian Brotherhood 1972) and then in *Tradition and
Education* (Assembly of First Nations 1988) some sixteen years later, is
essential to thinking through issues and needs at both of these levels.
These features of the policy discourse on Aboriginal education would set
the stage for RCAP's work.

Observations and Reflections

We conclude by suggesting some important themes and issues that emerge
from *Soliloquy and Dialogue*. Looking back on the discourse that developed
through the documents included in this collection, we see that discussion
of issues concerning Aboriginal education has been closely linked to discussion of governance. Specifically, the way in which the relationship
between Aboriginal and non-Aboriginal governments has been envisioned
in the discourse on governance has been reproduced in the discourse on
education. Substantively, there has been considerable movement in the
way in which the relationship between Aboriginal and non-Aboriginal
peoples and their governments has been reflected in the sphere of education. This is seen in the assimilationist paradigms that dominated the
policy fields of both governance and education in the pre-Hawthorn
period and in the influence of documents such as the Hawthorn Report
and the Penner Report, which were seminal to developments in both
spheres of Aboriginal policy. It is also evident in the rights-based discourse
on self-government and responsibility for Aboriginal education in the
most recent period.

Similarly, the policy discourse on Aboriginal education has developed in
concert with the policy discourse on multiculturalism and multicultural
education. Unlike the impact of governance, the impact of multiculturalism on the development of the discourse on Aboriginal education is never
explicitly recognized in the documents under review; instead, we can draw
parallels over time between ideas and events in the sphere of multiculturalism and in the sphere of Aboriginal education. An emerging trend is for
a stronger connection between issues of Aboriginal education and issues of
racism. This is paralleled by an increasing emphasis on equality and, more
generally, on human rights and dignity.

The development of a discourse on Aboriginal education at the national
level did not always proceed in tandem with its development at the

provincial/territorial level. Each province and territory developed in a way that was unique to its own experiences. Because of their constitutional responsibility for education, the provinces (and, in effect, the territorial governments) have been extensively involved in the discussion and development of policy with respect to Aboriginal education. This complicates attempts to trace the evolution of the discourse from a national point of view, as the discourse in each province and territory has proceeded at its own pace, influenced in many instances by ideas and events internal to its own geographical boundaries. It is very important to note that, while we find a cumulative body of work on education in some provinces (such as Saskatchewan and Alberta), provincial momentum is contained within provincial boundaries. We might logically assume that any advances made by, say, Saskatchewan, might be studied and built upon by, say, New Brunswick. There is, however, no evidence in the documents to suggest that this has been the case; rather, the discourse seems to have developed within each province and territory in isolation from developments in other jurisdictions.[2]

In each of the three phases of our review we considered the state of concern with consultation and institutional cooperation as well as the extent of interplay between these two possibilities in the policy process. We conclude that there have been advances on both fronts. There has been a push to more meaningful forms of consultation, and there is increasing concern with issues of peaceful coexistence through institutionalized cooperation. This provides an important reference point when considering RCAP's findings and recommendations concerning education.

Despite constructive developments concerning consultation and cooperation, progress in the discourse on Aboriginal education has been jeopardized by an inability to establish common meanings for key concepts. We see, in several instances, that different participants have adopted different meanings for key words. Concepts such as "control," "local," and "consultation" have been interpreted in a variety of ways. This has bred frustration among participants in the discourse and has contributed to the failure to achieve meaningful dialogue. This conclusion has implications for future deliberations concerning Aboriginal education. Imprecise language may, in some cases, threaten the ability to achieve dialogue.

How close has policy development in the area of Aboriginal education come to true dialogue? There were clearly some significant obstacles. Commensurate participation by all those affected is undermined when key participants move in and out of the discourse at different times and proceed on different tracks. Increasingly, many of the documents recognized the need for a process to ensure sustained discussion. This was, however, never achieved – largely, it could be argued, because of a lack of will on the part of governments. Finally, the achievement of a common vision is being frustrated because different players are using different paradigms. In particular, we've seen the federal government and Aboriginal organizations focus on education within the context of governance, while provincial governments focus on multiculturalism and human rights. We've also seen how different participants assigning different meanings to the same words creates confusion and undermines the ability to achieve a common vision.

More fundamental features of Canada and its mode of governance have also stood in the way of dialogue. The essential power relationship between the federal and provincial governments and Aboriginal peoples, the vagaries of funding for Aboriginal organizations, and the entanglement of Aboriginal issues with Canada's broader unity deliberations are just three of many influences on what has occurred.

In conclusion, our review suggests that a growing consensus has emerged about the need for dialogue and shared effort with regard to issues of Aboriginal education. Objectively, there are some signs of progress, such as the increasing participation by Aboriginal people in higher education. Nonetheless, on the eve of the creation of RCAP, we were all still looking for a common understanding both of words and of the means that we all might use to deal with the challenges of education for Aboriginal people.

Acknowledgments

This chapter is based upon Katherine Graham, Carolyn Dittburner, and Frances Abele, "Soliloquy and Dialogue: The Evolution of Public Policy Discourse on Aboriginal Issues," Royal Commission on Aboriginal Peoples (Ottawa, 1996). The alphabetical listing of authors in this overview of the earlier analysis reflects equal participation by all.

Notes

1 In criminal justice, for instance, the legal profession played a prominent role in the policy discourse. See Chapter 6 in *Soliloquy and Dialogue: The Evolution of Public Policy Discourse on Aboriginal Issues* (Ottawa: Royal Commission on Aboriginal Peoples, 1996).
2 Others have found evidence of borrowing in the year after the period covered by our review. See Fettes and Norton in this volume.

References

Alberta Ministry of Education. 1985. *Native Education in Alberta: Native People's Views on Native Education in Alberta*. Edmonton: Ministry of Education.
Alberta Task Force on Intercultural Education. 1972. *Report of the Task Force on Intercultural Education: Native Education in the Province of Alberta*. Edmonton: Task Force on Intercultural Education.
Assembly of First Nations. 1988. *Tradition and Education: Towards a Vision of Our Future, Vol. 1*. Ottawa: Assembly of First Nations/National Indian Brotherhood.
British Columbia Provincial Advisory Committee on Post-Secondary Education for Native Learners. 1990. *Report of the Provincial Advisory Committee on Post-Secondary Education for Native Learners*. Victoria: Ministry of Advanced Education, Training and Technology.

British Columbia Royal Commission on Education (Barry M. Sullivan, Commissioner). 1988. *A Legacy for Learners: Summary of Findings*. Victoria: Queen's Printer.

Canada. Department of Indian Affairs and Northern Development, Indian Affairs Branch. 1966-7. *Survey of the Contemporary Indians of Canada* (the Hawthorn Report). Ottawa: Information Canada.

–. House of Commons. 1988. *Bill C-93*. (Multiculturalism Act.)

–. Special Committee on Indian Self-Government. 1983. *Indian Self-Government in Canada: Report of the Special Committee* (the Penner Report). Ottawa: Queen's Printer.

–. 1969. *Statement of the Government of Canada on Indian Policy* (the White Paper). Ottawa: Indian Affairs and Northern Development.

–. Standing Committee on Aboriginal Affairs (John Reimer, chair). 1989. *A Review of the Post-Secondary Student Assistance Program of the Department of Indian Affairs and Northern Development*. Ottawa: Queen's Printer.

–. Standing Committee on Indian Affairs and Northern Development (Ian Watson, chair). 1971. *Fifth Report of the Standing Committee on Indian Affairs and Northern Development*. Ottawa: Queen's Printer.

Constitution Act. 1982. Section 35.

Dalhousie University Task Force on Access for Black and Native People (A. Wayne Mackay, chair). 1989. *Breaking Barriers: Report of the Task Force on Access for Black and Native People*. Halifax: Dalhousie University.

Gabriel Dumont Institute. 1991. *Literacy for Métis and Non-Status Indian Peoples: A National Strategy by the Gabriel Dumont Institute of Native Studies and Applied Research*.

Graham, Katherine A., Carolyn Dittburner, and Frances Abele. 1996. *Soliloquy and Dialogue: Overview of Major Trends in Public Policy Relating to Aboriginal Peoples*. Ottawa: Canada Communication Group. Also available on the CD-ROM *For Seven Generations: An Information Legacy of the Royal Commission on Aboriginal Peoples*. Ottawa: Libraxus, 1997.

Indian Chiefs of Alberta. 1970. *Citizens Plus*. Edmonton: Indian Association of Alberta.

Indian Tribes of Manitoba. 1971. *Wahbung Our Tomorrows*. Winnipeg: Manitoba Indian Brotherhood.

MacPherson, James C. 1991. *MacPherson Report on Tradition and Education: Towards a Vision of Our Future*. Ottawa: Department of Indian Affairs and Northern Development.

National Indian Brotherhood. 1972. *Indian Control of Indian Education*. Ottawa: National Indian Brotherhood.

Northwest Territories Special Committee on Education (Bruce McLaughlin and Tagak Curley, Co-chairs). 1982. *Learning: Tradition and Change*. Yellowknife: Government of the Northwest Territories.

Ontario Task Force on the Educational Needs of Native Peoples. 1976. *Summary Report of the Task Force on the Educational Needs of Native Peoples of Ontario*. Toronto: Government of Ontario.

Ontario Métis and Non-Status Indian Association. 1985. Education proposal by the Ontario Métis and Non-Status Indian Association.

Saskatchewan. Department of Education. 1985. *Reaching Out: Report of the Indian and Métis Education Consultations*. Regina: Saskatchewan Department of Education.

–. Department of Education. Native Curriculum Review Committee. 1984. *A Five-Year Action Plan for Native Curriculum Development*. Regina: Saskatchewan Department of Education.

Saskatchewan Human Rights Commission. 1985. *Education Equity: A Report on Native Indian Education in Saskatchewan*. Regina: Saskatchewan Human Rights Commission.

Saskatchewan Indian and Métis Education Advisory Committee. 1991. *Partners in Action: Action Plan of the Indian and Métis Education Advisory Committee*. Indian and Métis Education Advisory Committee.

Weaver, Sally M. 1993. "The Hawthorn Report: Its Use in the Making of Canadian Indian Policy." In *Anthropology, Public Policy and Native Peoples in Canada*, ed. Noel Dyck and James B. Waldram. Montreal and Kingston: McGill-Queen's University Press.

Yukon Joint Commission on Indian Education and Training (Mary Jane Joe, Chairperson). 1987. *Kwiya: Towards a New Partnership in Education*. Whitehorse: Yukon Territorial Government.

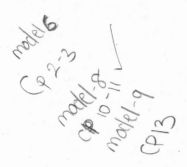

Part 2
Aboriginal Languages and Communications: Voicing the Promise

Aboriginal identities are shaped by many factors, but two of the most potent forces are the relationship with one's ancestral language and with one's self-concept as formed through the stories and images disseminated by media. Part 2 contains three chapters that address efforts to conserve Aboriginal languages and to bring Aboriginal voices into communications media. Such efforts are integral to the reassertion of control over the cultural processes of forming Aboriginal identities in the twenty-first century.

> There are many reasons why our generation of parents cannot speak our ancestral language. The residential school system's abusive campaign for the elimination of our languages and identity; non-Aboriginal foster and adoptive homes who sought to "take the Indian out of us," enrolment in "integrated" provincial schools which showed neither respect nor understanding for the importance of our languages and cultures; and, intermarriage. (Iris Lauzon in RCAP 1997)

It is now widely known that the decline of Aboriginal languages throughout the twentieth century did not occur by accident or through natural evolution. Charged with "civilizing" Indian children, government administrators and church officials understood well the pivotal role of language in the continuity of Aboriginal identity. With calculation and conviction, they imposed the use of English or French upon even the youngest children entering the doors of their schools. Children in residential schools were harshly punished for speaking their language precisely because language and communication processes lie at the heart of transmitting cultural values and unique worldviews from one generation to the next.

Because compulsory schooling was used to rob Aboriginal people of the intergenerational processes by which language and culture are passed on, the classroom has become the main site wherein Aboriginal people are battling to reinstate them. Despite funding levels that are grossly inadequate for the project at hand, Aboriginal people continue to pursue language revitalization, in part because Aboriginal languages are seen as inseparable from issues of Aboriginal identity. As the bearers of thought processes, Aboriginal languages encode unique ways of interpreting the world. When an Aboriginal language dies, a whole way of thinking is lost, both to the community and to humanity. The consequences of losing complex systems of Aboriginal knowledge are too painful to contemplate.

The difficulty of revitalizing a language, particularly an oral language, cannot be underestimated. There are numerous socio-technical processes that lay the groundwork for language instruction: documentation of oral languages, standardization of dialects and writing systems, and expansion of vocabularies in order to incorporate concepts that are new to the original language. These are expensive, time-consuming, and potentially divisive for language speakers, and they are only the starting point. Language curricula and resource materials have to be created, and language teachers have to be trained. All of these activities require intensive efforts by technical experts together with fluent speakers of a language.

Yvonne Hébert examines the language curricula used by First Nations schools and concludes that they are not oriented towards producing fluent speakers. Ruth Norton and Mark Fettes review the Aboriginal language policy statements of Aboriginal organizations, the policy positions by federal, provincial, and territorial governments throughout Canada, and the educational initiatives of each jurisdiction. The Yukon and Northwest Territories have adopted extensive policies aimed at strengthening Aboriginal language use. In most provinces, language policies look upon Aboriginal languages as second languages, often with only a few hours of instruction weekly. The province of Quebec is particularly interesting since the use of Aboriginal languages is supported in official policy.

Assimilative schooling has attacked not only language but also other processes of communicating. Government and Church officials who ran federally funded schools and, later, teachers in provincial schools took hold of the storytelling that systematically shapes the thinking and dreams of a people. Through school curricula, they have transmitted stories that claim to tell history, what is right and wrong, what it means to be successful, and what constitutes the very nature of the world. Stories, like language, embody culture. Stories of the sacred, of the past, and of everyday life are all part of the ongoing unfolding of a cultural map. But which stories are told and how, who tells them, who hears them, and the language and location of their speaking also reflect fundamental processes of control and power relations between Aboriginal peoples and the larger Canadian society.

Gail Valaskakis discusses how communities have lost the opportunity to tell their own stories. She analyzes the role of media in telling the stories of Aboriginal people in images and narratives. Considering the impact of mainstream media stories on how Aboriginal people come to form their identities, Valaskakis states the need for those images to be controlled by Aboriginal people. In the Far North, mainstream media have been an instrument of cultural erosion since the 1970s. In an effort to resist this tide, the Inuit have negotiated control of the mechanisms of storytelling through the Inuit Broadcasting Corporation. They have turned the tools of mass media into a form of storytelling that resonates with the oral traditions of the Inuit. In the process, broadcasting helps to preserve Inuktitut as a relevant, intergenerational medium of communication. In fact, Aboriginal communications societies in Canada have established Aboriginal language use as vital to their storytelling. But in many parts of Canada, Aboriginal peoples no longer speak their language. Where English and French have become common, the focus is on making sure that Aboriginal stories are not only told, but are told by Aboriginal people.

Aboriginal people in Canada are not alone in the struggle to maintain the integrity of their languages and communications. Indigenous languages and processes of transmission have been under attack all over the globe. The 1993 Draft Universal Declaration on the Rights of Indigenous Peoples, agreed upon by the United Nations Working Group on Indigenous Populations, devotes several clauses to recognizing the right of Indigenous peoples to "revitalize, use, develop and transmit to future generations their languages, oral traditions, writing systems and literatures," and further, "to all levels and forms of education, including access to education in their own languages" (United Nations 1993, 1-15). These provisions raise the profile of language retention and transmission from the realm of isolated local struggles to the arena of internationally recognized human rights. If the proposed declaration is adopted by nation-states, governments would be obligated to actively support language retention, rather than taking a passive stance as Indigenous languages lose ground.

Researchers such as Fishman (1990), Drapeau (1997), and others have studied language shift and how to reverse the decline of a language. The Royal Commission report examined this international phenomenon and noted that many language experts stress the importance of a multi-pronged approach that includes renewed intergenerational transmission as the key strategy (RCAP 1996, 3:614-17). Schools are only one element in a learning process that must take place on several fronts at once. If languages are to survive, then they must be transmitted as a first language from generation to generation, involving the whole family and the community.

Taken together, the three chapters in this section address significant dilemmas and issues facing Aboriginal people in reversing the effects of more than a century of deliberate and implicit assaults on Aboriginal language and cultural transmission in Canada. The will is strong, yet the pressures towards global uniformity are pervasive and unremitting. What is hopeful in these analyses is the clear demonstration that change is possible and that the primary power to revitalize Aboriginal languages and communicative processes lies within the grasp of families and communities, with support from public policy and access to appropriate resources.

References

Drapeau, Lynn. 1997. "Perspectives on Aboriginal Language Conservation and Revitalization in Canada." A research paper prepared for the Royal Commission on Aboriginal Peoples. In *For Seven Generations: An Information Legacy of the Royal Commission on Aboriginal Peoples*. CD-ROM. Ottawa: Libraxus.

Fishman, Joshua. 1990. "What Is Reversing Language Shift and How Can It Succeed?" *Journal of Multilingual and Multicultural Development* 11 (1&2): 5-36.

Royal Commission on Aboriginal Peoples (RCAP). 1996. *Report of the Royal Commission on Aboriginal Peoples, Vol. 3: Gathering Strength*. Ottawa: Canada Communications Group.

Royal Commission on Aboriginal Peoples (RCAP). 1997. Lauzon, Iris. Ojibway Language and Immersion Program for Pre-Schoolers. Winnipeg, Manitoba, 22 April 1992. In *For Seven Generations: An Information Legacy of the Royal Commission on Aboriginal Peoples*. CD-ROM. Ottawa: Libraxus.

United Nations. 1993. "Draft Declaration on the Rights of Indigenous Peoples." In *UN Commission on Human Rights: 45th session, Item 14 on the Provisional Agenda*. New York: United Nations Economic and Social Council.

2

Voices of Winter:
Aboriginal Languages and
Public Policy in Canada

Mark Fettes and Ruth Norton

> *Principles for Revitalization of First Nations Languages:*
> Language is our unique relationship to the Creator, our atti-
> tudes, beliefs, values, and fundamental notions of what is
> truth. Our languages are the cornerstones of who we are as a
> people. Without our languages our cultures cannot survive.
>
> As they belong to the original peoples of this country, First
> Nations languages must be protected and promoted as a
> fundamental element of Canadian heritage.
>
> The right to use our Aboriginal languages, and the right to
> educate our children in our languages, is an inherent Aboriginal
> and treaty right. The federal government has a legal obligation
> through various treaties, and through legislation, to provide
> adequate resources that will enable us to exercise this right.
>
> Language is a community resource to be planned and
> developed at the community level.
>
> Elders are the cornerstone of traditional education, and
> therefore must be accorded proper and fitting consideration
> for their expertise.
>
> All languages are to be accorded equal dignity and respect.
>
> – Assembly of First Nations (1990, 39)

It has been a cold 130 years for Canada's first languages, and the thaw is
still awaited. For a country in which language rights are now written into
the Charter of Rights and Freedoms, Canadian governments have shown
extraordinary disregard for the unique linguistic heritage of this land.

"The voice of the land is in our language" was the theme of the National
Elders' Gathering on Manitoulin Island in 1993. Throughout this week-
long meeting, Elders from hundreds of communities across Canada told
us that Aboriginal languages are spiritually interconnected with the land;
that they embody values and relationships; that survival and forgive-
ness, love and laughter, are all intertwined with the authentic language
of a place and people (Ojibway Cultural Foundation 1993). These facts are

recognized by First Nations and other Aboriginal peoples around the world, who throughout the centuries of colonization have tenaciously clung to language as one of their most precious resources (Fishman 1997; Maffi, Skutnabb-Kangas, and Andrianarivo 1997).

Yet this resource, in this country as in others, has been heedlessly squandered or deliberately destroyed. Most Aboriginal languages in Canada are now declining or endangered (Drapeau 1997). This precipitous decline of Aboriginal languages is no more "natural" or "inevitable" than the disappearance of Canada's fish stocks or rain forests: it is the outcome of a massive betrayal of treaty obligations and cultural responsibilities by federal and provincial governments. Conversely, a linguistic renaissance must be an integral part of the evolution towards local self-government and the restoration of spiritual and physical health to Aboriginal communities (Crawford 1996; Fishman 1996; Norton and Fettes 1997).

This chapter documents the concern and ideas expressed by Aboriginal organizations in Canada with regard to linguistic issues; the inconsistent and inadequate responses of federal, provincial, and territorial governments; and the developments that appear to the authors to hold out the greatest prospect of linguistic justice. In a chapter of such wide scope, it was impossible to do full justice to the range of effort and dedication displayed by Aboriginal language educators and activists across this country. We hope, however, that this brief summary will provide them with a useful tool in their efforts to secure support from communities and governments at all levels. It may also serve to remind us that our efforts on behalf of Aboriginal languages, wherever we are, form part of a wider struggle – one that can and must succeed.

In such voices from beneath the snow, we believe we hear the first vibrant stirrings of spring.

Speaking First: Aboriginal Perspectives
The diversity of Aboriginal identities in Canada led us to canvass a wide range of organizations and individuals for their views on language policy. This summary of our findings is divided according to current political realities but should not be taken as an endorsement of the status/non-status division or any other categories that unfairly label and discriminate against Aboriginal people. We support the right of all Aboriginal people to learn and use their ancestral languages, wherever they live and whatever their background. In our brief concluding section, we offer a vision of a language policy framework that could make this a reality.

First Nations
The Assembly of First Nations (AFN) began developing its language policy in 1988 (Jamieson 1988a, 1988b; Stacey-Diabo 1990), reaching a peak of

activity during the time of the Languages and Literacy Secretariat in 1992-3. The secretariat had a mandate to promote the following objectives:

- raise awareness of the importance of Aboriginal languages and literacy at the community level;
- encourage the development of literacy in First Nations languages, alongside the official languages;
- lobby the federal government for legislation to recognize, protect, and promote Aboriginal languages;
- lobby the federal government for additional funding for Aboriginal languages;
- carry out research on the present state of Aboriginal languages and literacy and develop strategies to preserve and strengthen them;
- research and establish an Aboriginal languages foundation.

In brief, the AFN's work was aimed in two directions: at First Nations governments, to encourage them to adopt effective language policies and strategies; and at the federal government, to create a national framework of legislative and financial support for the languages. In the first half of this program, the AFN's Languages and Literacy Steering Committee and its periodic language conferences (e.g., AFN 1991) helped to create a national network of language and literacy workers and advocates. Guidelines for community-based language policy were published by the AFN in 1992 and distributed nation-wide in both English and French (Fettes 1992). Two major reports, *Towards Linguistic Justice for First Nations* (AFN 1990) and *Towards Rebirth of First Nations Languages* (AFN 1992), included recommendations on the role of Aboriginal governments:

Language must be incorporated as an integral part of First Nations government through: adoption of First Nations official language bylaws; establishment of First Nations Language Commissions/Councils at the band, tribal or community level to implement language planning; promotion of Aboriginal language training programs for employees, administrators, as well as for leaders and community members who wish to become fluent in the Aboriginal language; promotion of day care and preschools that will provide immersion or bilingual language instruction. (AFN 1990)

Language and culture, the cornerstones of First Nation self-government, are to be protected and promoted in First Nations constitutions, self-government accords, and land claim agreements ... First Nations governments' fiscal negotiations with the federal government should include funding for language planning, promotion and development ... First

Nations governments should establish the position of Language and Culture Coordinator as an integral member of First Nations governments, under an advisory committee of community members and Elders. (AFN 1992)

The second prong of the AFN's language policy consisted of proposals for entrenching the status of Aboriginal languages within other levels of government. The following statements are representative:

The government of Canada must accord Aboriginal languages with official status, constitutional recognition, and accompanying legislative protection. Necessary funds must be provided by the federal government to ensure the development of language structures, curriculum materials, First Nations language teachers, resource centers and immersion programs. Aboriginal language instruction must be available from pre-school to post-secondary and adult education, and be acknowledged as meeting second language requirements at all levels. (AFN 1988)

First Nations language and culture must receive equivalent recognition, protection, promotion in the Canadian constitution, and through enabling legislation, as the official languages. The Canadian government must take steps to redress First Nations for suppressing language and culture, by providing support for promotion and protection of Aboriginal languages through [language planning and language retention activities, the publishing and recording of oral and literary works, native programming for radio, TV and newspapers, innovations and demonstration projects using new technologies, language studies programs]. Further, national and regional First Nations Language Commissions should be fully involved in planning and administration. (AFN 1990)

Mediating between these two levels of government, the AFN envisioned an Aboriginal Languages Foundation, which would coordinate activities at the national level:

A national clearing house on First Nations languages should be established with responsibilities that include: disseminating information on language revitalization programs and policies; monitoring international research on bilingual and immersion language training and disseminating findings to First Nations; maintaining a database on curriculum materials and resource personnel; publishing a First Nations Languages and Literacy newsletter for distribution to instructors of First Nations students, education authorities, and organizations and individuals interested in promoting Aboriginal languages and literacy. (AFN 1992)

This proposal was developed in a more detailed form by Verna Kirkness (Kirkness 1989) and then won support from the Native Council of Canada (Dunn 1989). Although we have been pleased to note recent political support for the idea of a national Aboriginal education institute (Canada 1996), such an institute would respond only partially to the challenge of language revitalization, which involves issues that extend far beyond the domain of the school.

Non-Status and Urban Indians

The Congress of Aboriginal Peoples (CAP; formerly the Native Council of Canada), the largest organization of so-called non-status and urban Indians in Canada, claims to speak for some 750,000 people. Away from their home communities, Aboriginal people face particular problems in maintaining or strengthening their languages. Speakers are far more scattered than they are on reserves, and they may have little incentive to participate in language retention programs. Furthermore, they have little opportunity to attend Aboriginal-controlled schools, and their children therefore depend on the provincial education system for the provision of mother-tongue programs.

Few studies have been carried out on the language skills and preferences of Aboriginal people off reserve, despite the fact that they number in the hundreds of thousands. Studies of census data (Burnaby and Beaujot 1986; Drapeau 1997) confirm that the non-status and urban Aboriginal population has a much lower average rate of language retention than does the on-reserve population.

CAP took steps to develop a language policy in the late 1980s (Dunn 1989). With no access to band-controlled schools, CAP placed much greater emphasis on the teaching of Aboriginal languages in provincial schools and universities, with effective Aboriginal representation on school boards and influence on the curriculum. It also stressed the issue of access:

> There was a strong recommendation that the "boundaries" for establishing various programs should be made on the basis of languages rather than on geographic location, political affiliation, or status. It was also proposed that implementation of policy and the development of programs be focused on Aboriginal language "interest groups" within larger non-Aboriginal communities on an equitable basis with those communities with an obvious Aboriginal majority. Aboriginal Language Councils were proposed as one vehicle that could serve to develop policy and program priorities for the larger co-ordinative bodies and avoid the impractical scenario in which literally hundreds of unconnected projects wasted resources and contradicted each other's efforts. The mechanism

of a bi-annual National Aboriginal Languages Conference was suggested as a vehicle for these councils to establish broad priorities while smaller regional offices served to help develop and resource specific community projects. (Dunn 1989)

In the same report, CAP voiced cautious support for the idea of an Aboriginal languages foundation (Kirkness 1989) and set out a number of conditions for its support, emphasizing equitable access to resources, participation in decision-making structures, and equal treatment in legislation for the off-reserve and urban Aboriginal population.

The 1989 report still reflects CAP's national language policy (M. Dunn, personal communication, 1993), and its conclusions were echoed in our research by some of the affiliated provincial and territorial organizations (PTOs). Among their recommendations were: increased funding for language instruction by federal and provincial governments; recognition and support for Aboriginal languages through legislation; inclusion of the languages in the school curriculum or in Aboriginal schools where numbers permit; and the introduction of a special tax deduction for contributions to organizations working for Aboriginal languages (Graham Tuplin, president of the Native Council of Prince Edward Island, personal communication by letter, 28 May 1993; Robert Hunka, executive director of the Native Council of Nova Scotia, personal communication by letter, 28 May 1993).

Similar concerns have been expressed by the National Association of Friendship Centres (NAFC), the most important source of language programs for the off-reserve Aboriginal population. This issue occupied almost a third of the NAFC's *National Literacy Survey* (NAFC 1990).

Métis

Métis organizations speak for a constituency that faces many of the same problems as do the rest of the off-reserve Aboriginal population, although the existence of distinct Métis communities on the Prairies increases the probability of language retention. This is supported by the findings of Burnaby and Beaujot (1986), who noted a higher proportion of mother tongue and home language among Métis than among the remaining non-status population. However, these authors also concluded, on the basis of age data, that the younger Métis generation was losing its language at an even faster rate than were other Aboriginal groups.

According to Audreen Hourie, "no firm policy statement" on the status and preservation of the Métis (Michif) languages has been made, although a Michif Languages Conference was held in 1985 and there has been ongoing work in recording Michif oral culture. "Limited funds have made the work very slow," she adds (Audreen Hourie, Manitoba Métis Federation, personal communication by letter, 15 June 1993).

The Saskatchewan community of Ile-à-la-Crosse has instituted a school-based Michif language program. According to the survey carried out by the Saskatchewan Indigenous Languages Committee, 28 percent of the people in this community speak fluent Michif-Cree (Fredeen 1991).

Inuit

Inuit organizations do not, in general, appear to have formal language policies. One possible reason for this is the existence of two relatively powerful and autonomous school boards, the Kativik School Board in Nunavik (Northern Quebec) and the Baffin Regional Division of Education in the Northwest Territories, which, together, serve over half the Inuit population. Both of these institutions have expressed a strong commitment to integrating the languages in schools and to ensuring that they remain a vital part of Inuit life. For example, the Kativik School Board recommends that students learn exclusively in the Inuit language during the first three years of their schooling and that they subsequently continue to study the language and culture in classes taught by Inuit teachers and Elders (Kativik School Board 1990a). The school board is also involved in developing an "academic mother-tongue curriculum" for adults (Kativik School Board 1990b). Concern exists, however, over the major gap in status between the Inuit language and the Canadian official languages, and the board has been urged to mobilize people behind a more ambitious language policy (Taylor 1990). Similar concerns exist in the Eastern Arctic.

The work of the school boards is complemented by that of cultural organizations such as the Avataq Cultural Institute in Quebec, which works for the preservation of Inuit language and culture at the community level. Direction is provided to Avataq by annual gatherings of Elders from all Arctic Quebec communities. Among its initiatives have been the formation of a language commission (Avataq Cultural Institute 1984), the organization of a language survey, and support for the publication of a 30,000-word dictionary of Inuktitut. Progress on other projects, such as a language laboratory for linguistic and terminology research and for training translators and interpreters, has been stalled for lack of funds (Avataq Cultural Institute 1992). Concern in Avataq for the future of Inuktitut remains high.

Linguistic and Cultural Organizations

Some of the strongest leadership on the language issue has come from Aboriginal organizations with a particular mandate in this area. Examples include the Sweetgrass First Nations Language Council, established in 1989 to provide overall leadership in the retention and revitalization of First Nations languages in Ontario; the Manitoba Association for Native Languages, founded in the mid-1980s to promote the retention and revitalization of Manitoba native languages; the Saskatchewan Indigenous

Languages Committee, composed of over sixty people from Aboriginal organizations throughout Saskatchewan, which, in 1991, published the *Sociolinguistic Survey of Indigenous Languages in Saskatchewan* (Fredeen 1991); and the Yinka Dene Language Institute, established in 1988 by the Carrier Sekani Tribal Council (a federation of thirteen Dene bands in north-central British Columbia), which develops programs aimed at restoring both fluency in Dene languages and knowledge of Dene history and culture.

All of these organizations have mission statements that are in broad agreement with the Principles for Revitalization of First Nations Languages (AFN 1990).

At the national level, the National Association of Cultural Education Centres links between seventy institutions, many of which play a major role in the maintenance and development of Aboriginal languages. In 1991 the association published a discussion paper that included a blueprint for "long-term focused and integrated language programs" as part of "a new approach and greater commitment on the part of all relevant Federal Government departments to the development of Aboriginal cultures" (National Association of Cultural Education Centres 1991).

Summary: Aboriginal Perspectives on Language Policy
Aboriginal organizations and governments do not always have language policies, but many have identified the survival of their languages as a priority. All are struggling with a severe shortage of human and financial resources, and with the lack of clear provincial and federal government policies. There is agreement on the need for language programs to be community-based and community-controlled, with Aboriginal culture and values at the centre. Métis and urban Aboriginal people generally face even greater difficulties than do those on reserve and in the North and, therefore, require special consideration in any comprehensive policy framework.

Legal and Political Frameworks
Aboriginal languages are not specifically referred to in the Canadian Constitution or in federal legislation. Only the Province of Quebec and the Territories have enacted legislation that directly relates to Aboriginal languages. Elsewhere in Canada their legal status is dependent on the interpretation of existing international, treaty, federal, and provincial law.

Legal frameworks are not, however, a reliable guide to the complexities of public policy. Even where legal guarantees exist, political practice may observe the letter rather than the spirit of the law; and where they do not exist, political practice may nevertheless provide a considerable measure of protection and support. The same remarks apply to policy declarations, which do not necessarily guide actual decision making at the administrative and financial levels. Such limitations need to be constantly kept in mind when reading the next sections.

A number of Canadian legal scholars, both Aboriginal and non-Aboriginal, have published thoughtful articles on the legal status of Aboriginal languages in recent years. They include, in chronological order: Morse (1989), Richstone (1989), Stacey-Diabo (1990), Slattery (1991), Nahanee (1991, 1995), de Varennes (1994), and Henderson (1995). Internationally, the concept of "linguistic human rights" is being further developed and applied to the situation of Aboriginal peoples in many different countries (Skutnabb-Kangas and Phillipson 1994). Norton and Fettes (1997) provide a brief review of the international, constitutional, and federal contexts.

Provincial Policy
Only two provinces, Prince Edward Island and Newfoundland, have to date adopted no policy measures whatsoever on Aboriginal languages. Seven of the remaining provinces have limited such initiatives to the formal education system, usually by establishing guidelines for the limited instruction of Aboriginal languages as "second" or "heritage" languages, without any broader policy objectives. This form of language policy, which does not differ markedly from practices in other industrialized countries (Churchill 1986), will be reviewed in a later section.

Quebec merits separate attention. The linguistic sensitivity of the majority francophone population appears to cut two ways, heightening reactions to the perceived threat of English but nurturing sympathy – at least in some circles – for other forms of linguistic and cultural distinctiveness. As a result, Quebec is the only province to have promised a certain degree of protection for Aboriginal languages in both legislation and policy. Unfortunately there is little evidence to suggest that this has a significant impact on programming, funding, or other forms of practical support.

The Charter of the French Language (1978) recognizes the right of Aboriginal people "to preserve and develop their original language and culture" and specifically excludes Aboriginal languages, Indian reserves, and the beneficiaries of the James Bay and the Northeastern Quebec treaties from the sections of the act designed to promote the use of French as a medium of instruction and public communication.

In 1983 the Quebec National Assembly adopted the following three principles, which have a direct or indirect bearing on Aboriginal languages:

(1) Quebec recognizes that its Aboriginal peoples are distinct nations entitled to their cultures, languages, customs, and traditions, with the right to direct the promotion of this distinct identity themselves.
(2) Aboriginal peoples are entitled to have and to control, according to

agreements with the government, the institutions that meet their needs in the areas of culture, education, language, health, social services, and economic development.

(3) Aboriginal nations are entitled to receive, under general laws or agreements with the government, public funds to pursue objectives they consider fundamental.

In 1989 the Social and Cultural Development Committee of the Aboriginal Affairs Secretariat produced a document entitled *Safeguarding and Promoting Aboriginal Languages in Quebec* (Quebec, Social and Cultural Development Committee, Sécretariat des affaires autochtones, 1989), a policy statement that recognized that "the federal and Quebec governments certainly share responsibility for the deterioration and limited use of [Aboriginal languages], since they have failed to provide all the support required to ensure their preservation," and it concluded that "steps absolutely must be taken immediately to protect the cultural and linguistic heritage of Quebec's Aboriginal nations that seek government help."

The document put forward the following guiding principles, in addition to those passed by the National Assembly:

(1) Aboriginal nations are primarily responsible for safeguarding and developing their languages.

(2) The government recognizes that it must support those who wish to learn an Aboriginal language.

(3) The government recognizes the equality of Aboriginal languages by deeming them worthy of support and preservation, with priority given to those that are still extant.

It went on to identify many possible objects of support, including communications programs (community radio, newspapers, videos, etc.); efforts to standardize vocabulary and spelling; the development of pedagogical tools (programs, guides, teaching materials); authors, interpreters, translators, writers and teachers of Aboriginal languages; the collection, recording, and dissemination of oral history and legends; and a variety of educational and political measures (Quebec, Social and Cultural Development Committee, Sécretariat des affaires autochtones, 1989). Some of these ideas were taken up in a subsequent collection of studies on the present status and future prospects of Aboriginal languages in Quebec (Maurais 1992).

However, in our research for the Royal Commission on Aboriginal Peoples (RCAP) we were told by the president of the Avataq Cultural Centre (Montreal/Inukjuak) that "contrary to the endless statements of both levels of government expressing concern and regrets for the state of Aboriginal languages, there is no program in place which can effectively claim to be resolving the problem" (Mary Palliser, president of Avataq Cultural Centre, Personal communication by letter, 17 June 1993).

Indirect confirmation was provided by a letter from the director of communications and public relations for the Secrétariat des affaires autochtones (Roger Richard, personal communication by letter, 28 May 1993), which estimated Quebec government expenditure on Aboriginal languages at $135,000 per year. This works out to approximately two dollars per person for the 65,000 Quebec residents who declared themselves to be of Aboriginal ancestry in the 1991 census. As noted in the following section, Quebec is also one of the few provinces not offering a general Aboriginal languages curriculum in its public schools.

Territorial Policy
The Yukon and Northwest Territories (NT) provide the only examples in Canada of sustained attempts to develop an effective political and legislative framework for Aboriginal languages (Fettes 1998). Only a brief review of these complex programs is possible here.

The NT is presently the only jurisdiction to have legislated official status for Aboriginal languages. The first Official Languages Act was passed in 1984 in response to federal pressure to bring the Territories in line with the language provisions of the Constitution Act, 1982. It declared Chipewyan, Cree, Dogrib, Gwich'in, North Slavey (Hare), South Slavey, and Inuktitut to be "official Aboriginal languages," and it empowered the NT government to extend its services in these languages. At the same time, a government task force on Aboriginal languages was established to consult with Aboriginal communities and make recommendations.

The *Report of the Task Force* (NT 1986) identified a wide range of measures to be undertaken or supported by the government, including amendments to the law, the appointment of language commissioners and a minister of Aboriginal languages and culture, the standardization of the Dene writing systems, the establishment of a genuinely bilingual education system, and greater visibility for Aboriginal languages inside and outside the government (NT 1986). In 1988 the Official Languages Act was revised in accordance with some of these recommendations. It gave all Aboriginal languages equal status with English and French and created a single languages commissioner, modelled on the office of the federal commissioner for official languages.

Other provisions of the act include the right to use any official language in the debates and proceedings of the Legislative Assembly; the possibility of having court proceedings take place in Aboriginal languages, although this right is not guaranteed; the provision, upon request, of sound recordings of legislative debates and important court decisions in Aboriginal languages and the availability of government services in Aboriginal languages where a significant demand exists. Beginning in 1984, a series of Aboriginal languages agreements with the federal government has provided much of the necessary funding for the implementation of these measures, at the level of approximately $3 million a year.

Unfortunately, the impact of these initiatives has not been as positive as might be expected. Reports by the languages commissioner (Harnum 1993, 1994) and an independent evaluator (New Economy Development Group 1994) point to numerous weaknesses in the NT's approach, most of them stemming from the use of federal legal and political frameworks as models for an entirely different situation. In particular, although the need for measures to revitalize and strengthen community languages was recognized by the task force, subsequent government measures have focused almost exclusively on institutional issues (NT 1991). In keeping with this approach, less than 10 percent of the Canada-NT Aboriginal Languages Agreement budget is destined for community language maintenance and revitalization, while over 30 percent is spent on programs related to translation and interpretation (in areas such as health and law) and close to 40 percent on school-based language programs (1992-3 figures).

Closer examination suggests that the relative strength of Inuit language and culture has also served to distract attention from the needs of the smaller Dene languages. Sixty percent of the NT's 35,000 Aboriginal people are Inuit, and at least a quarter of these use Inuktitut in their daily lives. The NT's focus on languages within the school system and on the provision of translation services may be appropriate for a flourishing language (a fair description of the Inuit language of the Eastern Arctic), but it is of limited value for communities with a declining or endangered language (i.e., virtually all of the remaining Inuit and Dene communities). Thus, in the Yukon, where no single Aboriginal language has more than a thousand speakers and fluency rates range from 75 percent among the Kaska to 13 percent among the Southern Tutchone (Cottingham and Tousignant 1991), the language program has focused, from the outset, on the needs of Aboriginal communities rather than, as in the NT, on official language rights.

The Yukon Languages Act, 1988, avoided declaring any languages official, although it provided the guarantees of French language services sought by the federal government. Framed to leave a wide array of policy choices in the hands of the territorial government, it declared that "the Yukon recognizes the significance of aboriginal languages in the Yukon and wishes to take appropriate measures to preserve, develop, and enhance those languages in the Yukon." It guaranteed the right to use "a Yukon aboriginal language in any debates and other proceedings of the Legislative Assembly" and provided that the government "may make regulations in relation to the provision of services in one or more of the aboriginal languages of the Yukon."

Unlike in the NT, however, the languages act in the Yukon has not been central to the program developed and implemented through the Canada-Yukon Language Agreements (1988-93 and 1993-8); rather, a small and innovative government office, Aboriginal Language Services, has pioneered a unique "bottom-up" approach, as summarized in the evaluation report for the first agreement.

The Yukon model for Aboriginal language preservation, development, maintenance, and renewal was based on the fundamental principle that the people are the proper stewards of their languages. The approach to the planning and delivery of programs and services was meant to be supportive and facilitative of Aboriginal people's articulation and implementation of their self-determined objectives, directions, and choice of activities as well as of the provision of effective public services to Aboriginal citizens.

The program model was designed when very little was known about what actually *causes* the revival and maintenance of a language within a community. Although numbers alone are not the most important factor, the Yukon model contained the idea of an unknown "critical mass" of language users and speakers which, once attained, is enough to precipitate the blossoming of language use by more people in more and more situations and to sustain retention of the culture. The intent of the program model was to support sufficient interaction to obtain the critical mass (Gardner 1993, 12).

The first step in the Yukon program was to conduct a field study that "provided a thorough understanding of the state of each of the eight primary Aboriginal languages in the Yukon" (Cottingham and Tousignant 1991). By contrast, a similar assessment appears never to have been conducted in the NT. The contacts and interest generated by the survey were used to involve First Nations in planning an Aboriginal languages conference in April 1991. Five participants from each community were subsidized by Aboriginal Language Services, but communities were encouraged to send as many participants as they could. The proceedings were reported in *Voices of the Talking Circle* (Yukon Aboriginal Language Services 1992) and included the identification of priorities for each language group.

Out of this initial phase came two innovations that have done much to define the Yukon program. One fluent speaker from each of the eight language groups was employed – on the advice of First Nations chiefs, councils, and Elders – as an interpreter/territorial representative. Although this has made administration of the program more difficult, the interpreters constitute a vital link to the communities, a visible presence for the language program, and a developing source of expertise. Then, following the conference, the Community Initiatives Funding Program was launched in order to support the language maintenance and revitalization programs, projects, and activities identified by each First Nation or language group

(Gardner 1993). According to the evaluator, the goal has been "a delicate balance between pro-active hands-on management and responsive tending to an organic model trying to support natural processes" (27). The greatest challenge has been to extract the government from management of the language program, leaving communities equipped with the knowledge and skills required to make it work within the processes of First Nations self-government.

Without reviewing the details of what has been accomplished and what challenges remain in the NT and the Yukon, it is clear that their approaches to Aboriginal language policy have been fundamentally different, and that the Yukon model is much better adapted to Aboriginal realities and priorities in most parts of Canada than is the NT model (Fettes 1998). Legislation is useful only as a means to an end. When it comes to define the ends themselves, it poses immense risks. Aboriginal peoples know only too well the icy constraints of laws formulated within a vastly different culture; the easy assumption of translatability is a false and dangerous one (Henderson 1995). If we turn our efforts instead to providing communities with the support they need to re-establish self-government in all spheres of life, then the ice will slowly melt, and we will see the languages emerge into the vigorous growth of spring.

Summary: Aboriginal Languages in Law and Policy
The legal position of Aboriginal languages in Canada is largely undefined, although Section 35 of the Constitution Act appears to provide the basis for a generous definition of Aboriginal language rights. The exceptions are Quebec, where Aboriginal languages are guaranteed a special role in northern Quebec, and the NT, where they are co-official with French and English. International law provides some support for measures to extend equal protection to all of the languages.

Few public governments have formulated a comprehensive policy on Aboriginal languages. The major exceptions are Quebec, whose progressive policy has not yet been backed up by an effective program; the Yukon, which has undertaken an extensive community-based revitalization program funded through an agreement with the federal government; and the NT, which is committed to implementing the provisions of its Official Languages Act, again with the help of federal funds.

Education Policy
Language policy encompasses many issues outside the education system. Nonetheless, educational issues have long been central to the linguistic concerns of First Nations and other Aboriginal peoples across North America (see Cantoni 1996). Frequently, these are also the only issues

that non-Aboriginal policy makers are prepared to deal with, however inadequately.

For our original paper for the Royal Commission on Aboriginal Peoples (RCAP), we did not have the time or resources to conduct a thorough survey of provincial policies on Aboriginal language education. Here we give a much fuller account, based on a longer and more detailed survey conducted by Mark Fettes in the summer of 1996.

The Federal Fiasco

Aboriginal languages provide a telling measure of the federal government's commitment to reform. More than a generation ago, *Indian Control of Indian Education* clearly set out the consensus reached by First Nations parents and community leaders: that "pre-school and primary school classes should be taught in the language of the community" for four to five years and that "transition to English or French as a second language should be introduced only after the child has a strong grasp of his own language." Furthermore, "in places where it is not feasible to have full instruction in the native language, school authorities should provide formal instruction in the local native language as part of the curriculum and with full academic credit" (National Indian Brotherhood 1973, 14-6). At this time (1973), the Department of Indian Affairs and Northern Development (DIAND) was noting in its annual reports "increasingly strong demands for professional and technical assistance" from over eighty communities involved in language programs.

Yet, as Anastasia Shkilnyk discovered in 1985 when she interviewed DIAND personnel in various regional offices, the initial policy of support for these programs was soon watered down to a fifty-dollar-per-capita grant to band-operated schools, earmarked for "cultural enrichment programs." From the mid-1970s on, DIAND collected no data on how these funds were actually spent or on band-controlled language programs; instead, language policy was left to the discretion of the regional offices, resulting in huge variations (Phillips 1985; Shkilnyk 1986). In most provinces, Shkilnyk found "no cooperation or communication between federal and provincial education departments with respect to the necessary 'infrastructure' for native language retention, such as teacher training, curriculum development, linguistic research, and community advocacy" (Shkilnyk 1986, 22). A DIAND official in Nova Scotia bluntly stated that "language is not a priority in education in this region. Our primary thrust and motivation is to provide a standard of education that is close to established provincial norms" (72). In Ontario, DIAND officials voiced a similar policy: "Although many Indian communities have requested support for native language immersion programs, especially in kindergarten and the first two grades, DIAND is not prepared to support the developmental costs of such programs at this time" (54).

The one remarkable exception reported by Shkilnyk was the Quebec Regional Office of DIAND, which

> began to support community-based activities in Aboriginal language retention as early as 1970. In spite of the lack of interest in (and financial resources for) languages on the part of DIAND's Ottawa headquarters, the regional office nevertheless managed to reallocate general education funds to give priority to language projects. Where funds were insufficient, DIAND-Quebec either entered into informal agreements with the provincial government to share the costs of particular projects or it sought funds from other government departments to supplement the contributions it could make ... In 1984-5, DIAND-Quebec funded language projects in seventeen Indian communities ... In the same year, its total budget for curriculum development in the Aboriginal languages amounted to approximately $1.4 million. (Shkilnyk 1986, 63)

The example of DIAND-Quebec makes it clear what the federal government could have done, had it the will and the foresight. Today many of those same Quebec communities stand out as leaders in the struggle to maintain Aboriginal languages. Meanwhile, with the federal government now intent on devolving many of its constitutional responsibilities to Aboriginal and provincial governments, it is becoming ever less likely that DIAND will adopt or pursue a global proactive policy with respect to languages. Hence it is to the provinces and territories that we now turn.

Provincial and Territorial Education Policies

Since the federal government adopted its integrationist policy in 1946, the provinces and territories have exercised increasing influence over Aboriginal education. Yet it is only within the last ten to fifteen years that structures and policies have been put in place that take the particular needs of Aboriginal education into account (Tanguay 1984; Kirkness and Bowman 1992). However imperfect these measures are, they do suggest that much-needed change is under way. Once again, Aboriginal languages provide a telltale indicator of how deep these changes may go.

From the early 1970s to the early 1980s, various policy declarations and even quite elaborate policy documents on Aboriginal education were issued by provincial ministries of education, but they were generally not followed by substantive action (Shkilnyk 1986). In the mid-1980s, however, a series of public inquiries and governmental reviews across the country revealed continuing Aboriginal failure in schools and prompted a wide range of reforms. As a result, provincial policies can be placed on a

rough spectrum from the uncoordinated to the highly centralized. It must
be pointed out, however, that everywhere a great deal of latitude is left to
school boards and to individual schools and teachers. Some provinces have
established criteria for the mandatory offering of Aboriginal language programs: for instance, Manitoba's school boards are required to offer Aboriginal language programs where twenty-three or more students request it,
while fifteen students constitute a similar threshold in Ontario (Canadian
School Boards Association 1992). Most provi⸍ ᵃs also provide a certain
amount of financial assistance to boards engagᵉ ᵎn developing curricula
and resource materials that meet approved curricᵤ standards. However,
in practice school boards continue to exert a huge iₙ ᵉnce on what programs are offered and under what conditions. It is therᵉ ᵉe not surprising
that one of the best concise overviews of Aboriginal langᵤ ᵉ education in
provincial schools has been provided by the Canadian Schoₒ ᵎoards Association (Canadian School Boards Association 1992).

At one end of the policy spectrum, in Quebec and Newfounᵤ ᵎd, Aboriginal education is still left entirely in the hands of regional or ᵎ ᵎrigi-
nal school boards (Kirkness and Bowman 1992). In practice, this ᵢᵢ ᵎs
that no provision is made for the urban and off-reserve Aboriginal popᵤ
tion and that levels of curriculum development and delivery vary greatᵎ,
from one community or region to another – much the same conditions
that characterized all the provinces twenty years ago. In Newfoundland,
the development of language programs by the Labrador school boards,
and by the Conne River First Nation, is wholly dependent on support
from the federal government (Canadian School Boards Association 1992).
In Quebec, virtually all language initiatives derive from the activities of
the Cree and Kativik School Boards (which operate under the James Bay
Agreement), the Naskapi Education Committee (which operates under the
Northeastern Quebec Agreement), Atikamekw-Sipi, and the Institut culturel et éducatif montagnais (Quebec, Ministère de l'Education, 1995).

The situation in Nova Scotia appears to be evolving to resemble that in
Quebec: a very low but gradually improving level of Aboriginal education
services in the public schools will soon co-exist with the establishment of
a single Mi'kmaq Education Authority for all thirteen First Nations in the
province. How this will affect provincial policy towards the Mi'kmaq language remains to be determined; however, the fact that Mi'kmaq, under
the Education Act, 1996, is recognized as meeting provincial second language requirements is a hopeful sign (Dorothy Moore, personal communication, 1996).

The Yukon has progressed somewhat further down this path, in that the
Education Act (Yukon 1990) not only provides for "the development of
instructional materials for the teaching of aboriginal languages and the
training of aboriginal language teachers," but also empowers the minister

to "authorize an educational program or part of an educational program to be provided in an aboriginal language" in response to a formal request from an education authority or Yukon First Nation. To date, only a limited number of second language courses are taught in Yukon schools; however, negotiations over the establishment of local and central Indian education authorities are progressing under the umbrella final agreement on self-government for all fourteen First Nations in the territory. The final balance between central and local responsibilities in education remains to be decided.

Despite a large Aboriginal population and several pioneering initiatives in Aboriginal language education in Manitoba in the 1970s, the province's Aboriginal education policy has not been clearly defined or energetically developed for a number of years, owing to a succession of institutional upheavals and, more recently, to the planned dismantling of the Department of Indian Affairs in Manitoba. A large number of somewhat dated curricular materials for language instruction are still in circulation, while an accredited Native language instruction program now operates through Brandon University and the University of Manitoba (Paynter and Sanderson 1991). With support from the ministry, the Manitoba Association for Native Languages continues to play an important networking and consultative role.

The fragmented nature of language policy in the NT can be seen in the fact that, for over a decade following the adoption of the first Official Languages Act, Aboriginal children could still be taught entirely in English from the time they entered kindergarten, irrespective of parental or community wishes. The revised Education Act (NT 1995), however, requires instruction in English to be accompanied by instruction in another official language (and vice versa) at all levels of the school system. The act also, in striking contrast to the centralist, rights-based philosophy of the Official Languages Act, delegates important aspects of language policy to the regional and community levels. District education authorities may decide for themselves whether to provide instruction through the medium of a particular Aboriginal language, in consultation with parents, Elders, and community leaders.

In British Columbia, a decentralized language program necessarily follows from the enormous diversity of Aboriginal groups in the province. Indeed, the unit for Aboriginal education in the Ministry of Education is now located in the Field Services Branch, emphasizing its primary goal of building partnerships between school boards and First Nations. Section 104 of the Schools Act, 1989, specifies that school districts can work with band councils to develop language programs, while British Columbia's new Second Language Policy establishes a procedure whereby school districts can submit locally developed language curricula for provincial approval. Since 1989, the Aboriginal policy unit, in consultation with such province-wide bodies as the First Nations Education Secretariat, has worked to persuade districts and bands to sign tuition agreements that set out the terms of cooperation on language programs (among others).

In recent years Saskatchewan has become the lead province in developing a centralized Aboriginal language curriculum for primary and secondary schools. Since 1982, policy development in the province has been driven by the Indian and Métis Education Advisory Committee (IMEAC) and its variously named predecessors (Saskatchewan, Department of Education, 1995), while teachers in both provincial and band-controlled schools are involved in evaluating curricular materials. Coordination is in the hands of the Indian and Métis Education Unit (previously, Indian and Métis Education Branch) of Saskatchewan Education, which has published the programmatic statements *Rationale and Recommendations for the Teaching of Indian Languages in Saskatchewan Schools* (Saskatchewan, Department of Education, 1988) and *Indian Languages: A Curriculum Guide for Kindergarten to Grade 12* (Saskatchewan, Department of Education, 1994). In March 1996, the Ministry of Education committed itself to "design a coordinated plan of action for Indian Languages development in cooperation with First Nation and Métis peoples," along with increased staffing in this area (Saskatchewan, Department of Education, 1996, 8). Despite the impressive level of activity in Saskatchewan, however, it must be said that recent policy documents place little stress either on the unique aspects of Aboriginal languages or on the need for communication and cooperation with Aboriginal communities (Saskatchewan, Department of Education, 1994, 1995). Although it is risky to judge the program on the basis of its written materials, we get the impression that its main thrust is to bring the teaching of Aboriginal languages in line with other "second" languages in the provincial curriculum. Given the limited success of most second language programs, this is not an adequate response to community needs.

These limitations have been more clearly recognized by Ontario, the first province to institute a centralized Aboriginal language curriculum (Ontario, Ministry of Education, 1986, 1987). In its curriculum guide the ministry emphasizes the importance of consulting with First Nations communities, in part "to ensure that the community's expectations do not exceed what the school is able to offer" (Ontario, Ministry of Education, 1987, 5). The stated goals of the program seem to represent a clear-headed assessment of what provincial schools are realistically capable of achieving: that is, a certain degree of language awareness and communicative ability, which in over 95 percent of cases will fall well short of fluency but may suffice to give students and their parents a sense of achievement (Ontario, Ministry of Education, 1986). The province has taken exceptional care to integrate its Native as a Second Language program with the general school curriculum, to the point of accepting it as an alternative to French instruction in the grades where the latter is compulsory (Ontario, Ministry of Education, 1989).

The language program in Alberta strongly resembles that in Ontario. The Language Services Branch of Alberta Education develops curricular frameworks, resource materials, and bibliographies for teaching Native languages in provincial schools. Among the branch's achievements are the provincial guidelines *Aboriginal Language and Culture Programs: A Curricular Framework for ECS-Grade 9* (Alberta, Department of Education, Language Services Branch, 1990) and *Teaching Native Languages in High School: A Teacher Resource Manual* (Alberta, Department of Education, Language Services Branch, 1993) as well as a number of specific curriculum guides and resources for individual languages. A separate branch of the ministry, the Native Education Project, provides funds to local school boards to develop learning resources. The boards, in turn, "cooperate with local Indian bands in the development activities" (Sokolowski and Oishi 1993). The Alberta curriculum statement goes further than either Ontario or Saskatchewan in stressing that "language must be taught *with* the culture, if not *for* the culture" and that "consultation and constant communication with Aboriginal communities is a prerequisite for success" (Alberta, Department of Education, Language Services Branch, 1990). We are unable to say to what extent these principles are observed in practice or whether there are meaningful differences between these provincial programs at the classroom level.

New Brunswick has recently developed a set of policy and curriculum documents for its Micmac and Maliseet Language Programs (New Brunswick, Department of Education, 1993a, 1993b, 1995). Although the guides borrow heavily from those developed for the centralized programs in Alberta, Ontario, and Saskatchewan, they also recommend a number of teaching strategies based on traditional Aboriginal values, including cooperative learning, storytelling, experiential learning, and talking circles, and they emphasize the role of the Micmac and Maliseet Language Committees in further developing the program. The province recently recognized Aboriginal languages as an alternative to French for secondary school language credits, but most school districts have so far refused to offer them as anything other than programs that pull students out of regular classes – a practice that is unpopular with parents and teachers.

Overall, the stated policy goals for Aboriginal language education in provincial schools typically include some or all of the following: social tolerance and understanding; ways of bridging two cultures; ways of valuing linguistic heritage; the acquisition of cultural knowledge; cognitive development through language learning; and language preservation. Not all of these goals are equally realistic. A few hundred hours of instruction in an Aboriginal language constitutes but a small counterweight to many thousands of hours spent on learning through the medium of English or French. Claims made for language preservation are particularly unconvincing: there is virtually no hard evidence to suggest that such instruction can, by itself, promote language revival or even support a community-based revival. Much experience from around the world suggests that, by encouraging symbolic language use by non-speakers, language instruction may indeed have some benefits in terms of social cohesion and self-esteem; but the struggle for language maintenance must be waged on other grounds, as many Aboriginal people are well aware (Fishman 1991; Shkilnyk 1986).

Other goals, too, may require a much more fundamental reorganization of schooling than anything the provinces have contemplated to date. Recent research on "minority" or "multicultural" education has clearly shown that cognitive and social goals can only be achieved by establishing horizontal power relations in the classroom (Cummins 1996). In order to build a "bridge between cultures" much more is required than a view of Aboriginal languages as a kind of cultural wallpaper to make Aboriginal students feel more at home. Strikingly, only the two territories have been willing to address the issue of genuinely bilingual schooling; that is, the willingness to use an Aboriginal language as a medium of instruction in public schools as an equal partner with French or English. Yet this, in our view, is what the voices of winter are calling for, if only people and their governments can learn to listen.

Summary: Aboriginal Languages in Education

Most provinces have taken steps to provide second language instruction in Aboriginal languages within the regular provincial curriculum. The conditions and methods of such instruction generally resemble those of other second languages and are clearly insufficient to achieve oral fluency or language preservation by themselves. Second language programs nonetheless constitute an important form of recognition, particularly where they are accepted as meeting compulsory second language requirements and are backed up by effective teacher training and curriculum development.

No province has expressed a willingness to provide regular instruction through the medium of an Aboriginal language. In public schools, such instruction is common only in the school boards of northern Quebec and the Eastern Arctic (and only for the first few years of schooling). In the absence of strong, balanced bilingual programs, the overall effect of schools on Aboriginal language use and transmission is likely to remain negative.

A Policy Framework for Language Renewal

Based on our research, we wish to offer a brief outline of the policy measures that we believe would best meet the national challenge of language renewal.

First, effective language programs must be developed, implemented, and controlled at the local level. Each self-governing Aboriginal community must establish its own linguistic goals and a strategy that involves all relevant aspects of community life, not only the school. In urban areas, and other areas where self-government is not yet a practical option, programs must be built around institutions under Aboriginal control (such as cultural or friendship centres). Aboriginal language skills, including literacy, would be developed within holistic programs that incorporate Aboriginal values, knowledges, and ways of relating with each other and with the world.

Second, the federal government should enact legislation recognizing the status and significance of Aboriginal languages and defining the linguistic rights guaranteed to Aboriginal people under Section 35 of the Constitution Act. The Aboriginal Languages Act should include provisions in the areas of legal services, communications media, and education, and it should establish the office of an ombudsperson (or commissioner) for Aboriginal languages. Provincial legislation may be required to further define the application of the Aboriginal Languages Act in areas of provincial jurisdiction.

Third, a single federal program for Aboriginal languages should be established within the Department of Canadian Heritage, and piecemeal federal funding of individual projects should be ended in favour of provincial and territorial funding agreements. These would resemble those presently in effect with the governments of the Yukon and NT but would involve broad-based regional Aboriginal language organizations as key partners in program design and implementation. Funding for the entire federal-provincial program should be increased to the level of the territorial agreements – approximately $200 per person per year, excluding teachers' salaries. Negotiation would be needed between the federal and provincial governments with regard to the provision and funding of school-based language programs under the education rights clauses of the Aboriginal Languages Act.

Federal policy on Aboriginal languages should be developed within the context of the framework for self-government and the legislative guarantees established under the Constitution and the Aboriginal Languages Act. The policy must incorporate the principle of community decision making and avoid setting global goals, focusing instead on cost-effective forms of financial and technical support for different program options. Provincial policy should be developed in consultation with provincial language organizations and include stable, multi-year funding within a continuous program of research, curriculum, and resource development, involving workshops and conferences, teacher training, and scholarship programs for students.

A national Aboriginal consultative body should be established to monitor the language program and to encourage private-sector involvement. This body would support national and regional conferences on a regular basis, operate a clearinghouse for materials and information, and oversee a carefully focused research program under Aboriginal control. A priority would be the completion of sociolinguistic surveys in all Aboriginal communities, yielding data on which realistic language programs could be based. Over the longer term, research is needed on language acquisition, transfer of language and literacy skills, and the economic and social aspects of Aboriginal language renewal.

The seasons turn. The bitter cold is losing its grip. It is time to take note of the signs of change: the stubborn shoots of green amidst the white, the returning sounds of life. In heeding the voices of winter, we prepare our spirits for the songs of spring.

Acknowledgments

This chapter is based upon Ruth Norton and Mark Fettes, "Taking Back the Talk: A Specialized Review of Aboriginal Languages and Literacy," Royal Commission on Aboriginal Peoples (Ottawa, 1994).

References

Alberta, Department of Education, Language Services Branch. 1990. *Aboriginal Language and Culture Programs: A Curricular Framework (Early Childhood Services – Grade 9)*. Edmonton: Department of Education.

–. 1993. *Teaching Native Languages in High-School: A Teacher Resource Manual*. Edmonton: Department of Education.

Assembly of First Nations (AFN). 1988. *Tradition and Education: Towards a Vision of Our Future*. Ottawa: Assembly of First Nations/National Indian Brotherhood.

–. 1990. *Towards Linguistic Justice for First Nations*. Ottawa.

–. 1991. *The Challenge. Report of the Aboriginal Languages and Literacy Conference*. Ottawa.

–. 1992. Towards rebirth of First Nations languages. Ottawa.

Avataq Cultural Institute. 1984. *Proceedings of the Inuit Language Commission*. Montreal.

–. 1992. *Avataq Cultural Institute: Its Role in Protecting Nunavik Inuit Culture*. Montreal.

Burnaby, B., and R. Beaujot. 1986. *The Use of Aboriginal Languages in Canada: An Analysis of 1981 Census Data*. Ottawa: Department of Secretary of State. Doc. no. S2-176.

Canada, House of Commons, Standing Committee on Aboriginal Affairs. 1990. *"You Took My Talk": Aboriginal Literacy and Empowerment*. Fourth Report of the Standing Committee on Aboriginal Affairs. Ottawa: Queen's Printer.

–. 1996. *Sharing the Knowledge: The Path to Success and Equal Opportunities in Education*. Ottawa: Queen's Printer.

Canadian School Boards Association. 1992. *CSBAction: A Special Report on Aboriginal Languages Teaching Resources*. Ottawa: Canadian School Boards Association.

Cantoni, G., ed. 1996. *Stabilizing Indigenous Languages*. Flagstaff: Center for Excellence in Education.

Churchill, S. 1986. *The Education of Cultural and Linguistic Minorities in the OECD Countries*. Clevedon: Multilingual Matters.

Cottingham, B.E., and J.P. Tousignant. 1991. *A Profile of Aboriginal Languages in the Yukon*. Whitehorse: Aboriginal Language Services.

Crawford, J. 1996. "Seven Hypotheses on Language Loss: Causes and Cures." In *Stabilizing Indigenous Languages*, ed. G. Cantoni, 51-68. Flagstaff: Center for Excellence in Education.

Cummins, J. 1996. *Negotiating Identities: Education for Empowerment in a Diverse Society.* Ontario, CA: California Association for Bilingual Education.

De Varennes, F. 1994. L'article 35 de la loi constitutionelle de 1982 et la protection des droits linguistiques des peuples autochtones. *Revue nationale de droit constitutionel* 4 (3): 65-303.

Drapeau, Lynn. 1997. "Perspectives on Aboriginal Language Conservation and Revitalization in Canada." In *For Seven Generations: An Information Legacy of the Royal Commission on Aboriginal Peoples.* CD-ROM. Ottawa: Libraxus.

Dunn, M., ed. 1989. *Language Retention Project Report.* Ottawa: Native Council of Canada.

Fettes, M. 1992. *A Guide to Language Strategies for First Nations Communities.* Ottawa: Assembly of First Nations.

–. 1998. "Life on the Edge: Canada's Aboriginal Languages under Official Bilingualism." In *Language and Politics in the United States and Canada: Myths and Realities*, ed. T. Ricento and B. Burnaby, 117-49. Mahwah, NJ: Erlbaum.

Fishman, J.A. 1997. *In Praise of the Beloved Language: A Comparative View of Positive Ethnolinguistic Consciousness.* Berlin: Mouton de Gruyter.

–. 1991. *Reversing Language Shift: Theoretical and Empirical Foundations of Assistance to Threatened Languages.* Clevedon: Multilingual Matters.

–. 1996. "Maintaining Languages: What Works? What Doesn't?" In *Stabilizing Indigenous Languages*, ed. G. Cantoni, 186-98. Flagstaff: Center for Excellence in Education.

Fredeen, S. 1991. *Sociolinguistic Survey of Indigenous Languages in Saskatchewan: On the Critical List.* Saskatoon: Saskatchewan Indigenous Languages Committee.

Gardner, L. 1993. *Walking the Talk. Implementation Evaluation of the Canada-Yukon Funding Agreement on the Development and Enhancement of Aboriginal Languages, 1988/89-1992/93.* Whitehorse: Aboriginal Language Services.

Harnum, B. 1993. *Eight Official Languages: Meeting the Challenge.* First Annual Report of the Languages Commissioner of the Northwest Territories. Yellowknife: Government of the Northwest Territories.

–. 1994. *Together, We Can Do It!* Second Annual Report of the Languages Commissioner of the Northwest Territories. Yellowknife: Government of the Northwest Territories.

Henderson, S. 1995. "Governing the Implicate Order: Self-development and the Linguistic Development of Aboriginal Communities." In *Les droits linguistiques au Canada: collusions ou collisions? / Linguistic Rights in Canada: Collusions or Collisions?* ed. S. Léger, 285-316. Ottawa: Canadian Centre for Linguistic Rights, University of Ottawa.

Jamieson, M.E. 1988a. *National Aboriginal Language Policy Study.* Ottawa: Assembly of First Nations.

–. 1988b. *The Aboriginal Language Policy Study.* Phase 2: *Implementation Mechanism.* Ottawa: Assembly of First Nations.

Kativik School Board. 1990a. "Mother Tongue Literacy: Inuttitut Language." Paper delivered to the Circumpolar Conference on Literacy.

–. 1990b. "Adult Education Inuttitut Literacy Program." Paper delivered to the Circumpolar Conference on Literacy.

Kirkness, V.J. 1989. "Aboriginal Languages in Canada: From Confusion to Certainty." *Journal of Indigenous Studies* 1 (2): 97-103.

Kirkness, V.J., and S.S. Bowman. 1992. *First Nations and Schools: Triumphs and Struggles.* Toronto: Canadian Education Association.

Maffi, L., T. Skutnabb-Kangas, and J. Andrianarivo. In Press. "Linguistic Diversity." In *Cultural and Spiritual Values of Biodiversity*, ed. D. Posey. Intermediate Technologies/Leiden University/United Nations Environment Programme.

Maurais, J., ed. 1992. *Les langues autochtones du Québec.* Dossiers de la Commission pour la langue française, 35. Québec: Publications du Québec.

Morse, B. 1989. "Aboriginal Language Rights." Appendix 8 in M. Dunn, *Language Retention Project Report.* Ottawa: Native Council of Canada.

Nahanee, T.A. 1991. *Aboriginal Language Rights in Canada.* Ottawa: Assembly of First Nations.

–. 1995. "Indian Challenges: Asserting the Human and Aboriginal Right to Language. In

Les droits linguistiques au Canada: collusions ou collisions? / Linguistic Rights in Canada: Collusions or Collisions? ed. S. Léger, 471-517. Ottawa: Canadian Centre for Linguistic Rights, University of Ottawa.

National Association of Cultural Education Centres. 1991. "Aboriginal Cultural Institutions Policy: Discussion Paper." Ottawa.

National Association of Friendship Centres (NAFC). 1990. *National Literacy Survey.* Ottawa.

National Indian Brotherhood. 1973. *Indian Control of Indian Education.* Ottawa: National Indian Brotherhood.

New Brunswick, Department of Education. 1993a. *Maliseet Language Program.* Fredericton: New Brunswick Department of Education.

–.1993b. *Micmac Language Program.* Fredericton: New Brunswick Department of Education.

–. 1995. *Curriculum Guidelines for Maliseet Language Courses.* Fredericton: New Brunswick Department of Education.

New Economy Development Group. 1994. *Evaluation of the Canada-NWT Cooperation Agreement for French and Aboriginal Languages in the NWT.* Final Report. Yellowknife: Government of the Northwest Territories.

Northwest Territories (NT). 1986. *The Report of the Task Force on Aboriginal Languages.* Yellowknife: Government of the Northwest Territories.

–. 1991. *Bringing Our Languages Home: Aboriginal Languages Conference.* Yellowknife: Government of the Northwest Territories.

–. 1995. Education Act.

Norton, R., and M. Fettes. 1997. "Talking Back the Talk: A Specialized Review of Aboriginal Languages and Literacy." In *For Seven Generations: An Information Legacy of the Royal Commission on Aboriginal Peoples.* CD-ROM. Ottawa: Libraxus.

Ojibway Cultural Foundation/Assembly of First Nations. 1993. *Wisdom and Vision: The Teachings of Our Elders.* Report of the National First Nations Elders Language Gathering, Manitoulin Island, 21-5 June 1993. West Bay/Ottawa.

Ontario, Ministry of Education. 1986. *Ontario's NSL Program: Teaching and Learning a Native Language as a Second Language.* Toronto: Ontario Ministry of Education.

–. 1987. *Native Languages.* Part A: *Policy and Program Considerations, Curriculum Guideline – Primary, Junior, Intermediate, and Senior Divisions.* Toronto: Ontario Ministry of Education.

–. 1989. *Policy/Program Memorandum No. 110: Interrelationship of Native-as-a-Second-Language (NSL) and French-as-a-Second-Language (FSL) Programs.* Toronto: Ontario Ministry of Education.

Paynter, F., and E. Sanderson. 1991. "A Regional Training Program for Native Language Teachers." Presentation at the Native American Language Institute Issues Conference, 22-5 September 1991. Winnipeg: Manitoba Education and Training.

Phillips, S. 1985. *Aboriginal Languages in Canada: A Research Report.* Ottawa: Department of Secretary of State.

Québec, Social and Cultural Development Committee, Sécretariat des affaires autochtones. 1989. *Safeguarding and Promoting Aboriginal Languages in Quebec.* Quebec: Sécretariat des affaires autochtones.

Québec, Ministère de l'Education. 1995. "L'éducation et les autochtones au Québec: Un portrait des nations autochtones." Document de travail, 1995-05-19.

Richstone, J. 1989. "La protection juridique des langues autochtones au Canada." In *Langue et droit: Actes du premier congrès de L'Institut International de Droit Linguistique Comparé / Language and Law: Proceedings of the First Conference of the International Institute of Comparative Linguistic Law,* ed. P. Pupier and J. Woehrling, 259-78. Montreal: Wilson and Lafleur.

Saskatchewan, Department of Education. 1988. *Rationale and Recommendations for the Teaching of Indian Languages in Saskatchewan Schools.* Regina: Saskatchewan Department of Education.

–. 1994. *Indian Languages: A Curriculum Guide for Kindergarten to Grade 12.* Regina: Saskatchewan Department of Education.

–. 1995. *Indian and Métis Education Policy from Kindergarten to Grade 12.* Regina: Saskatchewan Department of Education.

–. 1996. *Minister's Response to the Report of the Indian and Métis Education Advisory Committee: Indian and Métis Education Action Plan.* Regina: Saskatchewan Department of Education.

Shkilnyk, A.M. 1986. *Canada's Aboriginal Languages: An Overview of Current Activities in Language Retention.* Ottawa: Department of Secretary of State.

Skutnabb-Kangas, Tove, and Robert Phillipson, eds. 1994. *Linguistic Human Rights.* Berlin: Mouton de Gruyter.

Slattery, B. 1991. "Aboriginal Language Rights." In *Language and the State: The Law and Politics of Identity / Langue et état: Droit, politique et identité,* ed. D. Schneiderman, 369-74. Cowansville: Yvon Blais.

Sokolowski, J., and M. Oishi. 1993. "Native Language and Culture Programs in Alberta Provincial Schools: A Brief Overview. *Alberta Modern Language Journal* 30 (2): 3-14.

Stacey-Diabo, C.K. 1990. "Aboriginal Language Rights in the 1990s." In *Human Rights in Canada: Into the 1990s and Beyond,* ed. R.I. Cholewinski, 139-64. Ottawa: Human Rights Research and Education Centre, University of Ottawa.

Tanguay, S. 1984. *Recent Developments in Native Education.* Toronto: Canadian Education Association.

Taylor, D.M. 1990. *Carving a New Inuit Identity: The Role of Language in the Education of Inuit Children in Arctic Quebec.* Montreal: Kativik School Board.

United Nations Human Rights Committee. 1994. "General Comment No. 23 (50) on Article 27 / Minority Rights. Doc.CCPR/C/21/Rev.1/Add.5." *Human Rights Law Journal* 15 (4-6): 234-6.

Yukon Aboriginal Language Services. 1992. *Voices of the Talking Circle.* Whitehorse: Yukon Territorial Government.

Yukon. 1990. Education Act.

3
The State of Aboriginal Literacy and Language Education

Yvonne Hébert

In order to function in the symbolic worlds in which we live, worlds in which knowledge and skills are cultural creations, we must be proficient in the use of the symbol systems – written and spoken language, mathematics, signs, gestures – that are valued by our particular society. The forms that represent our worlds to ourselves and to each other shape our perception of those worlds. Looking at literacy as the ability to use symbolic systems that are culturally valued enables us to make a distinction between the ability to read and write and the ability to gain access to cultural resources, understandings, and underlying assumptions that constitute social reality in a literate world (see Illich 1987; Smith 1991; Chambers and Walker 1991). Adopting this dynamic conception of literacy permits us to recognize the importance of education and, especially, of literacy and language education. One of the main goals of education, then, is to transmit and provide access to symbolic knowledge; and language is the primary vehicle through which this occurs. For Aboriginal peoples, this involves (1) making sure that youths are functioning and contributing members of societal collectives and (2) maintaining particular culturally constructed knowledge systems.

Given the symbolic importance of the knowledge systems that permeate educational content and processes, Aboriginal language and literacy programs are essential to the development of future citizens of Aboriginal nations and of the Canadian state. We need future citizens who are secure in their being, their languages, and their cultures; citizens who are able to participate in the (re)construction of society; citizens who not only exercise their rights but also their responsibilities and duties while participating actively in society. If Aboriginal schools and programs are to attain this goal, then we must reflect on the very nature of literacy curricula as well as on administrative and pedagogical practices and their contribution to self-identity and group-identity formation among Aboriginal youths (see Hampton 1995).

This chapter analyzes a collection of Aboriginal first and second language curriculum materials for reserve-based language and literacy programs. Curricular data are drawn from a recently completed study of materials used in reserve-based Aboriginal language education and literacy efforts for the Royal Commission on Aboriginal Peoples (RCAP) (Hébert 1997). Sixty-nine exemplars of curriculum materials dealing with Aboriginal literacy and language education are analyzed in order to identify curricular and pedagogical issues in Aboriginal language and literacy education. Reviewing the information base of the larger study, I elucidate curriculum and teaching models in general, being especially attentive to philosophical orientations, goals, learner needs, and other fundamental elements. Further developing my analytic framework, I draw upon pedagogical models for language and literacy education, reviewing the shift from structuralist behaviourist methods to more recent experiential process approaches. Then I apply this philosophical, curricular, and pedagogical framework to the analysis of the Aboriginal curriculum documents, looking particularly at examples of statements of philosophy, goals, and objectives, in order to reveal patterns and tendencies.

Flowing from the analysis, my discussion deals with three important issues in terms of past and future needs: the isolation of curriculum and literacy workers; the strong influence of linguistics and language theories; and the struggle for curriculum as evidenced in the divergence between philosophical statements, curricular goals, specific objectives, and methods. I then highlight the need for innovation in each of these areas.

Information Base

For the purposes of this research, I have attempted to collect, consult, and analyze curriculum documents pertaining to Aboriginal languages and literacy. These include programs of studies, background reference materials (such as dictionaries and collections of stories), teachers' unit and lesson plans, and students' activity books and folders as well as other possible formats. These were requested from band-operated schools with Aboriginal language programs, and then they were supplemented with similar documents available from library searches and from personal collections.

As research technique, a documentary analysis is limited by the number and type of curricular documents that exist, are available, and/or can be collected. In this case, most of the curricular documents received and collected deal more with Indian on-reserve language and literacy concerns and less with Inuit, Métis, non-status, and off-reserve situations. This may be revealing of the non-existence and/or unavailability of curricular documents as well as of shortcomings of the data collection process. The literature review is similarly limited by the existence, availability, and ease of accessibility of written analyses of the situations under study. The broad literature review includes North American and international sources that provide assistance in elucidating, analyzing, and contextualizing the perspectives offered herein.

My previous experience with qualitative and quantitative research in the field of Aboriginal languages and literacy education also provides a basis for interpretation. This experience is situated within a process-oriented approach to knowledge building – one that seeks to promote thinking through problem solving as well as to enhance self-awareness, understanding of self, and respect for others.

Data Collection

Locating and collecting relevant curricular documents was more difficult than would first appear. There is no centralized registry of Aboriginal language programs or even of band-operated schools. The RCAP staff, as well as the regional offices of the federal Department of Indian and Northern Development (DIAND), were instrumental in compiling a list of Aboriginal language programs and band-operated schools that were likely to offer such programs. I then mailed out a total of 395 letters of request for curriculum documents.

Sixteen replies were received. Of these, two groups declined to participate, and five regretted that they had no Aboriginal language materials to send. Nine replies included the happy provision of materials, in some cases of considerably detailed materials, offering a wide range of possible curricular documents. Of these nine, one set of materials focuses on Native cultural content at the primary level (kindergarten through Grade 3) and does not specifically target Aboriginal literacy and language education. The other eight replies deal explicitly with Aboriginal literacy and language education. To these have been added curricular documents obtained from library searches or personal collections. Taken altogether, seventy-three curricular documents were provided and/or collected; of these, sixty-nine discrete curricular documents pertaining to Aboriginal literacy and language education are included in my review of educational materials. Without seeking to be exhaustive, I also examined program descriptions available from other sources (e.g., published research accounts and evaluation reports), as these also tend to be revealing.

In some ways, the response may seem minimal. Yet it should be taken into consideration that I cannot ascertain exactly how many Aboriginal literacy campaigns and/or language education programs exist in Canada. Given the variability in personnel and procedures involved, the comprehensiveness of the list of DIAND-funded programs cannot be ascertained, nor can it be taken for granted that letters of request mailed out actually reached the Aboriginal language instructors in all situations. Aboriginal language programs operating in provincial school districts were not included in this search, nor were Inuit, Métis, non-status, and off-reserve programs and situations. Nevertheless, the scope and quality of materials identified are sufficient to make useful inferences.

The documents collected are categorized according to intended audience and whether the language taught was the learners' mother tongue (L1) or second language (L2), with the latter being the most frequent situation for Aboriginal students. Support and reference documents that may be of use to language teachers and literacy workers form another curricular category. The level of detail varies from document to document, depending on whether they are course outlines, program guides, teachers' manuals, unit plans or modules, lesson or activity plans, teachers' plans, readers, story books, dictionaries, resource guides, or catalogues.

Data Significance

The correspondence received from those who provided exemplars is characterized by considerable pride in the materials developed. A preliminary review of these curricula reveal that, in nearly all cases, a key person is involved in their production. This person is often an instructor, sometimes a program coordinator or other administrator. It is also obvious that tremendous efforts have been expended in the production of literacy materials and that those for whom Aboriginal languages and literacy efforts assume major significance have shown great dedication and harbour great expectations. The correspondence received from those without materials to send is characterized by a sincere, poignant regret, with some correspondents also expressing a wish for assistance.

The difficulty in obtaining a broad sampling of Aboriginal curriculum materials underscores the nature of these educational endeavours. They are, for the most part, local or regional; this is as it should be, as it ensures that the voices represented are those of the collective tribal or band group concerned (Fyle 1990). This also means, however, that the curriculum materials have limited range, participation, production, and distribution. While a good number of units and readers enjoy some form of publication, key curricular documents such as teachers' lessons and unit plans typically do not circulate at all (except among a few trusted teachers).

Generally, teachers, including Aboriginal language teachers and literacy workers, benefit from examining each other's materials and exchanging teaching stories and techniques. When learning new teaching approaches and skills, coaching from other teachers is usually invaluable (Joyce and Weil 1986). Yet Aboriginal language teachers and literacy workers are often isolated, working alone, trying to respond to their students, the parents, the administrators, other educators, and the community as a whole. They come together only rarely, for workshops, courses, or conferences.

Recognizing the difficulties involved in collecting Aboriginal language and literacy curricula, which are of limited distribution and sometimes of an underground nature, I thank the RCAP staff who facilitated my work as well as the many Aboriginal schools and bands who generously provided curriculum materials.

Establishing an Analytic Framework

A curriculum typically contains a list of items of some sort that students are expected to "know," and it offers some form of advice to teachers on the appropriate means of "transmission." More specifically, a language or literacy curriculum makes general statements about content, language learning, learning purpose, experience, evaluation, and the roles and interactions of teachers and learners (Candlin 1984). A curriculum involves not only statements of philosophy, goals, and objectives, but also includes the results of decisions made regarding the identification of learners' needs and purposes, the selection and gradation of content, the organization of appropriate learning arrangements and learner groupings; and the selection, adaptation, and/or development of appropriate materials, learning tasks, and evaluation tasks (Nunan 1988). Curriculum, then, is concerned with meaning making and with knowledge building in both a very specific and a very broad sense.

Four families of alternative models of teaching are available to orient classroom activities and may occur singly or in combination (Joyce and Weil 1986). The *information-processing* family of teaching models considers concepts to be tools for organizing information and approaching problems. These models are designed to teach concepts and to help students become more efficient with regard to learning and creating them. The *personal* family of teaching models considers all learning to be ultimately focused on the education of the individual. It is expressed in the enhancement of the self through the shaping of individuals and groups that support one another's struggles to achieve self-responsibility and self-determination. The *social* family of teaching models considers people to be social creatures and holds that any group of human beings is greater than the sum of its parts. Within this model, students are confronted with problems that they must solve together, thus leading them to analyze their values and the public policies that shape justice and encouraging them to increase their social skills and understanding. The *behavioural systems* family of teaching models takes advantage of the human being's capacity to learn and modify behaviour by responding to tasks and feedback. Such models are used to teach information, concepts, and skills; to increase comfort and decrease phobias; to change habits; and to help students undertake academic and social tasks.

Language teaching models may look at language synthetically; that is, as small discrete elements to be taught and mastered step by step so that acquisition consists of a gradual accumulation of parts until the whole structure of language is built up. Other approaches may look at language analytically; that is, as chunks of language organized in terms of the purposes for which people are learning language and the kinds of language performances that are necessary to meet those purposes (Wilkins 1976). Yet other models may look at language experientially *and* globally, in a non-analytic and non-synthetic way, assuming that children learn a language by being surrounded by it, as in the "whole language" movement of first language education or as in the "communicative" approaches of second language education. In the latter case, curricula are planned according to situations, tasks, problems, concepts, or, more recently, "fields of experience" within five domains of daily life dealing with physical, social, civic, leisure, and intellectual dimensions (Tremblay et al. 1990).

A distinction may also be made between product-oriented curricula and process-oriented curricula. Analytic and synthetic types of curricula are product-oriented, since they focus on forms and on functions of language. They typically include a plan of language knowledge and capabilities to be acquired, such as the four skills of reading, writing, speaking, and listening. An alternative process-oriented approach has four organizing principles: focus, selection, subdivision, and sequencing (Nunan 1988), which view language knowledge as a cluster or complex of competencies that focus on how something is to be done and that include negotiation and creativity along with rules and conventions. Important within this approach are the learner's own experiences and awareness of learning; thus, the curriculum includes communicative tasks, learning tasks, and meta-communciative tasks in order to develop the learner's awareness. Such an approach views the learner's capacities as including the interpretation and expression of meaning.

Language teaching may also vary according to one or more methods or approaches. These vary from the structuralist, grammatical method, in vogue from the 1940s through the 1960s; to the cognitive method, which reacted to the behaviourist foundations of the structuralist method by moving from focusing on language behaviours to building and linking language concepts to one another; to contemporary communicative and multidimensional approaches to language teaching (see Kramsch 1984). A more complex and intricate curriculum model, the latter approach encompasses four syllabi; that is, communicative/experiential, culture, general language education, and language components (see the documents of the national study by R. Leblanc 1990; Tremblay et al. 1990; C. Leblanc et al. 1990; Painchaud 1990; Hébert 1990; Harley et al. 1990). These current approaches to language teaching move away from the assumption that a single method, strictly and rigidly followed, is a suitable curricular model for all teaching and learning situations (see Stern 1983a; Desmarais and Duplantie 1986; Savignon and Berns 1984). While the terms used above refer to second language teaching, first language teaching has also moved from rigidly defined structuralist methods of teaching reading and writing (which focused on discrete elements) towards more global approaches to teaching what are now said to be the language arts, typified by the whole language movement (see Brozo and Simpson 1991; Noyce and Christie 1989; Robinson et al. 1996; and Lundsteen 1989). Once the sole focus of literacy programs, grammar and skills development are now considered to be one part of language learning, which focuses explicitly upon more expressive, interactive uses of language.

Today, language teaching, especially for first languages, includes expressive writing; children's and adolescent literature; language across the curriculum; metalinguistic awareness and learning strategies; schemata theory; reader response theory; early literacy concerns; and, to a lesser extent, ESL/FSL in the mother-tongue classroom (see Cox and Boyd-Batstone 1997; Noyce and Christie 1989; Robinson et al. 1996; and Lundsteen 1989). At the secondary level, language teaching incorporates functional uses of literacy, literatures of other cultural groups, and the integration of language and social studies into a humanities approach (see Brozo and Simpson 1991). Given the broad range of pedagogical approaches now available, a mix of teaching techniques and strategies, rather than strict adherence to one method, is deemed best, as this takes into account the complexities of both learners and language.

Curricular Analysis of Goals and Objectives
Within statements of philosophy, we typically find belief statements concerning the nature of language learning and teaching, as well as the overall orientation to pedagogical process and to curricular content. We may also find statements concerning the nature of the target community and of collective identity. In the case of Aboriginal literacy, these would likely be statements about the nature of Aboriginal communities and identity formation among Aboriginal youth.

The purposes for language learning are usually presented in statements of goals and objectives, the former being more broadly stated than the latter. Sometimes such statements are closely followed by scope and sequence charts that reveal, in a grid-like fashion, how goals and objectives are linked to program structure and organizing elements as well as to such phenomena as activities, learning styles, and learner strategies.

Searching for Philosophical Statements
In searching for broad statements of educational philosophy (i.e., the

nature of language learning/teaching and an overall orientation to peda-gogical process and curricular content), I found that Aboriginal-as-a-second-language materials tend not to provide such statements whereas some mother-tongue materials do. Some examples may suffice to illustrate this pattern. The Cree L1 curriculum materials developed for use at St. Andrew's School in Kashechewan, Ontario, provide the following overall mission statement for the entire school – a statement that combines a view of education as situated within the academic, personal, and social domains: "Education at St. Andrew's School should give our children the knowledge, attitudes and skills to develop a sense of self-worth, confi-dence and pride as Native people; to develop a respect for others and the environment; to participate fully in community life; and to participate actively in Canadian society" (Goodwin 1991-2, 3).

A philosophical statement concerning language learning/teaching is provided in the same curriculum materials under the rubric "Cree Language Rationale": "Language and culture are intimately related. Lan-guage is the primary means through which culture is transmitted from one generation to the next. Positive attitudes towards Cree beliefs, tradi-tions and contemporary perceptions serve to develop self-esteem, self-confidence and pride in the Cree individual and in the Kashechewan First Nation. The continuing use of the Cree language – speaking, listening, reading and writing – fosters an increase in the knowledge and enjoyment of the Cree cultural heritage, which in turn leads to a greater awareness of the Cree person's and community's role in Canadian society" (Good-win 1991-2, 10). This rationale reflects the view that education should deal with the personal and social domains; the academic domain encom-passes the skills-based technical, information-processing view of language learning.

The Cree L1 program of the Wasaho First Nation High School of Fort Severn, Ontario, as seen in the Grade 9 materials, situates language learn-ing mostly within the personal and sociocultural domains, with a slight reference to literacy skills such as reading and writing: "The course will provide the students with the necessary tools to recognize their identity and the deep rich values of life, mainly by enhancing and preserving their native language. The course will enable the students to see the importance of speaking and writing their language with dignity and pride. They will be able to speak fluently and allow this language to reflect their identity and their culture" (Thomas 1993-4, 2).

Other philosophical statements dealing with Aboriginal language and literacy may be found in the testimonial literature in, for example, the Declaration on Aboriginal Languages and citations of Elders' concerns. The latter are widely circulated on the poster distributed by the Assembly of First Nations (AFN), *Nation Building through Aboriginal Languages and Literacy* (AFN 1993), which was developed as a result of the study *Towards Linguistic Justice for First Nations* (AFN 1990). Elders speak poignantly of the sociocultural and spiritual importance of their languages:

> Our native language embodies a value system about how we ought to live and relate to each other ... It gives a name to relations among kin, to roles and responsibilities among family members, to ties with the broader clan group. There are no English words for these relationships ... Now, if you destroy our languages, you not only break down these relationships, but you also destroy other aspects of our Indian way of life and culture, especially those that describe man's connection with nature, the Great Spirit, and the order of things. Without our languages, we will cease to exist as a separate people (Taylor in AFN 1993).

These views also find support in the philosophical and political statement *Indian Control of Indian Education* (National Indian Brotherhood 1972), in the National Indian Education Review's summary report on preliminary findings (Faries 1995), in other policy and political documents (see Shkilnyk 1985), in descriptions of Aboriginal language programs in British Columbia written by language instructors (Hébert 1984a), and in the research literature on Aboriginal languages (see Battiste 1993, 1987, and 1986). According to these documents, Aboriginal language education has collective, social, personal, and academic importance; languages are seen as having a dynamic, communicative, cognitive force that shapes knowledge, worldview, beliefs, and values; language use is seen as a form of self-government; and Indian language and culture are considered to be the source of pride in oneself and the foundation for self-identity – an essential element in a meaningful education that prepares students to assume social responsibility and to maintain cultural continuity.

While philosophical statements of views of education, of the nature of language learning and teaching, of pedagogy and curriculum, are not common in Aboriginal curriculum documents themselves, there is nonetheless a general consensus among Aboriginal Elders, teachers, and scholars that Aboriginal language and literacy education is situated within sociocultural and personal domains and, to a lesser extent, within the academic domain (be these for mother-tongue education [L1] or second language [L2] education). Rationales are articulated most strongly within the social domain. A tension may be noted with respect to the academic domain: when it is included, it is usually spoken of in broad social terms with regard to educational success; less frequently, it is discussed in terms of techno-linguistic skills.

Searching for Statements of Goals and Objectives in the L1 Materials
Statements of goals and objectives are plentiful in the data and, in some
cases, are explicit, specific, and copious. The Cree L1 Kashechewan materials developed at St. Andrew's School (Ontario) provide twenty goals to
help "our children to achieve their potential in intellectual, emotional,
cultural, spiritual, social and physical development." Here I extract and
present, in numbered sequence, those goal statements that focus on language and culture: "(1) Read, write, speak and listen effectively and accurately in English and Cree ... (7) Discover and appreciate their own Native
culture and the other Native cultures including the prominent social
groups in their community and in Canada" (Goodwin 1991-2, 5).

In a twenty-five-page section following these goal statements and a
statement of rationale (cited in the previous section), these statements
are specified and organized in tables of objectives and sample activities
according to the four skills: listening, speaking, reading, and writing.
Another objective deals with language awareness. It is assumed, in these
materials, that listening skills precede speaking skills, that oral abilities
(which include speaking and oral reading) precede writing, and that the
four skills are used in the development of language awareness (here taken
to be the appreciation of linguistic structures and stylistic elements of oral
and written literature). Figure 1 lists general objectives.

In analyzing these goals and objectives, I note that the school goals
encompass three of the four educational domains; that is, personal, social,
and the academic as information-processing rather than as behaviour-
modification. The language aims and objectives, however, focus mostly
upon the academic as syncretic linguistic skills based on the order of
language acquisition. Such a focus is permeated by the structuralist-
behaviourist model of language learning and teaching.

The other L1 materials examined present similar patterns. The Montagnais Betsiamites materials cover both elementary and secondary levels.
While the global objectives focus on meeting the pedagogical needs of students with quality materials, the general objectives are organized around
oral, reading, and writing skills, including grammatical and functional
approaches to the study of language. Terminal and specific objectives deal
with enlarging the student's verbal and written repertoire by reading and
listening to short texts; recognizing words and writing letters, syllables,
and words correctly as well as reproducing them; observing regularities in
word building and sound-grapheme correspondence; reconstructing meanings of oral texts; and using words correctly in the school context. Finally,
the specific objectives include notions and linguistic structure serving as
organizing elements such as animal names, body parts, colours, numbers
up to sixty, parts of the house, seasons, birthdays, clothing, shapes, daily
routines, hunting tools, prefixes, the diminutive suffix, and the first three

Figure 1

Four language skills: Objectives and sample activities

Listening skills
Develop general listening strategies
Appreciate differences in pronunciation and intonation
Understand a variety of speakers in a variety of contexts
Increase the complexity of language awareness

Speaking skills
Develop speaking confidence
Refine pronunciation and intonation
Formulate and express ideas
Speak to a variety of audiences
Increase the complexity of language used

Reading skills
Extend reading strategies
Develop fluency in reading
Read to learn
Read written material of increasing complexity

Writing skills
Develop confidence in writing
Formulate and express ideas
Develop accuracy in writing and a knowledge of literary conventions
Write increasingly complex material

Language skills and the appreciation of oral and written literature
Develop an appreciation of the linguistic structure and stylistic elements of
oral and written literature

Source: Extracted from Goodwin 1991-2, 15-40.

personal prefixes for nouns and verbs. Here, again, we see global, general, terminal, and specific objectives situated within the academic domain, and the marked prevalence of the four skills (listening, reading, speaking, and writing) in well developed and thoroughly articulated curriculum materials.

Searching for Statements of Goals and Objectives in the L2 Materials

The L2 curriculum materials also focus upon the academic domain in their statements of goals and objectives. To illustrate, I cite the brief introduction to the Course Outline for *Cree Language Course Outline*, Grade 5 to Grade 10, from the Peter Ballantyne Nation in Pelican Narrows, Saskatchewan: "Language is the teaching of listening, speaking, reading and writing skills. The following outline is to ensure that Cree language is viewed as a process related to all subject areas rather than an isolated subject. All lessons will be based on a specific theme" (Cluster n.d., 1). This statement equates language knowledge with the four skills, which are usually associated with a product-oriented approach to education; yet here they are associated with a process-oriented approach.

The Oji-Cree L2 materials from the Sineonokway Native School in Kasabonika Lake, Ontario, are teacher-generated lesson plans, whereas the materials reviewed above are unit-based lesson plans. The language objectives are short-term and very specific, with a skills focus. They are meant, for example, "to facilitate listening and comprehension skills, and to encourage vocabulary development related to fall activities," whereas objectives in other subjects have a child focus and are meant "to develop each child's awareness of himself/herself, and encourage him/her to become actively involved in practicing good health and hygiene." Or they have a conceptual focus and are meant "to provide varied opportunities to learn the concept of one-to-one correspondence to numbers 1-5" (Anderson n.d., 1-2).

The older L2 curriculum materials, such as the Yukon Native language materials (1980) and the Algonkian materials (1978-80) do not explicitly provide statements of philosophy, goals, or objectives. The Algonkian materials provide "teaching points" that focus on discrete linguistic forms, such as "where" questions, expressions of distance and direction, locatives, verb structure, and so on. In lieu of objectives, the Yukon materials provide very brief notes to the instructor about sounds, syntax, and vocabulary. Thus, both sets of materials have an exclusively technical, syncretic, skills orientation, as is typical of behaviourist-structuralist approaches to language teaching/learning, wherein the learning of small discrete items is somehow supposed to turn into longer spontaneous oral and written productions.

Thus there is a divergence between philosophical statements, the more comprehensive goals of language programs, and their specific objectives. The philosophical and goals statements tend to focus primarily on personal and sociocultural development, whereas the language aims and objectives tend to be technical in that they are oriented to skills, product, and structure. This is especially marked in the L2 materials and most certainly in the older materials, whereas the more recent materials, especially the L1 materials, provide indications of interactive, problem-solving activities, although the pedagogy involved in integrating these into the classroom is not made explicit.

Important Issues

In order to move towards more effective Aboriginal language and literacy programs, a number of policy issues need to be addressed. These are concerned with the isolation of language and literacy workers; the strong influence of linguistics and language theories; innovation for the future; and divergence between philosophical statements, curricular goals, specific objectives, and methods. A further discussion of the need for future innovation flows from the discussion of important issues and serves as a conclusion to this chapter.

These interrelated issues are central to literacy education in general. How to choose the most appropriate methods and materials, how to determine how these help learners, how to effectively assess what is learned, and how to make the best use of technology are the four key issues at the very heart of the literacy debate today (Robinson et al. 1996, 2-3).

Isolation of Language and Literacy Workers

That many Aboriginal language teachers and literacy workers are working in isolation, with little program support, is evident from the response received to the request for current information, the involvement in curriculum development, and the materials examined. Yet curriculum development, its implementation and evaluation, is a massive undertaking and cannot be done adequately in isolation. Ideally, curriculum developers are part of a team that may include members from both inside and outside the local cultural and educational communities. Moreover, curriculum developers need to be in a position to influence the preparation of the teachers who will be implementing the materials. Thus, Aboriginal language and literacy curriculum developers need to be in touch with each other; with the field of curriculum inquiry, which includes development, implementation, evaluation, and theory building; with the field of literacy and language education; with teacher preparation, both initial and continuing; and with other interested parties.

Moreover, the limited distribution of materials further exacerbates the situation, leading to possible frustration, discouragement, territoriality, and duplication. The underground nature of these curricular documents reveals the marginalized status of Aboriginal language and literacy efforts. It becomes important to legitimize the endeavours of Aboriginal language and literacy workers, communities, and educational infrastructures.

External Influences upon Aboriginal Language and Literacy Education

This isolation also masks a struggle for curriculum, for who determines and creates it, for whom it is destined, and for what social and individual purposes. In general, the competing voices of many stakeholders, be they parents, cultural communities, governments, the press, professional educators, the corporate world, or the general public, make claims on school curriculum. For Aboriginal parents and communities, the issue of voice is

acute, and they are increasingly making claims on curriculum and pedagogy, as this core group of stakeholders has historically had very little to
say about the place and nature of curriculum in the education of Aboriginal youth (see Barman et al. 1986, 1987; Battiste and Barman 1995). In
the past, Native education was largely influenced by external voices of
the state, the educational community, or, as we shall see here, prevailing
theories and approaches.

The strong influence of structuralism upon Aboriginal language and
literacy education leads to another policy issue. Historically, the scientific
study of language came about because of the work of notable early structur-
alists such as Bloomfield, Sapir, and Haas, who insisted that each language
be studied on its own terms. A remarkable advance in Western science,
this nonetheless led to an overdependency on the field of linguistics,
which has exerted considerable influence on the development of writing
systems, dictionary making, curriculum design, and teaching methods.
While this is generally the case in North America for all language education (see Lebrun 1993 for L1; Stern 1983a, 1983b, and 1982 for L2), the
influence of linguists has contributed to the emergence of numerous competing alphabets for previously unwritten languages – alphabets devised
by individual linguists according to their understanding of the languages
in question. Unfortunately, the resulting alphabet wars between loyal fac-
tions of Aboriginal groups brought about divisive tensions which, in turn,
prevented valuable collaboration from occurring between small groups of
literacy workers, thus further isolating them. The recognition that these
literacy processes in Aboriginal communities have occurred in relatively
short time periods helps to put in perspective these difficulties, which
resulted from the pressure to establish documentary bases for Aboriginal
literacy practices.

By comparison, literacy practices in most other languages occurred over
much longer time periods (sometimes several centuries), gradually evolving into shared understandings about written language. Dictionaries have
emerged in European intellectual traditions as authoritative sources on
which to develop language education programs. The prominence of bilingual dictionaries in both the Aboriginal language and one of the official
languages raises questions about who is the audience for these materials
and who is the source of the language. Bilingual dictionaries are typically
for non-speakers of one of the languages and/or for people who want to
compare the languages at issue. Even when the layering of different contexts is considered (e.g., the insertion of the European-derived notion of
"school" into oral societies), the production of such dictionaries seems to
be at odds with recognizing Elders as the authoritative sources of Aboriginal languages.

Aboriginal language and literacy efforts frequently involve a linguist, usually a structuralist, who exerts tremendous personal and disciplinary influence on the end product. Combined with behaviourist psychology, this structuralist influence also permeated the curricular and pedagogical dimensions of Aboriginal education, leading to a focus not only on grammar and skills, but also on drill, repetition, and boring exercises which, in and of themselves, cannot ensure oral and written fluency. It becomes important, then, to put the structuralist influence in perspective, to recognize its benefits and its limitations as well as its former domination in the field of majority language education.

Narrow, technical, syncretic approaches to language education (e.g., skills and product-orientations to language and culture teaching/learning) are largely incompatible with Aboriginal program philosophies and educational goals, which are situated within the personal use and social domains. While these have a place in language teaching/learning, a heavy emphasis on grammatical forms and on cultural transmission of the past is unlikely to bring about the preservation, maintenance, and revival of Aboriginal languages so as to achieve fluent communicative use and to ensure the transmission of cultural knowledge to young Aboriginals.

The time has come to move beyond the influences of linguistics and of technical approaches to language curriculum and to embrace more holistic, experiential, communicative, and multidimensional approaches. This has already occurred for first and second language programs in other languages, and these curricular and pedagogical approaches are eminently more compatible with the holistic nature of Aboriginal cultures (Hampton 1995; Calliou 1995; Regnier 1995).

Struggle for Curriculum
Different ideas of what curriculum is all about are represented in the visionary philosophical statements of the Elders and in the broad goals of education, as distinct from the specific objectives rooted in technical structuralist methods. Three very broad goals govern contemporary conceptions of education: (1) the young must be shaped to the current norms and conventions of adult society, (2) the young must be taught the knowledge that will ensure that their thinking conforms with what is considered to be real and true about the world, and (3) the development of each student's individual potential is to be encouraged. According to Egan (1996, 1997), these goals – socialization, rational reality, and individuality – are in conflict with one another and are the real reasons behind today's ineffective schools, for they result in an incoherent overall conception of education.

The first goal, the socialization of the young, is central to today's schools, which are seen to have a duty to ensure that students graduate with an understanding of society, their place and possibilities within it, and their acceptance of its norms, values, and commitments. In this conception of education, "the teacher is an important social worker, primarily valuable as a role model who exemplifies the values, beliefs, and norms of society; knowledge of subject matter cannot substitute for 'character,' wholesomeness, and easy and open communication with students" (Egan 1996, 12).

The second goal, that students' thinking should conform to what is "true" and "real" about the world, first articulated by Plato, requires that schools attend to the intellectual cultivation of the young in ways that go beyond simple social utility. From this perspective, an appropriate education enables young people, by means of the disciplined study of abstract forms of knowledge, to develop a rational view of reality, thus transcending conventional beliefs, prejudices, and stereotypes in order to see reality clearly and so be able to engage in a great cultural conversation about the world. Citing excellence as a goal and calling for students to be knowledgeable about their cultural heritage, proponents of this perspective would like to refocus the school on academics and construct the curriculum on intellectual and cultural grounds. In such a conception of education, the teacher embodies "an authority that comes from being an expert in the relevant subject matter" (Egan 1996, 15).

The third goal, individuality, stems from concentrating on the child, on what children are capable of learning at different ages, and on how learning might proceed most effectively. In this view, which influenced John Dewey and Jean Piaget, teaching methods are based on the careful observation and study of students and conform to the nature of students' development, learning, and motivation as they actively discover knowledge. Focusing on the individual and experiential development of the student, "the teacher in such a school is not an authority so much as a facilitator, a provider of the best resources, a shaper of the environment from ... which the students will learn" (Egan 1996, 18).

These three goals are also integral to contemporary conceptions of Aboriginal education. The third one, which focuses upon individuality and pedagogical process, is reflected in the mission statement of the Joe Duquette High School in Saskatoon, which endorses emancipatory education in "a healing place which nurtures the mind, body and soul of its students. The school offers a program of studies which affirms the contemporary worldview of Indian people. The school supports the uniqueness and creativity of the individual and fosters self-actualization in a cooperative environment" (Regnier 1995, 314).

Mission statements, however, typically incorporate more than one conception of education. In this school's approach, the first goal, that of socializing the young to accept the values of their society, is also incorporated, as the school's approach is based on Cree cosmology, which sees human beings and nature as unified, time as cyclical rather than linear, and which allows for a sense of ultimate meaning within a heritage open to cross-cultural possibilities (Regnier 1995).

The second goal, that students' thinking should conform to reality, can also be seen in an emphasis on Aboriginal epistemology, which focuses on exploring subjective inner spaces in order to arrive at insights into existence rather than on external knowledge and information. "What Aboriginals found in the exploration of the self became the basis for continued personal development and of Aboriginal epistemology ... Individuals and society can be transformed by identifying and reaffirming learning processes based on subjective experiences and introspection. For Aboriginal people, first languages and culture are crucial components in the transformative learning process. The three specific orientations of the transformation are: skills that promote personal and social transformation; a vision of social change that leads to harmony with rather than control over the environment; and the attribution of a spiritual dimension to the environment" (Miller et al. 1990, 4; Ermine 1995, 102).

In this conception, Aboriginal languages encode valuable indications of an inner space. For example, the Cree word for "mystery" refers to a higher power while, at the same time, connoting a humble connection between it and an individual's deeper self. In conceptualizing "mysteries," Aboriginal languages reveal a very high level of rationality, which can only come from an earlier insight into power. Aboriginal languages suggest inwardness, where real power lies. The last great frontier and the most challenging one of all is this inner space of the individual (Ermine 1995, 108), and it may well constitute the very essence of Aboriginal education.

The first goal, socialization, is also seen in redefinitions of Aboriginal education based on the iterative spiral structure of knowledge made explicit in the six-directional patterns of heaven, earth, east, south, west, and north (Hampton 1995); in the knowledge inherent in grandmothers' narratives (Sterling 1995); and in explicit cultural content, dealing with, for example, fishing, hunting, plants, and medicine as well as the relationships between the sun, the rain, and the branches on the tree (Archibald 1995). Teaching by example and with narratives grounded in nature, philosophized in the sacred circle and medicine wheel, Aboriginal education emphasizes the recognition of responsibilities, the perception of internal strength, a process of integrating elements with new meaning at every turn, and circular movement in both the natural and spiritual worlds (Hampton 1995; Calliou 1995; Archibald 1995; Sterling 1995). The recognition of values particular to Aboriginal education emphasizes respect for all things spiritual; the notion of service towards others; respect for diversity; the full flower of Aboriginal thoughtways; continuity with tradition; respect for personal power and autonomy; a sense of history; a relentless commitment to teaching and learning; the nourishment of vitality, which underlies strength derived from personal and tribal suffering and oppression; conflict, tensions, and struggles between Aboriginal and White education; the importance of an Indian sense of place, land, and territory; and the need for transformation in the relationship between Indian and White as well as in the relationship between individual and society (MacIvor 1995).

Yet, according to Egan (1996, 1997), these three basic goals of education are incompatible because the kind of sceptical, philosophical, and informed mind that emerges from rationality (the second goal) is a disruptive force in a world governed by those who seek conformity with society's norms and values (the first goal). To establish schools that can attain social harmony through successful socialization while cultivating scepticism is probably impossible. Conformity and scepticism do not go hand in hand. The third goal, which focuses on the pedagogical aspects of education, guarding the young from the socializing pressures of society in order to protect their free growth, is clearly at odds with both the conformists and the skeptics. Proponents of the third goal argue for relevance in an age-related, individualizing, psychological process; proponents of the second goal argue for basics as a time-related, epistemological process; and proponents of the first goal argue for education as a skills-related, homogenizing, narrowing process. Where all of these notions are advanced with varying degrees of intensity by the same or different stakeholders, a struggle to define the core of curriculum ensues.

Need for Innovation
Charting a path that reflects the distinct needs of heterogeneous Aboriginal learners, that draws selectively upon the most suitable approaches of the past while avoiding the errors that accompanied that experience, will require a great deal of thought and innovation. This new direction for Aboriginal language and literacy education would be grounded in an acknowledgment of a range of Aboriginal ways of learning, would draw upon a wealth of cultural knowledge, and would realize activist and responsible Aboriginal leadership in the co-construction of the future. Isolated efforts on the part of Aboriginal curriculum and literacy workers cannot stem the tide of increasing majority language dominance. A new direction is needed to overcome the encroachment of methods that codify and teach languages in sequential, objective, and analytic modes that are inconsistent with the holistic, experiential, and narrative modes of Aboriginal communication styles.

Relying upon outside expertise, even on an occasional basis, calls for sensitivity and selectivity so as to ensure the continuation of Aboriginal perspectives and communication styles. Seeking inspiration in well developed dialogic and narrative learning models developed by other cultural groups (see Lambert Stock 1995; Egan 1986) is appropriate, as is drawing on majority theories of learning and language. Being distinctively Aboriginal does not require creating all out of nothing. Creating new ways of teaching and learning Aboriginal languages will involve reaching outside tradition: the crux of the matter will lie in the ability to use varied sources to achieve pedagogical and curricular solutions that are unique to Aboriginal cultures.

The divergence between the frequently stated social and cultural goals of language education and the synthetic, skills-oriented emphasis of curriculum materials poses a challenge for language and literacy educators. Unless the tension is resolved, the results expected of Aboriginal language and literacy programs will be elusive.

Language education policy for the future must address the development of a broad-based strategic approach to Aboriginal language teaching, the articulation of pedagogies reflective of distinctive Aboriginal cultures, and the formulation of curriculum that supports expressive, interactive communication grounded in present reality. While the energy and spirit of Aboriginal Elders, parents, and educators are at the heart of innovative instructional efforts, the need for complementary policy and dedicated resources in order to achieve broadly held goals is clear and urgent.

Acknowledgments
This chapter is based upon Yvonne Hébert, "The State of Aboriginal Literacy and Language Education," Royal Commission on Aboriginal Peoples (Ottawa, 1995).

References
Anderson, Moses. N.d. *Oji-Cree Language Program*. Kasabonika, ON: Sineonokway Native School.
Archibald, Jo-ann. 1995. "Locally Developed Native Studies Curriculum: An Historical and Philosophical Rationale." In *First Nations Education in Canada: The Circle Unfolds*, ed. Marie Battiste and Jean Barman, 288-312. Vancouver: UBC Press.
Assembly of First Nations (AFN). 1990. *Towards Linguistic Justice for First Nations*. Ottawa.
–. 1993. *Nation Building through Aboriginal Languages and Literacy*. Poster.
Barman, Jean, Yvonne Hébert, and Don McCaskill, eds. 1986. *Indian Education in Canada*. Vol. 1: *The Legacy*. Vancouver: UBC Press.
–. 1987. *Indian Education in Canada*. Volume 2: *The Challenge*. Vancouver: UBC Press.
Battiste, Marie. 1986. "Micmac Literacy and Cognitive Assimilation." In *Indian Education in Canada*. Vol. 1: *The Legacy*, ed. Jean Barman, Yvonne Hébert, and Don McCaskill, 23-44. Vancouver: UBC Press.
–. 1987. "Mi'kmaq Linguistic Integrity: A Case Study of Mi'kmawey School." In *Indian Education in Canada: Vol. 2: The Challenge*, ed. Jean Barman, Yvonne Hébert, and Don McCaskill, 107-25. Vancouver: UBC Press.
–. 1993. "Maintaining Aboriginal Identity, Languages, and Culture in Modern Society." Royal Commission on Aboriginal Peoples, National Round Table on Education, Discussion Paper 5.
Battiste, Marie, and Jean Barman, eds. 1995. *First Nations Education in Canada: The Circle Unfolds*. Vancouver: UBC Press.

Brozo, William, and Michele Simpson. 1991. *Readers, Teachers, Learners: Expanding Literacy in Secondary Schools*. Toronto: Collier Macmillan.

Calliou, Sharilyn. 1995. "Peacekeeping Actions at Home: A Medicine Wheel Model for a Peacekeeping Pedagogy." In *First Nations Education in Canada: The Circle Unfolds*, ed. Marie Battiste and Jean Barman, 47-72. Vancouver: UBC Press.

Candlin, C. 1984. "Syllabus Design as a Critical Process." In *General English Syllabus Design*, ed. C.J. Brumfit. Oxford: Pergamon.

Chambers, Cynthia, and Laurie Walker. 1991. "Introduction." In *The Literacy Curriculum in Canada in the 1990s*, ed. Laurie Walker and Cynthia Chambers, 1-7. Proceedings of the Tenth Invitational Conference of the Canadian Association for Curriculum Studies, University of Lethbridge, 7-8 June 1990, Lethbridge.

Cluster, Susan. n.d. *Cree Language Course Outline*. Curriculum materials developed for credits for Grades 5-10. 12pp. Pelican Narrows, SK: Peter Ballantyne Cree Nation.

Cox, Carole, and Paul Boyd-Batstone. 1997. *Crossroads: Literature and Language in Culturally and Linguistically Diverse Classrooms*. Upper Saddle River, NJ: Merrill Education, Prentice-Hall.

Desmarais, Lise, and Monique Duplantie. 1986. "Approche communicative et grammaire." In *Propos sur la pédagogie de la communication en langues secondes*, ed. Anne Marie Boucher, Monique Duplantie, et Raymond LeBlanc, 41-57. Montréal: Centre éducatif et culturel et CEPCEL.

Egan, Kieran. 1986. *Teaching as Storytelling: An Alternative Approach to Teaching and Curriculum in the Elementary School*. London, ON: Althouse.

–. 1996. *The Educated Mind: How Cognitive Tools Shape Our Understanding*. Chicago: University of Chicago Press.

–. 1997. "Competing Voices for the Curriculum." In *The Struggle for Curriculum: Education, the State and the Corporate Sector*, ed. Marvin Wideen and Mary Clare Courtland, 7-26. Burnaby: Canadian Association for Curriculum Studies, Institute for Studies in Teacher Education, Simon Fraser University.

Ermine, Willie. 1995. "Aboriginal Epistemology." In *First Nations Education in Canada: The Circle Unfolds*, ed. Marie Battiste and Jean Barman, 101-12. Vancouver: UBC Press.

Faries, Emily J. 1985. *Summary Report on Preliminary Findings*. Secondary research program. National Indian Education Review, Phase 1. Ottawa: Assembly of First Nations.

Fyle, Clifford. 1990. "Mother Tongue Education in Third World Situations." In *Didactiques des langues maternelles*, ed. Gilles Gagné, Michel Pagé, and Elca Tarrab. Bruxelles: De Boeck-Wesmael, Éditions universitaires.

Goodwin, Philip. 1991-2. *Cree Language Curriculum Documents and Material*. Primary, Junior and Intermediate curriculum documents, developed by the Cree language teacher. For use at St. Andrew's School. Kashechewan, ON: Hishkoonikum Education Authority.

Hampton, Eber. 1995. "Towards a Redefinition of Indian Education." In *First Nations Education in Canada: The Circle Unfolds*, ed. Marie Battiste and Jean Barman, 5-46. Vancouver: UBC Press.

Harley, Birgit, Alison d'Anglejan, and Stan M. Shapson. 1990. *The Evaluation Syllabus*. Ottawa: Canadian Association of Second Language Teachers and M éditeur.

Hébert, Yvonne. 1984. *Native Indian Language Education in the Victoria-Saanich Region: An Evaluation Report*. (With audio-cassette). School Districts 61 (Victoria) and 63 (Saanich).

–. 1990. *Syllabus formation langagière générale*. Ottawa: Association canadienne des professeurs de langues secondes et M éditeur.

–. 1997. "The State of Aboriginal Literacy and Language Education." In *For Seven Generations: An Information Legacy of the Royal Commission on Aboriginal Peoples*. CD-ROM. Ottawa. Libraxus.

Illich, Ivan. 1987. "A Plea for Research on Lay Literacy." *Interchange* 18 (1/2): 9-22.

Joyce, Bruce, and Marsha Weil. 1986. *Models of Teaching*. Englewood Cliffs, NJ: Prentice-Hall.

Kramsch, Claire. 1984. *Interaction et discours dans la classe de langue*. Paris: Hatier-Crédif/ Lasalle, Québec: Hurtubise HMH ltée.

Lambert Stock, Patricia. 1995. *The Dialogic Curriculum: Teaching and Learning in a Multicultural Society.* Portsmouth, NH: Boynton/Cook.

LeBlanc, Clarence, Claudine Courtel, and Pierre Trescases. 1990. *Syllabus Culture.* Ottawa: Association canadienne des professeurs de langues secondes et M éditeur.

LeBlanc, Raymond. 1990. *A Synthesis: National Core French Study.* Ottawa: Canadian Association of Second Language Teachers and M éditeur.

Lebrun, Monique. 1993. Les programmes de français et leurs objectifs socioculturels. *Dialogues et cultures* 35: 80-90.

Lundsteen, Sara W. 1989. *Language Arts: A Problem-solving Approach.* New York: Harper and Row.

MacIvor, Madeleine. 1995. "Redefining Science Education for Aboriginal Students." In *First Nations Education in Canada: The Circle Unfolds*, ed. Marie Battiste and Jean Barman, 73-99. Vancouver: UBC Press.

Miller, John R., J.R. Bruce Cassie, and Susan M. Drake. 1990. *Holistic Learning.* Toronto: OISE Press.

National Indian Brotherhood. 1972. *Indian Control of Indian Education.* Ottawa: National Indian Brotherhood.

Noyce, Ruth M., and James F. Christie. 1989. *Integrating Reading and Writing Instruction in Grades K-8.* Boston: Allyn and Bacon.

Nunan, David. 1988. *Syllabus Design.* Oxford: Oxford University Press.

Painchaud, Gisèle. 1990. *Syllabus langue.* Ottawa: Association canadienne des professeurs de langues secondes and M éditeur.

Regnier, Robert. 1995. "The Sacred Circle: An Aboriginal Approach to Healing Education at an Urban High School." In *First Nations Education in Canada: The Circle Unfolds*, ed. Marie Battiste and Jean Barman, 313-29. Vancouver: UBC Press.

Robinson, Richard D., Michael C. McKenna, and Judy M. Wedman. 1996. *Issues and Trends in Literacy Education.* Boston: Allyn and Bacon.

Savignon, Sandra, and Margie S. Berns, eds. 1984. *Initiatives in Communicative Language Teaching: A Book of Readings.* Reading, MA: Addison-Wesley.

Shkilnyk. Anastasia M. 1985. *Canada's Aboriginal Languages: An Overview of Current Activities in Language Retention.* Ottawa: Department of the Secretary of State.

Smith, David. 1991. "Modernism, Hyperliteracy and the Colonization of the Word." In *The Literacy Curriculum in Canada in the 1990s*, ed. Laurie Walker and Cynthia Chambers, 108-18. Proceedings of the Tenth Invitational Conference of the Canadian Association for Curriculum Studies, University of Lethbridge, 7-8 June 1990, Lethbridge.

Sterling, Shirley. 1995. "Quaslametko and Yetko: Two Grandmother Models for Contemporary Native Education Pedagogy. In *First Nations Education in Canada: The Circle Unfolds*, ed. Marie Battiste and Jean Barman, 113-23. Vancouver: UBC Press.

Stern, H.H. (David). 1982. "Core French Programs across Canada: How Can We Improve Them?" *Canadian Modern Language Review* 39 (1): 34-47.

–. 1983a. *The Fundamental Concepts of Language Teaching.* Oxford/Toronto: Oxford University Press.

–. 1983b. "Toward a Multidimensional Foreign Language Curriculum." In *Foreign Languages: Key Links in the Chain of Learning*, ed. R.G. Mead, 120-46. Middlebury, VT: Northeast Conference.

Taylor, Eli, Sioux Valley First Nation. 1993. In *Nation Building through Aboriginal Languages and Literacy.* Poster. Ottawa: Assembly of First Nations.

Thomas, Alice. 1993-4. *Cree Course Outline, Native as First Languages.* For Grade 9, teacher-prepared materials. 30pp. Fort Severn: Wasaho First Nation High School.

Tremblay, Roger, Monique Duplantie, and Diane Huot. 1990. *The Communicative/Experiential Syllabus.* One of six final reports of the National Core French Study. Ottawa: Canadian Association of Second Language Teachers and M éditeur.

Wilkins, D. 1976. *Notional Syllabuses.* London: Oxford University Press.

4

Telling Our Own Stories: The Role, Development, and Future of Aboriginal Communications

Gail Guthrie Valaskakis

> Stories are not just entertainment. Stories are power. They reflect the deepest, the most intimate perceptions, relationships and attitudes of a people. Stories show how a people, a culture thinks. Yet, Native images, stories, symbols and history are all too often used by Canadians and Americans to sell things – cars, tobacco, movies, books.
>
> – Lenore Keeshig-Tobias in Slapin and Seale (1992, 98)

Stories are narratives – written or visual – and academic writing has long recognized that the narratives we express are windows on who we are, what we experience, and how we understand and enact ourselves and others. At the same time, communications research recognizes that media play an important role in providing information and opportunities for cultural and linguistic continuity, community cohesion, and social development. But recent work in communication and cultural studies suggests that, because we actually construct who we are in the process of identifying with the images and narratives that dominate our ways of seeing and representing the world around us, media also contribute to the formation of social identity. From this perspective, culture involves the shared practices and experiences that we construct and express in our social relations and communication. Identity is not formed, then, in internal conceptions of the self, but in the adoption of changing representations and narratives that we generate, experience, and express in our individual and social experience. These changing images and narratives emerge in the area of social struggle, in which visual and verbal stories are told. As a result, identity is continually contested and reconstructed in the discursive negotiation of the complex alliances and relations that constitute community. Our communities, like our discourses, are not cemented in unity or belonging, but in the dynamics of change and difference (Hall 1986, 1989). And communication is not just the glue that holds communities together. Communication is the dynamic ground in which individuals and communities are formed, and this process involves conflicting media images and the ideological messages they carry.

For Aboriginal Canadians, identities and cultures are formed and contested in a struggle over how Aboriginal peoples are represented and how these representations are appropriated by others in dominant political and cultural processes. The struggle over distorted images, access to voice, and the telling of one's own stories involves media makers (along with artists and academics) in a growing debate over what a Mohawk artist calls "the politics of primitivism" (Jacobs 1986). This is, to an equal extent, a struggle over the politics of media. As Bud White Eye of Native News Network reminds us: "Many of the myths and misperceptions that persist among non-Aboriginal people are perpetuated by no communication, poor communication, or one-sided communication. The depth and diversity of the Aboriginal perspectives must be communicated through both First Nations and 'mainstream' news media, to as broad a public as possible" (White Eye in Royal Commission on Aboriginal Peoples 1997).

Over the last three decades, Canada has built an extensive communications system that reflects the size and diversity of the country. It has begun to respond to Aboriginal demands for broadcasting that recognizes their cultures and respects their identities. Satellite technology, Aboriginal programming, and new communications policies have been vital to the development of Aboriginal media in Canada, particularly in the North. But today, Aboriginal communications programs are retrenching; service is far from extensive, especially in the South; and the voices of Aboriginal peoples are still largely absent in mainstream broadcasting.

This chapter looks at the Aboriginal experience of mainstream and Native broadcasting from a variety of perspectives, including discussions of Aboriginal representations in mainstream media's treatment of the 1990 "Mohawk crisis"; the historical development and current features of Aboriginal communications in Canada; and Inuit television programming and its role in supporting the cultural continuity of Inuit oral tradition. The final section of the chapter looks at the future of Aboriginal broadcasting in Canada, including the central issues expressed by Aboriginal broadcasters: policy and legislation, funding, access, training, and Aboriginal media resources.

The Power of Stories: Representation and Appropriation
In the book entitled *Through Indian Eyes: The Native Experience in Books for Children*, Slapin writes: "Like many others outside the Native world, I grew up with the prevailing stereotypes of the people. I learned that 'Indians' whoop and holler and run around in little more than war paint and feathers, brandishing tomahawks and dancing on one leg; they scalp, torture

and menace innocent settlers; they beat on tom-toms and live in 'teepees'; their language consists mainly of raising one hand shoulder high and grunting 'how' or 'ugh!'; and they are not women, men and babies, but 'squaws,' 'braves,' and 'papooses.' Little has changed since my childhood" (Slapin and Seale 1992, 1).

Slapin's reflections illustrate the stereotypes and cultural narratives that structure the interaction between Aboriginal and non-Aboriginal peoples, both historically and today. The impact of these images and the stories they tell transform each of us and the social world in which we live. George Gerbner (1994) once said, "If you write a nation's stories, you needn't worry about who makes its laws. Today television tells most of the stories to most of the people most of the time." And Angus and Jhally (1989, 2) tell us: "In contemporary culture, the media have become central to the constitution of social identity. It is not just that media have become important forms of influence on individuals. We also identify and construct ourselves as social beings through the mediation of images."

Since the earliest days of non-Native contact, the stories of Aboriginal peoples have been constructed and disseminated by outsiders, for outsiders. These stories are told in cultural narratives embedded in ethnographic studies, paintings and photographs, movies, novels and newspapers, and in radio and television programming that often distort the cultural and political reality of Native culture, heritage, and contemporary life through the silence or appropriation of Aboriginal voices. In the current environment, Aboriginal Canadians struggle with media that confine the past as they construct the future. The importance of understanding stereotypes and the role that media play in constructing and representing Aboriginal identity, community, and culture is illustrated through the Aboriginal experience during what television and newspapers called the "Indian summer" of 1990, when Quebec was absorbed in what mainstream media labelled "the Mohawk crisis" (Valaskakis 1994).

Media and Representation: The "Oka Crisis"

Native Canadians in the south almost live in little enclaves and we basically ignore them unless something extraordinary happens. I think that is why Aboriginal broadcasters are so important, because not only do they promote their own languages and cultures and instill pride in the young people again, but they also have the ability to teach southern Canadians what being a native in this country is all about, what these cultures are all about and the fact that it is really important to hang on to these traditions.

– Adamson in Royal Commission on Aboriginal Peoples (1997)

In 1990, Mohawk assertion of their traditional heritage and long-neglected land rights evolved into barricades on the Kanesatake and Kahnawake reserves in Quebec. Confrontations between townspeople, police, army, and First Nations focused on the immediate and local frustrations of a bridge blockade; the death of a policeman; the Canadian army occupation of the area surrounding the reserves; and the historical and national frustrations of Aboriginal rights to sovereignty, heritage, and the land. When "Mohawk Warriors" barricaded themselves in the alcohol treatment centre at Kanesatake, a stand-off involving reporters, police, army, and Indians began. It lasted seventy-eight days, and over 4,000 Canadian soldiers were deployed over the summer to support the police at the barricades.

Lynda Powless of the Native Journalists Association states: "Non-Native reporters showed us through their spotty and dismal understanding of the issues that led to and provoked Oka and subsequent coverage that they are not as well-versed in Native issues as they pretend to be" (Powless in Royal Commission on Aboriginal Peoples 1997). In fact, the incident at Oka is remembered in startling media images of rock-throwing townspeople and scuffling Indians, staring soldiers, and crying children. But in all the television, radio, and newspaper coverage, one image emerged as salient in the Mohawk crisis: the image of the "warrior" – bandana-masked, khaki-clad, gun-toting Indians who dominated the media accompanied by headlines such as "Rough Justice: After Oka Will the Violence Spread?" (*Maclean's*, vol. 103, no. 32, 6 August 1990); "Mohawk Militancy" (*Ottawa Citizen*, 15 September 1990); "The Mohawk Warriors: Heroes or Thugs?" (*Toronto Star*, 24 November 1990); "The Making of a Warrior" (*Saturday Night*, April 1991); and Aislin's political cartoon of the "Mafia Warrior" (*Montreal Gazette*, 30 April 1990). This representation builds upon the "war-bonneted warrior," the dominant image – and narrative – of Native men for the last century (Albers and James 1987, 35). With few exceptions, the media's warriors were exaggerated, monolithic representations of Aboriginal activists: the military masculine, criminalized through association with terrorism and epitomized in the ultimate warrior, code-named "Lasagna," who became both the darling of the media and a willing subject.

In contrast to the majority of media images, when the Mohawk barricades came down on 26 September 1990, 60 people left the treatment centre at Kanesatake: 27 Aboriginal men of various nations, and one non-Native 16-year-old; 16 Aboriginal women, 6 children, and 10 reporters. The Indians from the treatment centre – like the Mohawks who served on both sides of the barricades at Akwesasne through the spring of 1990; those from Kahnawake who blockaded the Mercier Bridge in the summer; the traditional women who sat in vigil in the Kanesatake pine forest through the previous winter; and Native Canadians who ran the office of the Mohawk Nation or practised the traditional Longhouse religion, or expressed strong views on land rights, or were simply Indian – were all yoked together as the media's Mohawk warriors. For the media, there was one dominant image, one dominant narrative throughout the incident at Oka: warriors and the militant story they tell. The incident at Oka illustrated (1) that Aboriginal peoples do not participate significantly in either the production or the dissemination of information to the majority of their own people or to other Canadians and (2) that non-Native reporters who lack background information on Aboriginal issues tend to reinforce stereotypical representations of Aboriginal peoples.

Media images of violent Indians are, like representations in other Aboriginal cultural products that the media construct, reproduce, and make available, a double-edged sword for Aboriginal peoples. As Robert Berkhofer (1979, 72) writes, "For most of the past five centuries, the Indian of the imagination and ideology has been as real, perhaps more real, than the Native American of actual existence and contact." From Edward Curtis's sepia photographs to *Dances with Wolves* and warriors, Native people struggle with who they are and the nature of their interaction with others in relation to the media's popular representations of, in the words of Margaret Atwood (1972, 102), the Indian as both tormentor and sufferer; the villain and the victim. Neither of these representations drawn from the social imaginaries of the savage as noble or evil allows newcomers to identify Aboriginal peoples as equal, as "real inhabitants of a land" (105), and as sovereign nations absorbed in the struggle concomitant with their tenuous position within a nation-state carved out in companies and charters, proclamations and promises.

Images of warriors also pose problems for Aboriginal people themselves. From sports teams to flags to clothes, warriors have been appropriated into the discourse and culture of First Nations peoples. As Aboriginal people struggle over claiming and disclaiming the image of the warrior – over the threats and promises of appropriated identity and power – the media play a central role in transforming the traditions and heritage of peace-keeping warriors of the Iroquois Confederacy and blurring the distinction between the activism of promoting the sovereignty of Indian land and treaty rights with the action of initiating paramilitary confrontation. In continually headlining one facet of the prism of this modern transformation of the Plains warrior, the media contribute to a powerful fictive identity which, for Native youth, is "the biggest thing since Rice Krispies" (Mike Myers in Henton 1990). Mohawk warriors have become dominating representations of guns and muscle, articulating ideology and identity that is not fully understood or shared by all community members, who struggle over contested ideologies and identities and the interest groups with which they are associated. This struggle, which makes consensus and decision making difficult and contributes to community factionalism, is fed by a lack of information from pervasive and independent Native media. As Lynda Powless of the Native Journalists Association suggests: "When you don't have an informed public, you have the kind of chaos that exists in Native communities, the kind of social rifting that is occurring and isn't being closed because people don't know what is going on. They hear the myths and the misunderstandings and the misinterpretations that build, and they create problems when you don't have a free press" (Powless in Royal Commission on Aboriginal Peoples 1997).

But the conflict over diverse ideologies and identities in Native communities today remains grounded in a unity of common culture and history, experience, and political purpose – in collective memory and the continual formation of community. It is the negotiation of relations of power expressed in contested ideology and identity that both binds and fractures Aboriginal communities in their struggle with an oppressive past and an uncertain future; and the recognition of this unity in difference, continually reconstructed in culture and experienced today in the struggle over representation and appropriation, reveals the meaning and importance of the media for Native peoples today.

In the post-Oka era, there has been a dramatic increase in the number of books, magazine articles, and radio and television programs about Aboriginal peoples; but the majority of this material continues to be written and produced by non-Native people. As Miles Morrisseau, editor of *Native Beat*, writes:

> There is no end to the stories that need to be told out there, and they are not being told. I think they are being told from a perspective that does not reflect Native reality. In order for Native people to achieve those goals, they have to begin to share their stories with one another and share their experiences and achievements and successes and failures, and whatever else, with one another. Along with everything else that was undermined and destroyed or wiped out were our communication methods, and our ways of speaking and telling were undermined as well. I feel that the Native media plays a role in rediscovering or re-inventing those things. (Morrisseau in Royal Commission on Aboriginal Peoples 1997)

Over the past three decades, broadcasting has emerged as a vital means for Aboriginal people to "tell their own stories." The evolution of Aboriginal broadcasting has been complex, uneven, and prolonged; but through programs and policies, Canada has created a unique framework for the development of Aboriginal communications.

Development of Aboriginal Broadcasting

The modern era of Aboriginal communications began in 1969, when the Telesat Canada Bill proposed the first geostationary satellite system in the world; and the government released a White Paper on Indian policy. As Aboriginal peoples united against this White Paper's assimilationist implications, some provincial Aboriginal organizations began communications units in order to carry on discussion with their people. In the early 1970s, these units and some government-sponsored communications projects in the North formed the basis for independent Native Communication Societies, the flagships of Aboriginal communications efforts for the past twenty years. In 1972, Cabinet approved funding for CBC's Accelerated Coverage Plan and for the Native Communications Program (NCP), which, in 1974, began to core-fund the Native Communication Societies through the Department of Secretary of State. Between 1971 and 1981, satellite experiments in Alberta, northern Quebec, and the Northwest Territories strengthened the resources of Native Communication Societies; and in 1980, the Canadian Radio Television and Telecommunications Commission (CRTC) issued the Report of the Therrien Commission on the extension of service to remote and undeserved communities (CRTC 1980). This report asserts that the government is responsible for ensuring broadcasting that supports Aboriginal languages and cultures, and it formed the basis for the federal government's first northern communication policy, which was issued in 1983. The report contains five principles calling for the widespread participation of northern Native peoples in all aspects of media programming, distribution, and regulatory practice on the basis of "fair access" and "consultation." These principles are implemented through the Northern Native Broadcast Access Program (NNBAP), begun in 1983 with a budget of $13.4 million per year to fund the production of local and regional Aboriginal radio and television through the thirteen (of twenty-one) Native Communication Societies located in the North. NNBAP has been cut over the years, but this program continues to be the major funding source for Aboriginal broadcasting.

In 1981, the CRTC licensed the Inuit Broadcasting Corporation and the undertakings of Native Communication Societies in the western Northwest Territories and the Yukon. But Native communities experience an increasing array of southern media. Canadian Satellite Communications Inc. (CanCom), a Pay-TV package of Canadian and American television and radio stations, was also licensed in 1981; commercial television is widely available across the North on an off-satellite basis; and video playback units are common in Native homes.

The current phase of Aboriginal communications began in 1990, when three critical developments changed the media environment for Native

Communications Societies. First, the Northern Broadcasting Policy was reframed as a Native Broadcasting Policy, with wider application of the principles cited in the earlier document. Second, severe funding cuts in 1990 and 1993 decreased the budget of the NNBAP; and the Native Communications Program was terminated. Societies below the 55th parallel Hamelin Line, which defines the Canadian North for purposes of policy, were set adrift. Funding for Aboriginal newspapers and radio in southern communities and for the National Aboriginal Communications Society (NACS) was eliminated altogether. Third, the federal government approved $10 million to establish Television Northern Canada, or TVNC, a dedicated satellite channel that provides television distribution to ninety-four Native communities served by Native Communications Societies. TVNC does not produce television programming but broadcasts approximately 38 hours of Aboriginal language and cultural programs; 23 hours of educational programs; 12 hours of children's programs; and a variety of re-runs in 15 Aboriginal languages (Roth 1994, 330). Ironically, the viability of the framework envisioned through the Native Broadcasting Policy has been strengthened in the area of program distribution through TVNC and weakened in the area of broadcasting (and newspaper) production through cutbacks to the NNBAP and the demise of the Native Communications Program.

Aboriginal media today consist of a wide range of loosely knit media services and resources. Catherine MacQuarrie tells us: "Aboriginal communications has actually been quite successful over the past 20 years. From early beginnings as newsletters or local radio initiatives, it has grown to be comprised of several hundred local radio stations, eleven regional radio networks, the beginnings of a national Aboriginal radio network, six television production outlets, a pan-Northern Aboriginal television network called Television Northern Canada, and numerous newspapers" (MacQuarrie in Royal Commission on Aboriginal Peoples 1997).

This sounds impressive; but the reality is that Aboriginal media resources are uneven, relatively limited, and largely restricted to regions of the North, where NNBAP-funded societies provide regional radio and television services to some 260,000 Aboriginal people and produce more than 260 hours of radio and television weekly in 30 of Canada's 53 Native languages (Smith 1988). Only 14 percent of Aboriginal peoples who live in southern Canada have access to community radio, and the great majority of these live in Quebec and Ontario. This cost-effective medium broadcasts 4,831 hours of music, current affairs, and public service programming, almost entirely in Aboriginal languages (Rowlandson 1988). But smaller western communities, southern rural and urban areas, and the Atlantic region remain underserved; and research suggests that the survival of the Native Communication Societies and other Aboriginal media has important implications for the visibility, viability, and even the definition of Aboriginal cultures and languages.

Audience research conducted by Native Communication Societies since 1984 indicates that Aboriginal audiences have acquired new knowledge and skills related to their languages, traditions, and contemporary lives through media (Hudson 1985, 4). The surveys suggest that most Native broadcasters favour regional news and current affairs broadcasting and that radio and television are important factors in providing Native audiences with access to information about community, regional, and national organizations and issues; about Native history and heritage; and about each other (Hudson 1985). On the basis of this data, other researchers support the Aboriginal audience position that Native media programming contributes to the status of Aboriginal languages and cultures, particularly among the young; strengthening cultural and generational bonds; increasing interregional knowledge; and reinforcing an understanding of Aboriginal cultures and lifestyles (Lougheed 1986; Stiles 1988). Survey data also indicate that, from the perspective of both the broadcasters and their audiences, Native media must be more effective in reaching the majority Aboriginal population, which is under twenty years of age.

The development of Aboriginal broadcasting is a patchwork of policies and programs, the efficacy of which is supported by empirical research. But Aboriginal communities themselves suggest the deeper meaning of Aboriginal broadcasting. The Inuit experience of television programming illustrates both the cultural disruption of mainstream media and the adaptive use of Aboriginal broadcasting to support linguistic and cultural continuity.

Aboriginal Culture and Media: Television and Inuit Oral Tradition
Aboriginal peoples in the Far North have long been aware that mainstream media transmit narratives that can assault Native identity, cultural and linguistic integrity, community cohesion, and local control of their social and political institutions. Rosemary Kuptana, former president of the Inuit Broadcasting Corporation, makes the following remark about the introduction of television in the Far North: "We might liken the onslaught of southern television and the absence of native television to the neutron bomb. This is the bomb that kills the people but leaves the buildings standing. Neutron bomb television is the kind of television that destroys the soul of a people but leaves the shell of a people walking around. This is television in which the tradition, the skills, the culture, the language count for nothing. The pressure, especially on our children, to join the invading culture and language and leave behind a language and culture that count for nothing is explosively powerful" (Brisebois 1983, 107).

The destructive role that mainstream media can play is suggested by Grantzberg, Steinbring, and Hamer. Their research on the impact of southern television among the Cree concludes: "Traditional conceptions of communication influence the way new media are perceived and used. The traditional conceptions seem to cause the Cree to be very susceptible to TV, to take it literally and seriously, to idolize the superhero characters, to read special messages into it concerning behavior requirements, and to be especially concerned about its potential harm to children. We cannot consider TV to be a uniform phenomenon cross-culturally. TV is a different thing to different people and its impact varies according to cultural traditions that surround it" (Grantzberg, Steinbring, and Hamer 1977, 157).

Inuit have worked for two decades to participate in the media reaching their communities, in part to counteract the exclusionary role of early northern media. In January 1981, The Inuit Broadcasting Corporation began transmitting Inuktitut television programming to communities scattered across the Arctic. This first Native broadcasting network in North America produces television news, dramas, documentaries, and children's programs. Inuit television productions are modern northern stories that reflect Native awareness of the role oral tradition plays in constructing and confirming Inuit cultural continuity and social cohesion.

Introduced in the 1920s, High Frequency radio solidified the interests of southern institutions. Broadcast radio was established in the mid-1930s, but the first Inuktitut program was broadcast in 1960. In 1967, television programming was introduced to the North through the delayed transmission of videotapes in four-hour packages with no Native-language programming. In 1974, the Canadian Broadcasting Corporation (CBC) received funding to provide radio and television to communities with populations of over 500 through the Accelerated Coverage Plan (ACP). Monies were allocated for hardware, not production, and much of the programming broadcast through the ACP was not relevant to northern Aboriginal people. In effect, in 1973, the Anik satellite system brought Inuit, whose communication remained primarily based in the interpersonal interaction characteristic of oral tradition, into full contact with a compelling new change agency "by parachuting telephone, radio and live television simultaneously into a region that is culturally different from that of the producers of both the technology hardware and software" (Roth 1982, 3).

The opportunity to develop Inuit television broadcasting was forged through smaller-scale communications projects and satellite-access experiments, which established Inuit regional production facilities, along with trained producers, directors, camera operators, and animators, and broadcast both local and network Inuktitut radio and/or television programs.

Importance of Inuit Oral Tradition

Not only are the traditional Aboriginal methods of information transmission and documentation in sharp contrast with European methods, but the content of the information is also radically different. Vast pools of knowledge encompassed in the oral tradition comprise unique bodies of knowledge with distinct Aboriginal content. The expression of this cultural material constitutes what can be referred to as the Aboriginal voice (Young-Ing in Royal Commission on Aboriginal Peoples 1997). In discussing the role of television among northern Algonquin Indians, Gary Grantzberg (1982, 48) writes, "The parallels between television and storytelling are quite obvious and it is not difficult to understand why, upon arrival, television quickly becomes a society's number one storyteller." He adds: "Storytelling, as well, is powerful. Not only is it an entertainment device, it is also a teaching, culture-preserving mechanism and even a relational device. Through the format of an entertaining, easily remembered story, characters and plots are carefully engineered to act as metaphors for concepts of morality, principle, and prediction" (Grantzberg 1982, 9).

Like books in southern culture, Inuit oral tradition provides what Marshall McLuhan (1960, 1) calls a "classroom without walls," in which "the young learned by listening, watching, doing the language and skills of their elders." Through socialization and the transfer of knowledge related to Inuit culture, oral tradition builds "consensus on the sharing of mutually affirmed and celebrated attitudes and values" (Carey 1967, 11). In contrast, written traditions tend to be "space-binding and favored the growth of political authority and secular institutions and a culture appropriate to them" (11).

Younger Inuit are increasingly literate in their own language and English or French; and the importance that publication has acquired in the dominant society provides a role for Native newsprint and books. But as Kate Madden (1990, 5) writes, "Certainly to the 1950s, and significantly today, Inuit culture is defined in large measure by its relative closeness to the oral tradition." At the same time, Nathan Elberg's (1984) fieldwork in a northern Quebec community suggests that the pressures of cultural change can reinforce the isolation and cultural distance of younger and older Inuit. He observes that, like the representation of Mohawk "warriors," the representation of "real Inuit" challenges the identity and self-esteem of younger Inuit, whose stories of urban difficulties are "as significant in understanding the life of contemporary Inuit as some of the older stories about cold and anguish collected in earlier decades are to understanding the culture of those times" (6). Shirley Cook, of the Native Communications Society of the Western Arctic, suggests the importance of IBC programming: "Over 90 percent of the homes in the northern communities have a television set. As a Native journalist, I know this can definitely be one way to maintain a strong sense of Aboriginal identity in our changing environment" (Cook in Royal Commission on Aboriginal Peoples 1997).

From the late 1960s to the present, studies of northern television have focused primarily on its impact as "an alien socialization agent" (Coldevin 1977), carrying disruptive cultural images (Grantzberg 1982; Caron 1977; O'Connell 1977; Wilson 1981). The benefits of electronic media are associated with community-level communication (Hudson 1977; Dicks 1977; Salter 1976). Research emphasizes media as factors in southern control of the North (Mayes 1972; Valaskakis 1979). Later studies consider the longer-term implications of southern media impact (Coldevin and Wilson 1985) and the role of Native communications projects in northern participatory development (Valaskakis 1992; Roth 1994).

No long-term research has been conducted on the impact of Aboriginal media in Native communities, but the Native Communications Societies have conducted audience surveys on patterns and preferences of television viewing. The surveys indicate that in most northern regions Native language use is widespread, especially among the old, who are often unilingual, and that "a high percentage of respondents from all regions tend to listen to or watch native language and native-oriented programming when it is available" (Hudson 1985, 4). Kate Madden has analyzed Inuit cultural expression in IBC programming. Her work suggests that the content of Inuktitut television provides young Inuit with the opportunity to see and hear the past that they share with their Elders and that the tempo, structure, and values of IBC programs draw upon Inuit oral tradition.

Inuit television spans the range of programming that is reflected in southern media: public affairs, documentaries, news, drama, and children's programming. But there is a difference between southern network programming and Inuit television. This difference is suggested in the following discussion of *Qagik*, a regular current affairs/news program that Madden (1990, 19) suggests is the most "'western' of I.B.C.'s programs:" "*Qagik* may look western. It even adheres to several characteristics applied to southern news. But it does it on its own terms. Its programs focus on items of geographic or psychological proximity to its audience (the Inuit and issues important to them) ... Visuals are important to *Qagik*, but the visual style is different" (Madden 1990, 14).

In the Inuit language, Qagik means "coming together," which, in Madden's analysis, is reflected in both its production values and content: "Consensus-building appears subtly in Qagik in the audio-video mix and in the program selection and dialogue," and the result is a non-linear approach to programming that more closely resembles the communication patterns of oral tradition: "Qagik demonstrates that IBC has managed to put together a news/current events show which espouses Inuit values. Its definition, organization and structure promote the Inuit value of personal autonomy through sharing information in cooperative, non-combative, consensus-building ways. It does not copy US/Southern Canadian conventions. If anything, it sets those conventions on their ear in the sense that the convention in Qagik seems to be allowing the organic to develop" (Madden 1990, 18).

At the other end of IBC's programming spectrum are cultural programs, a series that reflects subjects drawn from traditional Inuit life on the land. Programs such as *Clyde River Hunting Trip* "share a consistent storytelling style which displays characteristics consistent both with Inuit cultural values and distinctive features of oral culture" (Madden 1990, 19). Here, IBC builds upon the special characteristics of the medium to tell stories "almost totally through the visuals, natural sound, and asynchronous music" (22). "The story is told almost totally through visual elements shot in combination of subjective and objective camera perspective, predominantly through primary movement. None of the pieces has narration. Dialogue is minimal. Synchronous natural sound predominates. The pace of the programs is slow by US and southern Canadian standards" (19-20).

The full transfer of territorial control and administration in Nunavut will occur in April 1999. During this period of political change, Inuit are adapting television to tell stories, using visuals as a narrative device. As it did with earlier storytellers, this "serves as a connecting link to the Inuit traditions of the past, reinforcing them and demonstrating their relevance today" (23).

Inuit experience suggests that, as Robin Ridington (1990, 256) writes, "Electronic media may be used either to suppress the genuine experience and discourse of people in an oral culture or to document and share it." The future of Aboriginal communities depends forcefully on the Native capacity to document and share Aboriginal culture, language, and experience. Broadcasting provides a unique opportunity to accomplish this, but, as Native broadcasters recognize, the future of Aboriginal broadcasting in Canada is linked to developments in the areas of policy and legislation, access, training, funding, and Aboriginal media resources.

Paths to the Future: Aboriginal Communications
During the past twenty-five years of Aboriginal media development, satellites have become a critical force in Canadian broadcasting; and they have been joined by fibre optics in the development of telephone and data transmission. Newer satellites have greatly enlarged capacities, and current regulatory policy allows Telesat Canada to deliver communications services directly rather than through common carriers. These developments play important roles in the continuing strength of the Canadian cable industry and the trends towards competition (and, in the case of cable,

monopoly), privatization, and integration of telecommunications services. The Information Highway of telecommunications and computer connections is stretching across the country, and DBS satellites that broadcast directly to individual homes are promised in the near future. Debate continues over the definition, mandate, and role of public broadcasting and narrowcast, or specialty, broadcasting services. As telecommunications, computers, and the Information Highway encourage shifts in interaction, control, and culture, Aboriginal broadcasting and print media are increasingly more vulnerable and more important.

Aboriginal broadcasting in the North has demonstrated its effectiveness as a "first service" for Native audiences and its ability to perform as a full partner in the regional sectors of the Canadian broadcasting system. At the same time, limited but significant media initiatives and resources have begun to develop to support Aboriginal peoples across Canada. The communications services that Aboriginal media can provide are basic to Aboriginal participation in the cultural and political realities of Native and Canadian life.

The concerns of Aboriginal peoples related to communication are numerous and diverse; but reports, research, and comments from the Royal Commission on Aboriginal Peoples' public hearings focus on five central issues: policy and legislation, funding, access, training, and the development of media resources.

Communications Policy and Legislation

Policies and legislation have a crucial role to play in defining a unique presence for Aboriginal people in Canada's cultural industries. The 1990 Native Broadcasting Policy (NBP) (Canada, Department of Communications, 1990) is a vital step towards creating media institutions in Canada that acknowledge the Aboriginal population of this country. Furthermore, the Broadcasting Act, 1991, states that, through its programming and employment opportunities, the Canadian broadcasting system should "serve the needs and interests and reflect the circumstances and aspirations of the special place of Aboriginal peoples within that society" (Canada, Department of Communications, 1991, Section 3-1-d-iii). Yet despite repeated requests from Aboriginal communities and broadcasters and a recommendation by the Caplan and Sauvageau Report (1986, 519), Aboriginal language programming has not been protected in legislation. The consequences of this will be discussed below.

Aboriginal broadcasters look to the CRTC to define a supportive environment for the development of Native media. This includes (1) CRTC regulation that designates Aboriginal fair access to radio and TV broadcasting as a condition of licensing commercial and public broadcasters in regions with heavy concentrations of Aboriginal peoples and (2) pressing cable companies towards joint ventures or dedicated funding in order to support Aboriginal media production and distribution. The CRTC is also implicated in the issues of employment equity and funding, which depend on the commitment of the regulatory agency.

Funding

For Native broadcasters and journalists, the issue of funding is equally critical and complex. As Ray Fox of the National Aboriginal Communications Society (NACS) points out, the evaluations of the Northern Native Broadcasting and Access Program conducted by Lougheed (1986) and Curley (1993) show that the basic flaws in the program structure are inadequate funding, absence of funds for training, absence of funds for equipment renewal, and a greater need for independence (Fox in Royal Commission on Aboriginal Peoples 1997). With reference to the major government funding cutbacks to the NNBAP, Fox explains: "that is 26% of our funding that we have lost over the course of ten years."

In addition to the escalating costs of production, broadcasters face rising costs for program distribution, which, given the cost of satellite transmission and the elimination of distribution subsidies, is especially problematic for members of TVNC. Northern Aboriginal broadcasters are established as a first service for their target audiences within the regional context of Canadian broadcasting, and their funding does not reflect this reality.

The solutions include the provision of dedicated funding with commercial and public networks as well as joint ventures. Government agencies, including Aboriginal governments, also need to support the production and distribution of Aboriginal programming in both the North and the South, including their English and/or French versions. Aboriginal programming can be offered to current specialty channels and can, in the future, form the basis of an Aboriginal specialty channel carried on cable. In 1986, the Caplan-Sauvageau Report (Caplan and Sauvageau 1986, 520) suggested the establishment of a third national network, an autonomous Aboriginal language service similar to CBC and Radio Canada. In addition, Aboriginal media councils can be established to fund the development of Aboriginal communications in the South as well as in the North.

Access

At the current time, the Aboriginal voice is not widely available to Aboriginal people living beyond the area of TVNC, to the many Aboriginal people who live in the South, or the great majority of non-Native people. This silence is a reflection of Aboriginal media access, an issue closely associated with funding, policy, and legislation. Major concerns expressed by Aboriginal broadcasters and journalists focus on four interrelated areas:

(1) access to mainstream media to combat the negative representation and cultural appropriation of Aboriginal peoples and to provide Aboriginal perspectives and information on current issues involving Aboriginal peoples
(2) broader access to media networks in regions of the North that do not benefit from TVNC
(3) Aboriginal media for Native peoples living south of the Hamelin Line
(4) assurances of open access and media independence in Aboriginal communities.

Although these concerns have been noted earlier in this chapter, it is worth elaborating further on some of their complexities.

In many regions, Aboriginal broadcasting distribution agreements depend upon the good will of station or network broadcasters, be they public or private. Because they often operate in a broadcasting environment of conflicting audience and commercial interests, Aboriginal programming can be substituted, pre-empted, and marginalized in late-night slots. Unless Aboriginal broadcasting becomes a priority in regions with Native target audiences through the establishment of regulations that require this as a licensing condition, things will not change.

Aboriginal language broadcasting is a clear priority for the majority of the Native Communications Societies because they understand the crucial difference that Aboriginal media can make to the preservation, retention, and revitalization of Aboriginal languages. It is a tragic and well known fact that many Aboriginal languages in Canada are struggling for survival and that some are close to extinction. Language research, as discussed in the chapter by Fettes and Norton in this volume, indicates that languages are more likely to be retained when used in daily interaction in the total cultural milieu – the home and school and in the broadcast media. This means that Aboriginal media have a crucial role to play in the retention and renewal of Aboriginal languages.

Difficulties in gaining access to broadcasting opportunities mean that Aboriginal language transmission occurs mainly in northern areas, where Aboriginal languages are still vibrant and in daily usage. For example, the Inuit Broadcasting Corporation broadcasts entirely in Inuktitut; Wawatay broadcasts two hours of television and thirty hours of radio each week to thirty-five communities in northern Ontario (Martin in Royal Commission on Aboriginal Peoples 1997). Equally important to an understanding of Aboriginal nations today is the knowledge that language is intimately, but not uniquely, associated with culture. Aboriginal media also play a vital role in providing information within the changing cultural and linguistic realities of Native communities. Many Aboriginal people in urban areas and in the South no longer retain their languages. In this context, Aboriginal media take on a broader importance, a reality recognized in the 1990 Native Broadcasting Policy, which defines a Native undertaking not only in relation to the preservation of Aboriginal languages and cultures as proposed by commercial broadcasters, but also in relation to Native ownership and control, Native target audience, and Native-oriented programming.

Without an Aboriginal broadcasting network in southern Canada, there are limited options for Aboriginal language broadcasting. Opportunities on cable and on provincial public networks are important. Without broadcasting agreements, there is no solution to the problems of Aboriginal media access in communities beyond TVNC, except investment in additional broadcasting technology – a prospect that should involve the federal Department of Communications in assessing the need and planning the extension of service.

Aboriginal media in southern Canada, where the majority of Aboriginal people live, has developed on a localized level through the efforts of community volunteers, organizations, and entrepreneurs. At the current time, the issue of fair media access below the 55th parallel cannot be addressed without access to at least start-up funding for Native newspapers, radio stations, media production, and media resources through an Aboriginal Media Council. The development of joint ventures in communications through Aboriginal and other business initiatives would provide the basis for media that can be self-supporting.

Since the 1970s, Aboriginal broadcasters have lobbied for regional and national distribution of Native programs in order to extend Canadian understanding of Aboriginal lifestyles, problems, and positions. But the Aboriginal voice will be heard only if it is included as a regular part of the Canadian media landscape. This requires there being a wide range of Aboriginal employees in production and management positions within southern and northern media institutions as well as on management or policy boards of public cultural industries, including the CRTC and the CBC. Although the framework for Aboriginal employment has been established through the federal policy on employment equity, Aboriginal employment equity requires both that the CRTC monitor employment equity action plans and that it regulate licensing on that basis.

Training

Broadcasting and journalistic training is a long-standing issue of concern to Aboriginal peoples involved in the media. With the exception of the Native Communication Arts Program of the Saskatchewan Indian Federated College in Regina, attempts to build Aboriginal training programs at colleges or universities have been limited and short-lived. The great majority of Native journalists and broadcasters are trained "on the job" through Aboriginal media.

Media training is an important part of the work of Native Communication Societies, but the NNBAP has never had a special budget for training. As a result, training has been conducted largely on an ad hoc and in-house basis. There is a clear need to establish stable and accessible training for Aboriginal broadcasters and journalists.

Media Resources
Over the past decade, limited and tenuous resources have developed to support the infrastructure of Aboriginal media in Canada. Central among these is the National Aboriginal Communications Society, which, before its core funding was eliminated, organized the first national Native communications conferences in Canada. The Dream-speakers Film and Video Festival now constitutes the only annual meeting of Aboriginal film and video artists.

The Native News Network of Canada is an example of the media resources that are required to build an Aboriginal communications system in Canada. Incorporated in 1992, the Native News Network has never been adequately funded to achieve its goals of linking Aboriginal news media into a central news-distribution system that provides both coverage and local reaction to Aboriginal issues and activities (Smoke in Royal Commission on Aboriginal Peoples 1997). The development of a national Aboriginal news network is essential to providing accurate and authentic information to Aboriginal and non-Native media, particularly in the era of the Internet and the World Wide Web.

Native people recognize that computer and telecommunications technologies offer central resources for Aboriginal media access to, and distribution of, Aboriginal and non-Native news and information. The efficacy of electronic bulletin boards or computer networks has been demonstrated, as has the effectiveness with which these resources can be used to gain access to and distribute regional, national, and international information. But the reality is that, notwithstanding the attempts of Industry Canada to extend Internet access in Aboriginal communities through its Schoolnet and Community Access programs, most Native communities do not currently have appropriate infrastructure or affordable access to the Information Highway. There is a critical and timely need for the funding and knowledge to provide Internet connections, hardware, software training, and maintenance to support distance education, telehealth, and social services in Aboriginal communities.

Concluding Comments
The future of Aboriginal identity, culture, and community is intricately interwoven with the future of Aboriginal broadcasting; and the potential for understanding, dialogue, and development that Aboriginal access

to mainstream media can sustain is equally important to the future of Canada.

Canada draws a certain history and identity from its relationship with Aboriginal Canadians, who stand at the periphery of its institutional borders. If Aboriginal Canadians are part of Canada's political reality, then technology is central to its social history. Like the transcontinental railroad of an earlier era, communications technologies and the cultural industries they spawn continue to shape the Canadian experience. For Aboriginal Canadians, the experience forged through the media is too often one of exclusion, stereotypical inclusion, or appropriation. Aboriginal broadcasting can provide a basis for cultural and linguistic continuity and social development in Aboriginal communities. But because we actually construct who we are in the process of identifying with the images and cultural narratives that dominate our ways of seeing and representing the world, Aboriginal media and Native perspectives in the mainstream media are also central factors in the formation of culture, identity, and community, both Aboriginal and Canadian.

Acknowledgments

This chapter is based upon Gail Guthrie Valaskakis, "Telling Our Own Stories: The Role, Development, and Future of Aboriginal Communications," Royal Commission on Aboriginal Peoples (Ottawa, 1995).

Parts of the section "Media and Representation: The 'Oka Crisis'" have appeared in: Gail Valaskakis, "Rights and Warriors," *Ariel: A Review of International English Literature* 25, 1 (1994): 60-72, and in "Rights and Warriors: First Nations Media and Identity," in *The Mass Media and Canadian Diversity*, eds. Stephen E. Nancoo and Robert S. Nancoo (Mississauga: Canadian Educators' Press, 1997).

References

Albers, Patricia C., and William R. James. 1987. "Illusion and Illumination: Visual Images of American Indian Women in the West." In *The Woman's West,* ed. Susan Armitage and Elizabeth Jameson, 36-50. Norman and London: University of Oklahoma Press.

Angus, Ian, and Sut Jhally. 1989. *Cultural Politics in Contemporary America.* New York and London: Routledge.

Atwood, Margaret. 1972. *Survival: A Thematic Guide to Canadian Literature.* Toronto: Anansi.

Berkhofer, Robert F. 1979. *The White Man's Indian.* New York and Toronto: Random.

Brisebois, Debbie. 1983. "The Inuit Broadcasting Corporation." *Anthropologica* 25 (1): 105-15.

Canada, Department of Communications. 1990. Native Broadcasting Policy, 10 September. Ottawa.

–. 1991. The Broadcasting Act.

Caplan, G.L. and F. Sauvageau. *Report of the Task Force on Broadcasting Policy.* Ottawa: Supply and Services.

Caron, André. 1977. "The Impact of Television on Inuit Children's Cultural Images." Paper presented at the Annual Meeting of the International Communication Association, Berlin.

Carey, James. 1967. "Harold Adams Innis and Marshall McLuhan." *Antioch Review* 28 (2): 5-39.

Coldevin, Gary O. 1977. "Anik I and Isolation: Television in the Lives of Canadian Eskimos." *Journal of Communication* 27 (4): 145-53.

Coldevin, Gary O., and Thomas C. Wilson. 1985. "Effects of a Decade of Satellite Television in the Canadian Arctic." *Journal of Cross-Cultural Psychology* 16 (3): 329-54.

CRTC 1980. *The 1980s: A Decade of Diversity – Broadcasting Satellites and Pay-TV.* Report of the Committee on Extension of Service to Northern and Remote Communities. Ottawa: Canadian Government Printing.

Curley, Austin, and Associates. 1993. *Evaluation Report: Northern Native Broadcast Access Program.* Ottawa: Department of Secretary of State.

Dicks, Dennis J. 1977. "From Dog Sled to Dial Phone." *Journal of Communication* 27 (4): 120-9.

Elberg, Nathan. 1984. "In Search of Real Inuit." Paper presented to the Fourth Etudes Inuit Studies Conference. Montreal: Concordia University.

Gerbner, George. 1994. "There Is No Free Market on Television." *Hofstra Law Review* 22: 879-84.

Grantzberg, Gary. 1982. "Television as Storyteller: The Algonquin Indians of Central Canada." *Journal of Communication* 32 (1): 43-52.

Grantzberg, Gary, Jack Steinbring, and John Hamer. 1977. "New Magic for Old: TV in Cree Culture." *Journal of Communication* 27 (4): 154-8.

Hall, Stuart. 1986. *Journal of Communications Inquiry* 10. Special Issue dedicated to the work of Stuart Hall.

–. 1989. "Cultural Identity and Cinematic Representation." *Framework* 36: 68-81.

Henton, Darcy. 1990. "The Mohawk Warriors: Heroes or Thugs?" *Toronto Star*, 24 November, D1, D5.

Hudson, Heather. 1977. *Northern Airwaves: A Study of C.B.C. Northern Service.* Ottawa: Keewatin Communication Studies Institute.

–. 1985. *The Need for Native Broadcasting in Northern Canada: A Review of Research.* Ottawa: Department of Secretary of State.

Jacobs, Alex Karonialkiteae. 1986. "The Politics of Primitivism: Concerns and Attitudes in Indian Art." *Akwekon* 2/3: 1-3.

Lougheed and Associates. 1986. *Report on the Native Communications Program and the Northern Native·Broadcast Access Program.* Ottawa: Secretary of State.

Madden, Kate. 1990. "The Inuit Broadcasting Corporation: Developing Video to Sustain Cultural Integrity." Paper presented at the Annual Meeting of the International Communication Association, Dublin.

Mayes, R. Greg. 1972. "Mass Communication and Eskimo Adaptation in the Canadian Arctic." MA thesis, McGill University, Montreal.

McLuhan, Marshall. 1960. *Explorations in Communication.* Boston: Beacon.

O'Connell, Sheldon. 1977. "Television and the Canadian Eskimo: The Human Perspective." *Journal of Communication* 27 (4): 140-4.

Ridington, Robin. 1990. *Little Bit Know Something: Stories in a Language of Anthropology.* Vancouver: Douglas and McIntyre.

Roth, Lorna. 1982. "The Role of Canadian Projects and Inuit Participation in the Formation of a Communication Policy for the North." MA thesis, McGill University, Montreal.

–. 1994. "Northern Voices and Mediating Structures: The Emergence and Development of First Peoples' Television Broadcasting in the Canadian North." PhD diss., Concordia University, Montreal.

Rowlandson, John. 1988. *Aboriginal Community Radio in Canada: A Report on the National Native Community Radio Survey: Aboriginal Communications and Broadcast Program.* Ottawa: Department of Secretary of State.

Royal Commission on Aboriginal Peoples (RCAP). 1997. Testimony at RCAP public hearings: Adamson, Mary Jane, Inuvialuit Communications Society, at Inuvik, NWT, 6 May 1992; Cook, Shirley, at Yellowknife, NWT, 8 December 1992; Fox, Ray, National Aboriginal Communications Society, Vancouver, BC, 15 November 1993; MacQuarrie, Catherine, at Yellowknife, NWT, 9 December 1992; Martin, Lawrence, at Moose Factory, ON,

9 June 1992; Morrisseau, Miles, at London, ON, 11 May 1993; Powless, Lynda, at London, ON, 11 May 1993; Smoke, Dan, at London, ON, 11 May 1993; White Eye, Bud, at Toronto, ON, 3 November 1992; Young-Ing, Greg, at Vancouver, BC, 4 June 1993. In *For Seven Generations: An Information Legacy of the Royal Commission on Aboriginal Peoples.* CD-ROM. Ottawa: Libraxus.

Salter, Liora. 1976. "Community Radio – Five Years Later – Concept and Development in Review." Presentation to the Conference of the Canadian Broadcasting League. Halifax: St. Mary's University, August 12.

Slapin, Beverly, and Doris Seale, ed. 1992. *Through Indian Eyes: The Native Experience in Books for Children.* Gabriola Island, BC: New Society.

Smith, Greg, and Associates. 1988. *Review of Native Broadcasting.* Ottawa: Canadian Radio-Television and Telecommunications Commission.

Stiles, J. Mark. 1988. *Native Broadcasting in the North of Canada.* Ottawa: Canadian Commission for UNESCO, Report 54.

Valaskakis, Gail. 1979. "A Communication Analysis of Interaction Patterns: Southern Baffin, Eastern Arctic." PhD diss., McGill University, Montreal.

–. 1992. "Broadcasting and Native Northerners." In *Seeing Ourselves: Media Power and Policy in Canada*, ed. Helen Holmes and David Taras, 202-16. Toronto: Harcourt Brace Jovanovich.

–. 1994. "Rights and Warriors." *Ariel: A Review of International English Literature* 25 (1): 60-72.

Wilson, Thomas C. 1981. "The Role of Television in the Eastern Arctic: An Educational Perspective." MA thesis, Concordia University, Montreal.

Part 3
Innovations in Education Practice: Renewing the Promise

While the last three decades have been marked by the resilient struggle of Aboriginal people to regain control of education, the 1990s have produced concentrated efforts to rethink Aboriginal education and to articulate what is "Aboriginal" about Aboriginal education. With Aboriginally centred education research still emerging, and with education practice being highly decentralized, the vibrancy of Aboriginal education is to be found in communities. This section, consisting of four case studies and a review of learning and teaching styles, highlights the efforts of Aboriginal people to reclaim the theory and practice of educating Aboriginal children and youth.

The case studies presented here share experiences of innovative practice – challenging existing systems, creating new designs and strategies, and translating hopes and dreams into realities. They affirm that Aboriginal education is more than an abstraction. It is made real in the daily acts and decisions of thousands of Aboriginal Elders, parents, and educators who bring particular values, knowledge, and ideas to the development of children. Aboriginal dimensions of education come alive in the efforts of schools and communities to make education work in profound ways – to prepare students as Aboriginal citizens and as citizens of a world changing beyond our ability to grasp, except in broad contours.

Written from different contexts, the three community case studies by Brenda LaFrance, Sheila Watt-Cloutier, and Lorna Williams, respectively, speak from a commitment to transform classroom conditions that render learning lifeless and oppressive to so many Aboriginal students. Each of the case studies has its own focus. In "Culturally Negotiated Education in First Nations Communities: Empowering Ourselves for Future Genera- tions," LaFrance introduces the science and math curriculum developed by the Mohawk of Akwesasne. The Mohawk Thanksgiving Address stands as its focal point, from which lessons radiate out into program content and process. This is an outstanding example of culturally based curricu- lum, developed with the cooperation of many community members, Elders, and resource people both inside and outside the community. Williams, on the other hand, talks about the challenges of working in the urban context, where schools have students from many First Nations backgrounds. In response to this diversity, a variety of initiatives have been developed to respect individual cultural traditions and also to build bridges among First Nations and with non-Aboriginal people.

In "Honouring Our Past, Creating Our Future: Education in Northern and Remote Communities," Watt-Cloutier presents the work of the Nunavik Educational Task Force, which asked fundamental questions about the nature of education in the Kativik School Board in northern Quebec. The task force started with the understanding that "the effective- ness of education is measured by how well it prepares people to handle the problems and opportunities of life in their own time and place" (Watt- Cloutier, this volume, p. 114). Contrasting the efficacy of traditional education with the southern-style education of today, Watt-Cloutier reit- erates the conclusion of the task force report in suggesting that creative approaches to empowering youth should guide the rethinking of Kativik school programs. There is much to learn from Watt-Cloutier's case study since, under the James Bay and Northern Quebec Agreement, the Inuit of Nunavik have had considerable latitude to design and implement their own programs. Aboriginal peoples in other parts of the country have advocated such flexibility for designing their own school systems, yet Watt-Cloutier warns that control must be accompanied by careful analy- sis, program development, and evaluation.

In order to transform learning, the classroom has to expand outward to include the community. Parents and Elders must become active planners and decision makers in education, and education can no longer be con- fined within the walls of an institution. In the case studies, there are examples where the conventional separation between the school and the community is challenged, whether by learning with Elders on the land in Nunavik, taking water samples from the St. Lawrence River in Akwesasne, or holding a traditional feast with multicultural students in a Vancouver school gym.

While the innovations discussed in each case study hold out hope for recreating Aboriginal education systems, the authors are also open in speaking about the struggles they have faced in trying to transform promise into achievement. Two recurrent themes are the pervasive presence of provincial governments in setting curriculum standards and in regulating funding, and the intrusiveness of Euro-Canadian ideology, which characterizes the learning experience in formal education. For Watt-Cloutier, the basic organization of education in Nunavik reflects a southern model that infiltrates the curriculum and day-to-day activities of educators. To rethink education means to plant Inuit values and goals at its deepest levels.

The Akwesasne Science and Mathematics Pilot Project has taken up the challenge identified in Watt-Cloutier's chapter, placing Aboriginal values, specifically those of Mohawk culture, at the heart of its curriculum. The Akwesasne project has produced a bicultural, provincially accredited curriculum. By helping students to see that values pervade all knowledge, students become aware of the connection between values, ideas, and experience. Yet the continuance of the curriculum development work has been in jeopardy since the "pilot project" exhausted its funds. The lack of sustained funding for innovative curriculum development has shackled Aboriginal education for decades, causing great frustration because of the cost to the present generation in delaying the implementation of Aboriginal curriculum.

In a large urban context, there is cultural and ideological diversity. The city often brings together Aboriginal peoples from different cultural traditions. Yet, despite the rhetoric of respect for diversity in multicultural, racially diverse school systems, the dominant position of provincially accredited curriculum and practices ensures that school environments continue to emphasize ideas that reflect Western knowledge and belief systems. Creating a space in which Aboriginal perspectives are consistently expressed is an ongoing struggle. Many initiatives depend on special funding that must be secured within a competitive environment – one in which funds are either limited or shrinking. As Williams points out, in order to secure funds to create Aboriginal programs, the learning needs of Aboriginal students must often be framed in terms of student deficits. Stereotypes are perpetuated, and the underlying logic of provincial curriculum and schooling practices remains unchallenged.

A fourth case study is unique in its content and national scope. Many educators and community representatives told the Royal Commission on Aboriginal Peoples (RCAP) about their efforts to produce curriculum with few resources and a mere trickle of funding. Recognizing the importance of adding to the pool of available resources, RCAP designed an education project that would extend beyond the life of the commission itself. Its curriculum innovation is an education guide based on the RCAP CD-ROM, *For Seven Generations*, a searchable database containing 60,000 pages of testimony (largely by Aboriginal people), five volumes of the RCAP final report, 200 research reports, and other publications issued during the life of RCAP. As a flexible resource, the CD-ROM gives students and teachers access to Aboriginal voices and concerns across a wide range of subject areas. In "The Information Legacy of the Royal Commission on Aboriginal Peoples," Marlene Brant Castellano describes the development of this curriculum initiative and the potential it holds to introduce students to the perspectives of Aboriginal people from all regions and nations in Canada.

The final chapter, "Issues of Pedagogy in Aboriginal Education" by Kathy Hodgson-Smith, reviews research literature on efforts to identify a distinctive Aboriginal learning style. The goal of such research has been to provide a basis for devising more effective methods of Aboriginal in-school education. As Hodgson-Smith reports, the results have been mixed, and strong evidence of a distinct "Aboriginal learning style" has not materialized. Some Aboriginal educators have questioned the motives behind such research and caution that teachers may stereotype Aboriginal students based on what they have heard about learning styles. Hodgson-Smith points out the limitations of previous research, which has examined teaching as science, reflecting the world from the outside in; instead, she challenges us to explore pedagogy from a perspective that recognizes teaching as an act of love and to rethink the world from the inside out.

The research reviewed by Hodgson-Smith, taken together with the case studies, highlights shifts in the directions of Aboriginal education over time. The learning styles research that she reviews produced inconclusive results through the 1970s and 1980s. During the same period Aboriginal educators were turning their attention to improving the quality of education by creating program designs that incorporated traditional values and pedagogies. Convergence between research that legitimizes knowledge and local innovations that chart new paths has yet to be achieved.

The case studies in this section bring to the fore the energy and imagination with which the transformation of Aboriginal education is being pursued in practice. There is no question that the task is difficult. In specific instances, governments have funded innovations that nourish the vigour of Aboriginal identities and knowledge for coming generations. Yet when attempts are made to implement these innovations as part of the ongoing curriculum, they are overshadowed by the institutionally sanctioned knowledge of provincial curricula, whose legitimacy is paramount. They wither, and, if they survive, they have to fight for basic nourishment. It is a testament to the commitment and vision of Aboriginal Elders, parents, educators, and community leaders that innovation persists and that the promise of education for future generations continues to be nurtured.

5
Culturally Negotiated Education in First Nations Communities: Empowering Ourselves for Future Generations
Brenda Tsioniaon LaFrance

Numerous studies and commissions that examine "Indian Education" have been conducted over the past two centuries. However, the larger society has continually failed to recognize that schooling involves cultural negotiation. People of colour worldwide have always recognized the need for education – that is not the debate. The divergence occurs around the concept of "education."

First Nations people have long understood that education is a lifelong continuum of experience gleaned from interaction with one another, with all of nature (seen and unseen), as well as with all of the cosmos. For Mohawk people of the Haudenosaunee culture, this is reflected in the Thanksgiving Address that reminds us of the role assigned by the Creator to all living entities as well as of our thanks that the cycle of life continues. The underlying philosophy of this simple Address forms the basis of our approach to life and its experiences. Our experience with past and current Western schooling, however, is that it separates "education" from living: so the experience alienates us from our surroundings and, therefore, our culture. What Western schooling has done is to essentially provide students with their "formulas," "theories," "laws," "facts." Then there is a test, generally written, that proves to the teacher that the student has grasped the concepts.

In many instances the learning is not related to the students' everyday lives or culture. Students are taught to individualize their understanding. Our Thanksgiving Address and our culture says that "we come to one mind." However, Western education says "come to my mind" (Western expert in any given field); "to his mind" (Darwin's theory); "to their mind" (any given theory accepted by a collection of Western experts). There is no "our mind." Consequently, we cannot, culturally, be educated in a Western way and remain who we are: there are just too many minds!

First Nations peoples venture into the twenty-first century, many with cultures and teachings intact; many struggling to protect, preserve, and pass on the spirit of their respective nations. Mohawk people are no different. The struggle for survival by First Nations peoples has magnified the need for the culturally appropriate instruction of youth.

Schooling continues to play a major role in this survival. We are acutely aware of, and we accept, the fact that education – either through schooling or life experience – involves cultural negotiation. This acceptance is shown throughout First Nations territories, and one only needs to visit institutions operated by First Nations people for First Nations children. The negotiation process involves the formulation and presentation of the educational environment, curriculum, activities, and the like for First Nations schools. This process has been difficult for many, including the Akwesasne. It has taken the better part of two decades to slowly develop, and it follows much local debate, self-examination, and cultural self-consciousness. That it has taken this time to become socially acceptable to First Nations is in itself a testimony to the painstaking effort of cultural negotiation.

Evolution of the Akwesasne Science and Mathematics Pilot Project

The Akwesasne School Board decided to approach schooling from a cultural perspective and to undertake the blending of Mohawk and Western education. There has been much anxiety and uncertainty in this approach to learning, since it involves relatively unknown territory. However, the board has risen to the challenge and, in a leap of faith, has continued to support the integration process in the hopes of improving students' personal success.

Many Mohawk parents and Elders support teaching from the perspective of Mohawk ancestors, the "science and mathematics" that will enable youth to walk forward in this world with, on the one hand, the First Nations teachings and wisdom and, on the other, an understanding of the Western way of knowing. Only then will youth be able to see the relevance of Western education to their way of life. In this chapter, I report on our efforts to create a unique curriculum.

The Western world will be required to be flexible enough to accept the validity of integrating its concepts and views into Indigenous teachings and wisdom. Canadian society needs to appreciate the gains that may accrue from this approach to learning. This type of schooling would enhance understanding of other worldviews and would illustrate how culturally integrated schooling can broaden educational experience.

The absence of First Nations students within institutes of higher education ultimately creates a void in policy-making professions that have the ability to transfer the harmonious, Earth-based concepts of First Nations to Canadian society. Also, with First Nations being on the eve of self-government, there is an overwhelming call for scientific and technical professionals to deliver services for First Nations administration. Across Canada, the educational attainment of First Nations people is generally less than that of the overall Canadian population. While the number of high school graduates at Akwesasne has increased significantly, few local students have successfully completed courses of study, including science and mathematics at the university level.

Prior to 1988, elementary students at Akwesasne were taught from forty-year-old textbooks. Principals/supervisors hired by federal officials lived in Peterborough, about four hours away by car. There was no formally adopted curriculum that guided the teacher and ensured that the previous grade's work was reinforced and built upon. Two of the elementary schools were considered to "be in Quebec," the third "in Ontario"; teachers seemed to be primarily recruited from Quebec or New York State. From their elementary school, students attended the secondary schools of Ontario or New York State. With no firm base, it was predictable that students either did not achieve or left school prior to graduation.

In 1985, the Mohawk Council of Akwesasne (MCA) initiated a study of the educational system as the first step towards local control. The study examined the reserve's three elementary schools and included a section for General Vanier Secondary School (GVSS) because 20 percent of its student body consists of Aboriginal students. Representatives from the three school committees formed a Tri-School Steering Committee that examined the local control study results and reviewed statistics.

In late 1986, this same committee became the Akwesasne Mohawk Board of Education (AMBE) and, in 1987, signed an agreement with the Department of Indian Affairs to assume local control of local education. The first goal had been met. This exercise was an indication of the Canadian federal policy of self-government. This policy empowered reserve communities to examine system components and to work towards aligning them in their best interests.

The 1985 study of the educational system indicated appalling conditions: at the secondary level, the principal said "not many of the Native students opt for the Advanced level of study which would prepare them for university or college. Most of the Native students select the General or Basic levels" (AMBE Local Control Study 1985). In 1991, the principal said of Mohawk students at GVSS: "they are ready, they are good – they can compete." This reflects well on the concerted efforts of the AMBE and GVSS.

We are moving away from past trends, which involved educating Mohawk students for positions off the reserve. For us, the final success of education is the production of socialized citizens who meet the needs of the community. AMBE recognizes the current/future need for developing a local pool of scientific, health, and technological professionals.

Environmental preservation and infrastructure development have become of the utmost importance, given that pollution has raged through our First Nation. Various chronic care and emergency health facilities are under construction, and they complement the minimal care facility, Iahkhisotha, that became a reality in 1990. Most local health care providers are paraprofessionals; now we need to provide Mohawk health care professionals.

It was a tenet of the Akwesasne Science and Mathematics Pilot Project that all twenty-first-century careers will require the knowledge provided in the disciplines of science and mathematics. In this era of self-government, it is imperative that future leaders, providers, and citizens be educated in all areas, including the hard sciences and mathematics. At the same time, education must not supplant the values and knowledge of Aboriginal peoples; rather, it must enhance what is practised in the community. It must be attractive, practical, and appropriate to the culture in which it is applied.

As educational institutions and families guide Aboriginal students into the future, they must do so in a practical manner: youth are no longer being educated to take their place in a non-Native society; they are being educated to take control of their future in a Native society. With these goals in mind, the Aboriginal Health Professions Program of the University of Toronto, the Akwesasne Mohawk Board of Education of the Mohawk Council of Akwesasne, and the General Vanier Secondary School of the Stormont, Dundas, and Glengarry Public School Board undertook the Akwesasne Science and Mathematics Pilot Project.

This project was designed to address, through curriculum design, the Akwesasne Mohawk way of attending school. Its mandate was to experiment with various types of career awareness programs that could prove successful in encouraging student enrolment in academic courses. A significant focus of the project was to explore the teaching and learning strategies that are most effective with regard to Mohawk youth and to help achieve full understanding of the Akwesasne Mohawk "way to go to school."

While local role models do exist, many have been educated, from kindergarten to university, in the United States: Henry Lickers, biologist; James Ransom, civil engineer; Ken Jock, biologist; Wallace Ransom, agronomist; Wesley Laughing, industrial engineer; Leah Tarbell, computer engineer. Mohawk medical personnel employed in our community health services include Ben Kelly, MD; Beverly Jackson, nurse practitioner; Jeanine Rourke, BSN; Maxine Caldwell, biologist; Rebecca Brown, laboratory technician; Angus Pyke, pharmacist, Cecelia LaFrance, X-Ray technician; and several nurses who have completed RN training. The fact that many of these professionals have received their educational training in the US would entail a study in itself and may serve as one possible solution to the problems in Canada's First Nations schools.

A brainstorming session was held with several of these people in order to gain input into this project's design; they continued to be consulted and utilized throughout the project. Limited funds from federal and provincial governments as well as from private foundations have enabled research to be conducted, and a First Nations science and mathematics curriculum for Grade 7 through Grade 9 that meets Ontario curriculum requirements was designed. Additionally, special experiential programs and educational research were incorporated to examine the potential positive influence on student achievement, retention, and pursuit of higher education.

Interestingly enough, even though – being the first curriculum of this type in First Nations territory – this project had national and provincial implications, provincial funding trickled down from the Ontario Ministry of Citizenship and Culture as an anti-racism exercise. Efforts to secure funds from the Ontario Ministry of Education were unsuccessful. Yet the Ministry's internal review process cited this as a project of high merit for First Nations students.

The underlying premise of this project was that the promotion of science and mathematics knowledge must be culturally relevant in order to spark interest and enthusiasm among First Nations youth. The overall goal was to promote self-confidence and self-esteem in Mohawk youth by introducing and reinforcing Aboriginal contributions to the fields of health, science, and technology and, thus, demonstrating the historical and current importance of science and math in First Nations culture. This strategy included developing a portable culturally appropriate science and mathematics curriculum for First Nations and Ontario youth (Grades 7 to 9) through using an experiential, integrated approach to learning that increases student self-confidence and self-esteem as well as multicultural understanding. The expected outcome was increased achievement levels among participating First Nations students and increased First Nations student enrolment in science and math throughout university.

Extensive Aboriginal and non-Aboriginal institutional consultation occurred and continued to occur with regard to curriculum design and experiential programs. Community-based educational institutions that specialize in the provision of cultural education also assisted in conceptualizing curriculum and experiential programs. A curriculum working group composed of teachers, parents, students, and cultural advisors monitored and commented on the curriculum process, and it suggested resources and approaches to proposed topics. The resulting draft curriculum then served as a discussion document with other Mohawk people.

A pilot project steering committee set the overall direction for the project and was composed of members of the Stormont, Dundas, and Glengarry Public School Board; the Akwesasne Mohawk Board of Education;

the University of Toronto; the Department of Indian and Northern Affairs; and General Vanier Secondary School (an off-reserve public school).

Several advisors from the Native and non-Native scientific world were involved in the development of the project. They provided guidance and support on an as-needed basis. These people include: John Fadden, Onchiota Museum; Dr. Michael Closs, University of Ottawa; Joe Bruchac, author; Dr. Ed Barbeau, University of Toronto; Dr. Mary Fadden, Cornell University; Jim Murphy, Learning Hands, Inc.; Dr. Thom Alcoze, Northern Arizona University; Dr. Charles Moore, Northern Arizona University; Dr. Steve Harris, Queensland University; and Dr. Pam Harris, Queensland University.

To date, the Akwesasne community members have contributed much in-kind support, including the time to attend meetings that involve local Elders, spiritual leaders, Mohawk professionals, teachers, parents, and students; local government environmental staff (for project design); archival staff (for research); health professionals (for project design); council members' time (for committee meetings and project input); and space, equipment, supplies, and field trips.

In this way, at least one of the project's goals was being achieved: Elders, spiritual leaders, and Mohawk people in general began to reassert their rightful place in the education of their youth by assisting in the curriculum design process and by participating in classroom projects. Over time, they may ultimately be requested to seek out and to assist in documenting the oral history, teachings, stories, legends, and mythology so that it may be continually incorporated into the curriculum.

Staff met with a team of local Elders, historians, and spiritual leaders to debate curriculum content and approach as well as to help write and review curriculum themes based on Mohawk culture. The meetings provided participants with the opportunity of struggling to "come to one mind." Each individual was respected for the particular gift that she/he brought to the discussions. In this way staff developed story, legend, and mythology files with local Elders, spiritual leaders, and historians; they developed science themes that integrate earth, trees, animals, birds, agriculture, food, water, cosmology, and Mohawk ways of knowing; they developed math themes that incorporate number systems, cultural values, sacred circles, ceremonial significance, space, time, measurement, and Mohawk concepts of distance; they also developed geography and conservation themes, along with language arts themes, that resonate with the Mohawk worldview.

Curriculum

To provide the reader with the essence of the Akwesasne Mohawk way to go to school, let's share a dream that is struggling to become a reality.

Envision youth empowered by bringing to life and validating their ancestors' Aboriginal wisdom. At Akwesasne, we are using the Mohawk Thanksgiving Address, which has been recited for centuries. It acknowledges and expresses appreciation for the natural world and the duties that are fulfilled in order to maintain existence. This forms the basis of the science curriculum design and embraces the Mohawk concept of the relatedness of all creation while exploring the internal and external environments of all living things. The Aboriginal concept of "ecology" is examined and compared to that of the dominant culture.

Our Mother Earth is studied through the discovery of what constitutes "earth," or soils, and Aboriginal uses of soils are explored from an agricultural perspective as well as from an Aboriginal potter's perspective. Plant life is surveyed from a holistic Aboriginal perspective – how it assists Mother Earth, people, and animals (ecology); its medicinal characteristics; its use as natural dyes; and the Haudenosaunee connection between the Three Sisters – corn, beans, and squash – and its cultural significance. Western classifications are also incorporated into the units.

Water is looked at from an Aboriginal ecological perspective, and its chemical composition and properties are also studied. Animals form the basis of the Haudenosaunee clan system, or family organization, which is incorporated into the curriculum, as are classification systems and ideas concerning cells and cell functions. The study of "energy" includes units on the Haudenosaunee teachings of the Four Winds, Thunder, Lightning, and Sun, along with overall notions of conservation and ideas stemming from Western science. The cosmos is incorporated into the curriculum through experiential teaching in the Aboriginal and Haudenosaunee concept of oneness with the universe. The moon, stars, and other galaxies are intertwined with Aboriginal mythology to demonstrate the intricate thought of our ancestors concerning cosmology.

Field trips and experiential programming are integrated into the science curriculum to demonstrate how Aboriginal and Western concepts have been incorporated. Where appropriate, the mathematics component incorporates Western curriculum requirements with their Aboriginal equivalent for each unit. This component involves a survey of Aboriginal number systems and the origin of number words, the limits of counting, mathematical thought of the Haudenosaunee agricultural and hunting society, Mesoamerican geometry, the Mayan concept of zero, Inca and Mayan calendrics and computational techniques, the Inca counting board and uipus, and notation devices. Mr. James Murphy (Cherokee), Dr. Charles Moore, and Dr. Michael Closs, all mathematicians who have extensively studied Aboriginal mathematics, serve as advisors to the project. Problem solving and research skills are fostered in much the same way as were the analytical skills of Elders.

A teaching/learning assessment of Mohawk youth and their teachers was designed to determine the most effective learning and teaching processes. The analysis served to assist in finalizing curriculum design. Additionally, we like students to discuss different modalities of learning and to develop the skill to operate in alternative learning modes. This skill enables students to consciously observe and adapt, depending on the requisite modalities.

It appears that First Nations ancestors used intense and extended observation to study science and mathematics. There was a high degree of respect for the individual during the learning process, which enabled the child to observe until he/she felt confident to undertake the task independently.

The initial trial was conducted in private, and this privacy was universally respected. Once the task was successfully completed, it was repeated and lauded in public. Learners cooperated and assisted each other in achieving their goals. The concept of failure was not introduced to the learner; rather, it was accepted that learning was a lifelong process and that knowledge acquisition continued until death. Such knowledge brought with it an obligation to share it and pass it on.

Present-day learning and teaching seems to continue to follow this pattern. In a basket-making course this winter, Henry Arquette began the class by assisting students with initial layout and design. After a short demonstration, he allowed the student to work independently until she/he asked for help. As a group, the students would work on their project until they had a problem. Other students would provide assistance without question and then go back to their work. When a student fell behind, the others would pitch in to bring him/her to the same place. So this "coming of one mind" approach to learning resulted in spurts of achievement that brought everyone to the same place. This was followed with more spurts until everyone finished together.

Programs can serve to provide a survey of career opportunities as well as to gain further insight into Mohawk culture. They can also serve to delve into the need to incorporate Western ways of knowing into our culture and everyday lives. Such experiential ways of learning improve the likelihood that students will seek higher education.

Career Awareness Options

A major component of the pilot project consists of special programming designed to achieve several objectives. The goal is to plan and design annual project activities that will encourage students to undertake the study of an advanced science and math curriculum by introducing and reinforcing Haudenosaunee and other Aboriginal contributions to the fields of health, science, and technology.

Many youth living within First Nations territories are unaware of the career options available to them, even though they may see adults who have succeeded in their careers. By demonstrating those options in an experiential fashion, and stressing their importance and relevance to Aboriginal culture, an opportune setting is provided within which youth can integrate First Nations ways of knowing with Western ways of knowing and vice versa.

The initial stage of this opportune setting is student recognition of a science and mathematics curriculum designed by their families. They see this because it is threaded throughout the curriculum and so becomes normal. Also, programs and services can serve to entice students to attend institutions of higher learning. Visits to universities enable youth to gain familiarity with campus living and to glimpse the commitment necessary for gaining knowledge in various fields. During their high school years, students can be helped to understand that a university campus can be initially confusing but will eventually become familiar. The mystique of institutions of higher learning is thus minimized, and such a venture becomes achievable.

There are several year-round and summer programs available to students in Grades 7 to 8 and Grades 9 to 12. These programs may not be specifically geared to First Nations students, but they are established to interest students in both college/university and science and technology. Native school counsellors need assistance in linking with these existing programs, especially First Nations special services and programs at the university level.

Field trips can be designed to provide students with the opportunity to experience and meet Aboriginal and non-Aboriginal health professionals in their work environment. This is a primary area for students to experience a well-balanced mixture of Aboriginal and non-Aboriginal practices and teachings.

Other types of programming our project has employed include presentations by Steven Fadden from the Six Nations Onchiota Indian Museum about Haudenosaunee and other Aboriginal contributions to the world – from a traditional and Western scientific perspective. Local laboratories provide tours of their facilities in order to demonstrate available careers. In remote areas, videotapes can be used. Our project has been implemented in Iahkhisotha, a local chronic care home, to establish a junior volunteer program and tours related to health career awareness. Various health professionals share insights into their careers.

We had projected the implementation of a mentorship program. We know that there are many people to whom, in our walk through life, we turn for support of various sorts. We felt it important that mentors develop a support network for First Nations students. These mentors would be committed to providing required emotional, academic, and spiritual support to the student. This support may be required not only for the student, but also for his/her family members, many of whom may not have had the opportunity to experience post-secondary education. The mentors need to make a commitment to be available to the student, to encourage and support the student in his/her chosen path, to provide spiritual guidance should the student request it, to assist the student in opening the doors to a wholesome career, and to encourage the student to seek experiential career opportunities for professional growth and development.

We found that the type of mentorship program most suitable to Akwesasne was a "job shadowing" program. Students could, through available school programs, follow a mentor through a typical work period in order to gain insight into the type of work experience undertaken in a particular profession. Some are self-evident mentorships. Because our reserve, as with many others, is facing environmental degradation, students can participate in environmental projects.

An activity incorporated into the Grade 8 curriculum was a water quality project that monitored the water life and the water conditions along the heavily polluted St. Lawrence River. Local universities and governmental agencies participated in assisting the students to conduct the various tests and analyses required. This activity was incorporated into the draft mathematics and science curriculum for Grade 8. Haudenosaunee and First Nations beliefs permeate the exercise and so ensure that the values of Aboriginal people are reinforced. Another project designed for Grade 8 curriculum was a joint effort with the Akwesasne's Environmental Division that will design and implement an indoor aquaculture project for Grade 8 that included historical Mohawk fishing practices.

National organizations often have educational components that can be brought to the community. For example, the Aboriginal Trappers Federation of Canada agreed to assist the project by organizing a field trip to a trapper's cabin (an established trapline) for Grade 7 students. This enabled the unit on animals to include personal experience with various aspects of hunting, trapping, and fishing; animals in their natural habitat; trap sets and snares; and skinning, preparing, and tanning hides. The rites of hunting, trapping, and fishing were described and demonstrated to the students, emphasizing the need to respect life and the interdependency of all of nature, including human beings.

The American Indian Science and Engineering Society (AISES) has a wealth of programming to encourage middle school and high school students to enter careers in science and technology. Our middle school and high school students participate in the annual AISES science fair and have the opportunity to mingle with other Native students in the United States and Canada as well as with Native science and technology professionals.

Exposure of students to our Mohawk and other First Nations professionals, especially in science and technology, is important for role modelling.
Those individuals who work quietly on a daily basis to serve the health,
environmental, and scientific needs of the community have not yet been
used as role models for youth. We sought funding for a video and poster
project to first identify those individuals who have, for many years, studied Haudenosaunee science and mathematics, and then those who have
pursued careers in the health, science, and technological fields.

Some high school graduates have entered colleges or universities and are
quite successful. These students, in person or through video, can share
their post-secondary experiences by talking about what college/university
life is like, what their career goals are, how they expect to achieve them,
and where they would like to be in five years.

In addition, First Nations experts can be invited into the classroom to
share their knowledge about a particular field. For example, in Mohawk
society, the late Jake Thomas was an expert in Haudenosaunee Cosmology
(and other topics); Jan Longboat is an expert in herbal healing; Tom Porter
is an expert in the circle of life and Haudenosaunee mathematics; and Jake
Swamp is an expert in the environmental responsibility of all Aboriginal
peoples. These presentations can also be videotaped for future use. Mohawk
Elders have much to say about science and technology, and it is again time
to promote a linkage between Elders and youth.

Most First Nations communities hold gatherings at least once a year.
For education, the primary goal of a gathering could be to demonstrate
to students the strong linkage between Western science and Aboriginal
science. Also, the importance of First Nations students entering science
and technology must be emphasized. Experts in the field of Aboriginal
ways of knowing could be invited to present and participate in student
discussions. Topics could include: traditional teachings, Aboriginal contributions to the world, the ancient wisdom of all Aboriginal peoples, and
melding Western and Aboriginal ways of knowing. These are but some
suggestions of the sorts of topics that could result in the building of a base
of First Nations professionals who are capable of walking in balance in
both worlds.

Research and Evaluation
The next step involves a process for measuring success and ensuring continuing growth. The project chose to use a culturally appropriate participatory research and evaluation approach to measurement in order to enable
self-evaluation. This type of approach was adopted in order to empower
the participants and community to develop their own terms of reference.

The stakeholders determined the research and evaluation issues/ques-
tions; chose the agenda of inquiry and the methods; and participated in

the data collection/analysis and interpretation of the data. They also decided how the results would be used. Our longitudinal study looked at six major areas: self esteem/confidence, including the problem of "drop-out" in its widest sense (e.g., students in school but not "fully present"); the current level of student learning – math, science, general/overall; the incorporation of "Mohawk" into schools; teaching and learning styles as well as course content; Mohawk/Native and non-Native relationships; and transition issues (e.g., student adjustment and adaptation to non-Native public schools). There was an interest in looking at the portability of this curriculum with regard to other Native and non-Native schools.

One reason our research and evaluation was successful was that we have made early linkages with university researchers who are interested in working with First Nations programs. Good researchers are careful to guarantee that the focus of the research comes from the First Nations community.

The research included the involvement of a combination of internal and external resource people. A community field researcher was hired by the project to carry out its fundamental tasks and processes. Two university researchers from Queen's University participated with project staff and other stakeholders to determine the overall approach, processes, and fundamental tasks.

We discovered that this pilot project's educational perspective had several implications. For schools in general, this perspective can provide an environmental education model based on First Nations culture that explores Western values from an alternative cultural base. Science, as a way of knowing, can successfully meld with Aboriginal ways. The two worlds can come together. This perspective on education places science within the broader context of ways of knowing and places the practice of science within specific contexts related to connections with our Mother Earth. This may provide more incentive to pursue this area of learning at a time when decreasing science enrolment is reaching a critical stage. Math and other courses can essentially be integrated and approached in the same manner.

For other First Nations communities this is one model of curriculum that is based within the culture and that has specific cultural references. Western concepts are brought into play to reinforce certain teachings and practices. Projects of this type can also provide an important framework for building participation in school programming and curriculum design in First Nations communities.

The path is not easy. Each answered question raises many more unanswered ones. Many of us at Akwesasne have been fostering the re-emergence of our way of going to school. Elders, as always, are willing to share; scholars are willing to write; educators are open to new ideas. Now we will see if our children are willing to learn.

Acknowledgments

This chapter is based on Brenda Tsioniaon LaFrance, "Culturally Negotiated Education in First Nations Communities: Empowering Ourselves for Future Generations," presented at the Round Table on Education convened by the Royal Commission on Aboriginal Peoples in 1993. The material was compiled from three previous publications, two prepared by the Akwesasne Science and Mathematics Pilot Project, *Empowering Ourselves: Making Schooling and Education One*, presented to the American Anthropological Association, November 1992; and *Aboriginal Science and Mathematics Pilot Project, Proposal 1992-3*, prepared for the Aboriginal Health Professions Program, University of Toronto. The *Local Control Study* prepared for the Mohawk Council of Akwesasne in 1985 was the historical source for the evolution of local control of education at Akwesasne.

Since the presentation of this paper to the Royal Commission on Aboriginal Peoples, the Akwesasne Mohawk Board of Education has quietly implemented and continued to field test the several developed units. The school board finalized and partially field-tested the entire curriculum. The primary funding source, the Department of Indian and Northern Affairs, did not fund the project beyond a five-year period. The Human Resources Development Canada guidelines prohibited continued funding of existing staff. The teachers, some of whom were the curriculum developers, use the units with much success. There is a move to renew the educational system based on the "Akwesasne Mohawk way to go to school." Major efforts began in fall 1997 and continue today. Like the turtle, our spirit moves steadily forward, and so will our view of "schooling."

6
Honouring Our Past, Creating Our Future: Education in Northern and Remote Communities
Sheila Watt-Cloutier

Education in Nunavik: The Past

Education is a means of learning, the way a people prepare themselves for life. All cultures and all peoples have education, but its form and effectiveness varies. The effectiveness of education is measured by how well it prepares people to handle the problems and opportunities of life in their own time and place. As the challenges of life change, education must also change – or the people will turn to self-destruction and perish physically and/or spiritually. Life has greatly changed for Aboriginal peoples, and our future depends on our ability to create new ways to prepare our children for life.

For thousands of years Aboriginal peoples had a very effective education. We knew how to prepare our children to handle the challenges they would face when living on the land. The harshness of our environment imposed a discipline that produced resilient, proud, and self-reliant people. Then things changed. Contact with the southern culture brought a flood of new things and new ways of life. People and decisions from far away places began to have more impact on our lives than the people around us and the disciplines of the land that we knew and understood. It was no longer clear what our own time and place was or what we now had to learn in order to control our own lives. The path of education we had successfully followed for countless generations did not prepare us for these new things.

Southern culture traditionally uses schooling as the principal means of education. Traditions seem right and natural to those who follow them, and seeing that we did not have schools, people from the south concluded that we needed them. The idea of institutional learning was new to us, and it was difficult for many of our people to understand and appreciate. However, if schools would help prepare our children for the changes they were facing, then most parents were willing to let their children be educated in the southern way. For those who were not willing to go this route, the government held back family allowance cheques, making it difficult for parents to feel like they had a choice in the matter.

In Nunavik, northern Quebec, initially the schools were set up and run by the governments in Ottawa and Quebec City. The government schools were basically "outpost" versions of southern schools. Their programs had nothing to do with our language, culture, or the adaptive challenges faced by our people, but they did provide an entry point to southern culture for some of our youth. They had mixed results. They enabled some of our youth to move more freely into the ways of the southern culture, but they did little to bridge the gap between our own culture and situation. Rather than making us stronger, they tended to undermine our confidence and identity.

Having said that, however, and having been part of that process and presently a survivor of that particular generation, I can say with a fair amount of clarity and certainty that, although the programs and processes we were a part of were irrelevant and at many times undermining, we nevertheless received an education that had a certain degree of rigour. Although a different culture was imposing this rigour upon us, we could identify with it through relating it to the upbringing we had received from our parents and the land. Most fellow Inuit of my generation will agree that in spite of the "deprogramming" efforts of the governments and religious orders at the time, the challenge and discipline of school programs did, to a certain degree, prepare us to handle some of the issues that lay ahead.

Certainly there are many negative effects from those years, depending on the places we were sent and the circumstances we faced, and we must deal with these issues on a daily basis as we come to terms with our past. The impact of the past situations should not be underestimated. However, the assimilation attempts of the governments, albeit unknowingly, did instill into us some confidence that we could actually learn as well as the next person. When they said, "learn our stuff and learn it well," this at times demoralized us, yet it also instilled in our psyche a sense that we were equal in our learning abilities. And learn we did, at times surpassing our southern peers. Many will agree that this rigour and challenge no longer exists in our schools and that we have gone from the extreme of a paternalistic system to the extreme of a system that challenges our youth so little that it undermines their intelligence. Time and time again we hear that our students are not learning well in either their mother tongue or the second languages. The watering down of programs, the lowering of standards and expectations is a form of structural racism that we must make every attempt to stop. There is a balance of respect and challenge that can be met, and we must make it a priority to find it.

Academic standards and rigour have been lowered in the name of respect for the "different learning styles" of Aboriginal peoples. Certainly there are cultural differences and value systems that must be respected at every level. However, these kinds of generalizations must be used with caution. What follows the lowering of standards is the lowering of expectations of all involved, including students, teachers, and parents. The low self-esteem that we are living with today did not occur overnight, and we must work to rectify it in every possible way. I caution academics about being too quick to make assessments and generalizations in an area in which very few Aboriginal people have participated in the basic research concerning the learning styles of our people. There are many questions about such research, and, in my opinion, we must avoid hasty conclusions. Until relevant quality programs have been in place in our schools for some time, and until benchmark studies are carried out to determine the effectiveness of such programs, it would not be wise for non-Aboriginal people to conclude anything about Aboriginal learning and schooling.

New Opportunities and Constraints

In Nunavik, the James Bay and Northern Quebec Agreement of 1976 gave our people a certain degree of regional autonomy, including the responsibility for operating our own school system. This provided an opportunity to create an educational service that matched the needs of our people. Unfortunately, neither we nor the governments involved anticipated what would be required to reshape the institutional system of learning we had inherited into something that would prepare our children to deal with their new environment as effectively as our grandparents had been prepared to deal with theirs.

There were some obvious things we could do, such as providing early education in our own language and building more schools so that children would not have to be sent away from their families to learn. These things were done, but operating the system, training Inuit teachers, building new schools, and extending services to every community took up almost all of our time and attention. These were significant accomplishments, but there was little time or energy left to think about the real educational needs of the community or how best to meet them. Even when needs were identified, the system could not always follow up, since it never had enough program development capability to design and produce effective programs.

We accepted the southern institutional programs as the standard because that is what schooling meant to us – it was what southern society did in their schools. In addition, our school board was accountable to the Quebec government through its Ministry of Education, not to our own emerging regional government. As a result, what our school system provided was a watered down, superficially adapted version of the official Quebec curriculum. This has little to do with the real challenges our people are facing.

The result is a system that does not adequately prepare our youth for life in either the North or the South. Many youth are demoralized and dispirited. Parents are told that they must be involved and encourage their children to do well in school because education is important, but they can make little sense of what they are being asked to support and they don't know what to do.

The problem is not that people have not worked hard. Many dedicated people, both Aboriginal and non-Aboriginal, have worked very hard to create the school system we have today. The problem is that, despite all the hard work, the education system is not producing the results we need.

The story is the same for many of our Aboriginal communities, whether they be Indian or Inuit. Having recently been involved in round table discussions on education where all the Inuit regions of this country were represented; and also frequently linking up with Indian nations in Canada and the United States, it is clear to me that the educational problems being experienced are very similar and, in many situations, identical.

The hunger for challenge is so evident in our youth that, in order to see it, you only have to look at the popularity of arcade halls or the popularity of video games in people's living rooms. Our youth are not looking to exercise their fingers or hand-eye coordination as they play these games; they are looking for ways to challenge and build their character, the very thing that traditional skills offer but that is denied to them by most of what is offered in the schools or elsewhere.

People do not learn the most significant things unless they are challenged. Parents and educators often see student success as being the most important thing. Institutions such as schools are good at providing success, and they can often do that by simply reducing the challenge (e.g., by watering down the programs until success is guaranteed). Easy successes are not worth much in human development terms. Certainly, there are more students graduating as more high school programs are offered in the communities; however, the statistics remain very high for dropouts in most northern regions.

In a recent article in *Arctic Circle*, this is what was expressed about dropouts in the Baffin region: "Of the 250 or so students who enter Grade 7 in schools throughout the Baffin region each year, statistics from the Baffin Divisional Board of Education show that only about half a dozen are likely to graduate with advanced Grade 12 diplomas. Most will drop out, some to take menial jobs, many more to do nothing much at all" (Coleman 1993). Furthermore, the achievement level of those from our northern communities receiving their high school leaving diplomas is clearly questionable when they enter post-secondary institutions in the South.

The question is whether they are really achieving anything, whether they are really being empowered by the system. People are "empowered" when they have learned to control the development and maintenance of their own powers – when they know what to do to continue their learning and development without being told what to do. Educators call this lifelong learning. Our Elders call this wisdom, and it is what we all want for our children so that they may control their lives rather then being overly controlled by external forces such as alcohol/drugs, institutions, processes, and people.

New Ways

In our Native heritage, learning and living were the same thing, and knowledge, judgment, and skill could never be separated. The Native way of teaching is holistic. When a young man is taught to hunt and be on the land, the technical skills of handling the gun or harpoon are taught at the same time as are the character skills of courage, respect, determination, persistence, and patience. When a young woman is taught to prepare and sew skins and materials for clothing, she is also taught the appropriate character skills to go along with her creativity. In the institutional way of learning, these things are frequently pulled apart and never reassembled. Schools spend much of their energy teaching and testing knowledge; yet knowledge by itself does not lead to wisdom, independence, or power.

If education does not genuinely empower children, then pretending that it does will only confuse them further. And it may even help to break their spirits because they will think it is their fault that they can find so little meaning in it. If education is done badly, then it can do more harm than good. No matter the intent or cultural slant, if programs are designed and delivered without respecting and challenging the full creative potential and intelligence of children, then they will crush rather than liberate.

It has long been recognized that there is a link between the quality of education and the future of a people or a nation. The greatest strength of a nation is the resourcefulness and wisdom of its people. The industrial models of education that have dominated most of the world for the past century are slowly starting to change. People are concerned about the dispiriting effect that schools frequently have on children, about the latter's dependency and lack of wisdom. Another reason for concern, however, is the rapid pace of change and the growing complexity of the things with which people must be able to deal if they are to survive. All the more reason for our communities not only to be able to survive the change, but also to be slightly ahead of the game, to know as much as possible about what lies ahead in order to keep control of our changing lives. The change has been rapid in the South, but we in the northern regions often state that we have gone from the "stone age" to the "space age" in a matter of four short decades.

start

ᐅAlthough our problems are more severe than most, people everywhere are having difficulty adjusting their education systems to new needs and conditions. For the past thirty years, southern society has, to little effect, been attempting to reform and realign education in North America. Once they are established, large institutions are very difficult to change. Our present education system in the remote areas is doubly disadvantaged. We are using a degraded copy of a system that not only does not address our needs as a people, but that no longer adequately addresses those of its own people. We have no choice but to find our own way.

This does not mean that we should ignore the educational methods and accomplishments of the South. There is no point in reinventing the wheel if a wheel is called for. However, we must be able to assemble the parts into a whole that meets our needs. To do this we must have a clear sense of what our needs are, and we must understand learning and instructional design well enough to be able to choose and build with the best educational "parts," wherever in the world they can be found.

In Aboriginal culture our Elders are our source of wisdom. They have a long-term view of things and a deep understanding of the cycles and changes of life. In our past it was very easy to see whether a person had wisdom or not. Living on the land required high levels of independent judgment, initiative, and skill. The challenges were real and immediate, and it was very obvious to everyone when someone did not yet know what they were doing.

With the introduction of communities and southern institutions, it became more difficult to know if someone had wisdom. In our past we had a high respect for anyone among us who knew what to do in different situations. The Elders, skilled hunters, artisans, and healers among us were all highly respected. So it was natural for us to respect the newcomers who seemed to know how to survive and how to make their organizations work. Their power looked like wisdom. But because we did not understand their manner of survival, their organizations, and what was involved in running them, we could not really know whether they were wise. We now know that it is a mistake to automatically assume that people who work for institutions have wisdom. Organizations can be very powerful, but they operate by dividing actions up into many small pieces. This makes it possible to quickly train a lot of people to carry out their own small part of very complicated activities. This means that life becomes much easier, but it also means that people may never understand the whole and never have a clear idea of what they are doing or why. We did not understand these things at the time.

The idea that personal wisdom was not necessary for survival never occurred to our people. Everything in our past told us that people without wisdom could not survive for long. Guaranteed survival seemed like a good idea to our people, just as it did to most others throughout history, given the same choices, and the people who could manage it seemed to have great wisdom and power. The traders, missionaries, police, and government officials found us easy to impress. Our traditional way of life was very hard, and, when the teacher was the land, the risks were great and wisdom took a long time to develop. Our people now had an option, and we started looking to the newcomers to be our teachers. We did not often understand why the new ways worked, we just trusted that if we did what we were told and were patient, things would work out.

When the teacher is the land, patience and wisdom go together. The best hunters had a lot of patience, not just in hunting but in everything. When the teacher is the land, patience usually works. Things can usually be figured out in time, as long as one is a careful observer. Our people thought that it would be the same with the new ways. They would eventually figure out how these things worked and would be able to run things themselves. To this day this has not happened. There was no wisdom or independent judgment to be gained. Patience and trust just got us deeper and deeper into things that were controlled by other people, things we did not understand. Our growing dependence was encouraged by the newcomers (and by their governments and institutions), who were prepared to control our lives for us.

The learning of wisdom started to diminish, as did the ability to be independent in one world or another. This has led many of our people to despair, and without the inner resources that are developed by constructive independence, people became vulnerable to different kinds of destructive dependencies. The use of alcohol/drugs became a way of life for many, although few people understood why.

Understanding Freedom: Giving It Away
Much turmoil and pain surrounds our communities, as the use of alcohol and drugs has become the most popular means by which the majority of the people choose to attempt to change the quality of their experience. With this choice, however, has come disastrous consequences: loss of life, morbidity, socioeconomic costs, and, most devastating and insidious of all, loss of personal powers and, ultimately, loss of freedom.

As the dependency-producing institutions continue to thrive, our people are led to further dependencies on substances, processes, people, and systems. People can become destructively dependent on anything that is a substitute for wise management and control. Organizational services as well as individuals often create dependencies in order to fill their need to be needed, to be in control of others. Furthermore, they are often threatened by any sign of growing independence because it would eliminate their reason for being. This makes it much harder for those who are dependent on them to break away and regain their freedom.

One only has to look at the growth of the programs, agencies, and institutions in our communities, most of which show no real evidence of change. If anything, many things are getting worse. As social problems increase, more social workers are hired. As the crime rate increases, so do the police forces and court halls. As accidents and diseases increase due to addictions, so do medical staff and facilities. The list goes on.

Unfortunately, many dependency-producing institutions make the big mistake of growing with the problem and, thus, of embracing dependencies/addictions rather then confronting them and finding concrete ways to empower people. The school systems that do not make true empowerment and independence the key themes of their programs are adding to the problem rather then solving it. Many educators may argue that socioeconomic problems prevent the school system from doing its job effectively. However, I and my Inuit colleagues who have been involved in looking deeply at the problems affecting our people believe that the lack of relevant and empowering programs in our schools not only perpetuates the problems but also undermines independence. Granted, it is difficult for educators to teach effectively if our children's basic needs are not being met. However, we can no longer use this as an excuse for maintaining the status quo. We cannot wait until communities heal before making changes to our institutions, especially to our education systems. Many things can be happening at the same time.

Everyone is trying to do what she or he perceives to be helpful in addressing these dependency problems, but most are dealing with only one piece of the problem, and, really, they are doing so to no avail. The problem of dependencies must be treated as a whole. The problem of alcohol and drugs cannot be dealt with by focusing only on alcohol and drugs. The larger issues of healing, life skills, being in control of one's life and destiny, freedom and living with freedom must be dealt with in order to effectively begin the process of changing from dependence to independence.

As we prepare for independence and self-government on a political level, so must we prepare for personal independence and empowerment, otherwise we will not achieve true self-government. Independence is not just an ideal. It is profoundly practical.

Autonomy as a goal of learning for individuals is the attainment of the capability to make judgments and decisions necessary to act with personal independence and freedom. An autonomous person need not wait for instructions [and is able to take] the given circumstances and constraints into account. Autonomy allows the decision maker to account

for these external constraints and to insert them into a clearer representation of reality as a basis for decision making. Autonomy provides both
a key to not being overwhelmed and a basis for self-fulfillment. (Botkin
et al. 1979)

An Education that builds bridges, that makes fuller learning more possible, that extends a young person's potential for independence is, in today's
terms, an "empowering education" that is a goal worth striving for. And
it is a goal that is possible. (Perrone 1991).

People can be well educated even though they have never been to school.
Education is a means of learning, and there are many formal and informal ways to learn. Schools are just one kind of tool that can help bring
about some types of learning. Schools can be very helpful if they are well-
designed and capably staffed, but the important thing is not the school –
it is learning, especially learning to be independent.

There are many advantages to freedom and independence, which is why
much of history is a story of people's struggle for greater freedom. Freedom
allows you to make more choices in life and makes it easier to adapt to different and uncertain situations. Freedom requires skills and does not just
happen. Everyone has some of these skills, but, like any kind of fitness,
freedom skills will develop or decay, depending on whether and how they
are exercised. Due to the long history of Aboriginal peoples being treated
in a paternalistic manner, to being controlled (i.e., to having given up
our personal powers), we are much more susceptible to, and, in fact, have
been groomed for, dependence upon many substances, processes, people,
and systems.

The loss of personal autonomy and the development of freedom-oriented
skills are linked directly to addiction. Dependence must be countered by
independence, by personal freedom. Freedom requires understanding,
skill, and motivation – all of which can be developed in appropriate circumstances and undermined in inappropriate circumstances. Preparing
people to make wise personal decisions, to exercise foresight and judgment, is a vital task for any society, but it is a task not well understood
and, worse, often poorly done.

Empowerment
In our communities, as elsewhere in the world, the importance of preparing youth for responsible self-direction is widely acknowledged and comes
up at almost every meeting dealing with educational and social issues.
However, most people do not know where or how to start the process of
empowerment. Many of the learning arrangements that we have accepted
from the South not only cannot deliver, they actually undermine the

process. Merely adding on some new programs or courses will not work. No small amount of tinkering with the system will do the trick, we can accept no more bandage solutions that only perpetuate the problems. In order for us to break free from despair and to take back our personal powers as Aboriginal peoples, we must now look at the big picture and think seriously about restructuring and refocusing our existing learning and living arrangements.

Empowerment cannot happen and wisdom cannot be nurtured effectively unless there is a wise, empowering structure in place to support it. Many students fail not because they do not have the ability to learn, but because the system has failed to teach them. As one of the adult educators from our region states with regard to standards of adult education programs: "Adult education must be a preparation for the real world. The Adult student must come to see the difference between a pass level and an acceptable accuracy level – the working level required in the real world. You do not hold a job very long by getting it right only 60% of the time. Drive a car with a 60% accuracy level and you will not live very long. Inuit adapt very quickly to the concept of 'accuracy level.' For generations they have known that a small margin of error is often a matter of survival" (Simm 1993).

Of course, this is not to say that you define the students solely by their ability to pass tests with a high level of accuracy, for academic testing in itself can at times be debatable (depending on the circumstances). The point here is to offer quality effective programs to our students, to expect their best, and not to reduce the demands that are made on them, as is so often done. It means finding a way to engage our children in significant striving so that they experience real achievement, not merely "success." Time and time again our students express that they would like to be more challenged and that they do not feel empowered by their school experience.

The students are even more critical of the language and culture programs that are provided in our schools. The lack of relevant challenge, and the lack of relevance to the real world, even extends into our own cultural and language teaching. School has reduced culture to handicrafts, something easily managed within the structure of the school program. Students complain that they learn very little and are always repeating the same things. Culture teachers say that they are not given the time, space, resources, materials, or respect necessary to do the job. Culture programs have not received the resources, attention, and support that they need in order to be effective. The way in which the programs are structured into the system does not give them the power to reach youth and to instill in them a sense of pride in their heritage.

Our youth are confused and torn between modern conveniences and traditional ways. In all our communities there is a longing among our youth to rediscover their roots. In the past we had our parents and Elders to teach us, but the land was our greatest teacher. Learning to live on the land, overcoming the difficulties with intelligence, ingenuity, patience, courage, a sense of humour, and cooperation is what taught our spirit and shaped who we were as a people. We can teach about this in the classroom, but we cannot acquire the spirit. The only place this can be learned is on the land, and we must find ways to ensure that all youth have the opportunity to rediscover that spirit so that they can develop the wisdom and inner strength they will need to meet the challenges of our rapidly changing world.

The language issue is often confusing, and the problem is how to ensure that Aboriginal languages are preserved while second languages are developed. Our languages are an essential part of our heritage, and our language programs must reflect the same quality as would traditional methods of language teaching. However, it takes more then language to become wise, and language without wisdom is hollow. It must involve more than simply putting Native pictures into the books. It is the Native spirit that has to be there. Without the spirit, the program has no energy to offer to the children. For example, legends should be taught by Elders telling the stories and explaining the meaning behind them, not by children colouring pictures in a so-called legend book.

With regard to the language program, students definitely want more challenge, relevance, content, and application. To provide high-level engagement for each individual child, the system must have a purpose, a structure, and an appropriately challenging program that responds effectively to the needs, aspirations, and potential of the children, the parents, and the community.

As Aboriginal people, we have an advantage over many other cultures in that we do not have to return to the holistic view of life because we never really left it. As we gain more autonomy over our own affairs, we can apply this view of life to planning, developing, and evaluating our education systems and schools. An example of such a framework is provided by the Four Worlds Development Project in Lethbridge, Alberta. Our own thinking on hidden curriculum has been greatly influenced by their work in *Holistic Education: Exposing the Hidden Curriculum*:

> In a holistic model of education, curriculum refers to everything that the student learns. Commonly the word curriculum has been used to describe the program that the staff of an educational institution is implementing in a conscious way. What the students learn from the education program is, however, only a small part of what they learn. It is, in fact, the part that is often forgotten within a short time after it is learned. What is not forgotten is what is learned about one's identity and role, and the identity and role of others in the program. How people treat each other and

their environment, and the attitudes, values and feelings that are encountered are also not forgotten.

This is what is sometimes called the hidden curriculum because people experience these things without realizing how much they are learning. The hidden curriculum is learned in the playgrounds and in the hallways. It is learned from the way the teacher manages student behaviour and from the way the desks are arranged. It is learned through the attitudes of parents and other community members about the school and it is these very things, learned through the hidden curriculum, that are likely to influence a person's identify, sense of worth and view of the world. These factors will have a direct connection with later or concurrent alcohol and drug abuse. (Four Worlds Development Project 1984)

The Four Worlds analysis goes on to discuss how a disempowering hidden curriculum can be replaced by a holistic education founded on empowerment and respect. A wise education is not something that is done to people, it is something that people must learn to do for themselves. This involves the whole community and starts with a collective vision of the future. Formal education is just a tool, a way of making something happen. The only way to choose what kind of tool is needed is to decide what you want to build.

Solutions: Taking It Back

Designing an effective education system involves a process of translating community needs and aspirations into effective programs and operations. There are different stages to this process, and each must be conducted carefully if the system is to work well. There is little point in having a clear vision that matches community purposes and needs if there is no effective way of realizing it. On the other hand, there is no point in having high-quality programs and operations if they have nothing to do with the purposes and needs of the community. It would be like being lost but making good time on the journey.

It is not enough simply to look at the programs and the organizations and services that they design and deliver. More in-depth analysis is needed. Different aspects of the organizations must be considered:

- the system's ability to create and follow a clear purpose and vision based on the needs of the communities it serves
- the system's ability to create effective strategies and methods to make the vision a reality
- the system's ability to deliver high-quality programs that faithfully reflect its strategies and vision
- the system's organization and structure.

Community and personal needs must also be considered. In the model we use, there are three general categories of community needs: self-government; culture preservation and development; and development of the community and regional infrastructure. There are four general categories of personal needs: self-management skills; heritage skills; global cultural access and analytical skills; and community and economic skills.

Examining these needs provides a good starting point for those wishing to look deeply into the problems of our education systems. There is a holistic relationship between all the needs, and each category is essential. Each skill supports and is supported by the others. Self-government depends on the self-management skills of individuals and vice versa. The community will be able to preserve and develop its unique culture only if this goes hand in hand with the development of heritage skills on an individual level. The community and regional infrastructures depend on the global cultural access and community/economic skills of individuals and vice versa. Community and individual development are inseparable.

By looking at all of these different needs and finding ways to take action to attain them, we can, as Aboriginal peoples, break our cycles of dependence and regain control over our lives.

The development of an appropriate and effective education system cannot wait for full self-government. Effective self-government requires high levels of knowledge and skill among the population and leadership, and this is the task of education. Our education system must be developed in parallel with, or even slightly ahead of, our emerging self-government as part of an overall plan. Since the movement for self-government is in advanced stages, our education system must be capable of rapid development.

Education systems in the South are not built for rapid change, and it would be a mistake to copy southern structures. The demands of education today are too complex to be handled by a single factory-like agency that processes youth through a fixed curriculum. The program of instruction is the core of education, and the rapid development of education is determined by the rate at which a system can develop and deliver high-quality educational programs. The design and development of good instructional material takes a great deal of time and effort. Just as it would be foolish for us to try to develop and build our own snowmobiles and airplanes in our regions, so it would be foolish to try to develop all the components of our education programs if they already exist elsewhere. The range of things our children must experience in order to learn our traditional language and skills as well as those skills that will enable them to gain access to global culture, is beyond the capacity of a single school program.

There are endless opportunities for us as we shop around for the best educational tools for our people. There are programs and curricula followed by southern alternative schools and private schools that are not mainstream but that still prepare students to enter post-secondary institutions. In our northern and remote areas, we have similar opportunities to create our own systems – systems that better meet the needs of our communities. For example, there are many advantages to interactive learning through modern technology, such as computers and multimedia, where the learner is actively participating in her/his own learning.

One of our Elders spoke about learning, saying: "Children do not learn language writing the words on a blackboard. They learn it by watching someone do something, like skin a seal." Have the child skin the seal and you have interactive learning. As stated earlier, there are countless ways that we can use modern technology to bring out the best of our culture and apply it to today's challenges. Traditionally, learning has never been a big mystery to the Aboriginal peoples. It is the giving away of our powers and wisdom to the new ways and institutions that has created such confusion, ultimately leading us into the dependencies and despair that we are currently experiencing.

There are incredible challenges ahead of us as we seek ways to break free and to regain our autonomy. However, we do not have the inertia of long established institutions to contend with, as we are small in number and still have a natural respect for wisdom.

As difficult as it may be, governments, institutions, and individuals now must start to let go and allow the process of empowerment to begin as we, the Aboriginal peoples, take back control and rediscover our natural ability to teach our children, using the best of our heritage skills and applying them to today's challenges. As easy as this may sound, from our experience in our region it is the most difficult challenge that our people are going to face. As for the "letting go" on the part of the institutions and people that have been in control for a long time, that is easier said than done. The relinquishing of control will require open and honest dialogue on the part of both the Non-Aboriginal and Aboriginal nations if we are to genuinely empower ourselves and to regain control over our lives. It will require political commitment, leadership, and determination. It can be done, and I have every confidence that it will be done.

Acknowledgments

This chapter is based upon Sheila Watt-Cloutier, "Honouring Our Past, Creating Our Future," presented at the Round Table on Education convened by the Royal Commission on Aboriginal Peoples in 1993.

Parts of the chapter come directly from the Nunavik Educational Task Force final report, *Silatunirmut: The Pathway to Wisdom*, authored by Sheila Watt-Cloutier, Minnie Grey, Johnny Adams, Jobie Epoo, and Josepi Padlayat, for Makivik Corporation. *Silatunirmut* provides a comprehensive and detailed discussion of issues and solutions presented in parts of this short paper.

References

Botkin, James, Mahdi Elmandjra, and Mircea Malitza. 1979. *No Limits to Learning: Bridging the Human Gap: A Report to the Club of Rome.* Oxford: Pergamon.

Coleman, Greg. 1993. "The Inherited Dream: Looking for Nunavut's Lost Generation." *Arctic Circle* (Spring): 14-19, 34-5.

Four Worlds Development Project. 1994. *Holistic Education: Exposing the Hidden Curriculum.* Lethbridge: Four Worlds Development Project.

Nunavik Educational Task Force. 1992. *Silatunirmut: The Pathway to Wisdom.* Makivik Corporation.

Perrone, Vito. 1991. *A Letter to Teachers: Reflections on School and the Art of Teaching.* Oxford: Jossey-Bass Education Series.

Simm, Ray. 1993. "Critique of Adult Education – Kativik School Board." Paper given to the Nunavik Educational Task Force, 5 May.

7

Urban Aboriginal Education: The Vancouver Experience

Lorna Williams

> In Bella Coola when I was lonely I'd just go up and watch the bald eagles. I had lots of friend animals. Here there is nothing.
>
> – Student, age 9

The Vancouver School District is a large urban school district with 53,000 students and more than 4,000 employees. It is located in a multicultural, multilingual city. The English-as-second-language (ESL) population is more than 50 percent. In some schools there can be forty different languages spoken.

Vancouver currently enrols almost 2,000 First Nations children who have moved here from all over Canada, the United States, Central America, and South America. Many of these families have moved to the city to seek better health, education, employment, and housing, or to escape ongoing violence. In 1980 Vancouver First Nations students were enrolled in 36 percent of the schools clustered in the northeast sector, in the northwest area, and around the Musqueam reserve. At that time, services could be concentrated in schools with significant enrolments of First Nations students. Today, the pattern has changed. In 1993, First Nations students are enrolled in 83 percent of the schools in the district. Schools without support for First Nations students are requesting assistance for academic, family, social, and cultural programs.

Providing appropriate educational services for the urban Aboriginal population is a complex undertaking that requires an understanding of the many interacting forces in the lives of students. This chapter will document the historical evolution and current profile of services developed in response to the needs of First Nations students in the Vancouver School District. I will also discuss the way in which Israeli educator Reuven Feuerstein's mediated learning approach (Feuerstein 1993) was integrated into our programming. And I will reflect on the experiences of First Nations education in the district over the past fifteen years and on the challenges we continue to face today.

I was hired as a Native Indian consultant in 1984. I added the word "education" to my job title to emphasize that the position was focused on education, not on my heritage. In my first week on the job, notes began to appear on my desk from colleagues, directing to me all the Aboriginal students who came to their attention, be they English-as-second-language (ESL) or special education people. Yes, I wanted to be involved, but Aboriginal children had the right to be provided with all the appropriate services. I realized that the district had to guard against ghettoizing and isolating First Nations students. Simply, my task was, first, to provide direct service in program development, curriculum support, and advocacy and, second, to entrench and provide knowledge about ourselves as First Nations throughout the district.

Initially I was concerned that my rural reserve education and teacher training experience might not be adequate in an urban provincial school district. As a member of the Lil'wat First Nation, I had worked in my home community of Mount Currie, where we pursued our quest to design and implement an education system that would serve our new reality in our homelands. Now, looking back, it is clear that the knowledge and experience gained in Mount Currie served as a solid foundation upon which to build.

Context

I'll begin by considering the varying circumstances of First Nations students in the Vancouver School District. While it is true that there are First Nations students living in financially stable families, many more exist in conditions of poverty and experience multiple social difficulties. When families break up due to domestic violence, it is often the mother who moves with her children. Living in the city without the support system of the extended family, she must rely on her children to assist in managing life in the city. Most recently, we have seen a trend towards grandmothers caring for their grandchildren.

When families move from communities on reserves, the social, health, and educational services change from federal to provincial jurisdiction; thus there is a shift in the delivery of service. Parents often do not know how to gain access to services. Furthermore, there is a perception that institutions and agencies are not there to help, and there is a fear that children will be taken away. Institutions are seen to be insensitive, to lack any understanding of how to help First Nations families. There is a reliance on First Nations-operated service organizations, but their funding is always tenuous and short-term. Moreover, with the shift towards self-government and the increased participation of First Nations in determining how funds will be spent in health, Headstart, and post-secondary initiatives, urban Aboriginal people have often been excluded from decision-making processes and benefits. Decisions regarding the distribution of funds have largely been made by British Columbia on-reserve leaders who may not take into consideration the large population of Aboriginal people from the Prairie provinces who now live in urban Vancouver.

In the 1992-3 school year, our records show that there were forty-three students enrolled in Grade 12, but by June 1993 only twenty-four students were still in school. Students retained were in the schools that had First Nations school support workers and that had a heightened awareness of First Nations student needs. In discussions with parents, students, and staff in First Nations programs and services, students consistently report that their greatest challenge is the racism they experience. Moreover, expressions of racism escalate whenever there is high profile conflict between First Nations and Canada, as tensions spill over into the school system.

In the past few years the number of young children leaving elementary school has increased. More and more First Nations youth are living on the street. Here they fall prey to gangs and crime. In many cases, school is the only safe haven; but the behaviour of First Nations students is often not acceptable in school, and this results in suspensions or non-attendance. Children living in poor families come to school hungry and without proper care. According to a study of the Downtown Eastside, where many First Nations people live, the incidence of substance abuse is increasing, and the number of children in the school system with birth-related drug and alcohol syndromes has increased fivefold in the last five years.

The challenge is to develop respectful, collaborative, and cooperative partnerships. In 1992, one family was dealing with fifteen separate ministries and community agencies. Due to the complex social issues a child must contend with, there is a risk that teachers and schools are overreaching their responsibility. If a child comes to school hungry and exhausted, it is difficult to ask her/him to engage in active school learning. Although to teachers the competing challenges a child can face seem to be insurmountable, they are still required to find a way to meet her/his educational goals.

The strategies employed by an urban school district, then, must be flexible and multifaceted. The beliefs and values held by all personnel must be consistent throughout all levels of the institution. The commitment for educational excellence for all children, whatever their particular challenge, is a strong motivating force. The programs and services must always have the child at their core.

Historical Responses by the Vancouver School District

Residential schools began to close in the 1960s, and Aboriginal students were bused to public schools in neighbouring White communities. Prior to the 1960s there were few Aboriginal students attending public schools. This sudden increase caught the public school system off guard.

In 1974, Vancouver hired four home-school workers to assist the district and First Nations parents and students with the educational process and to develop a cooperative relationship with Vancouver's Aboriginal community. In 1976 Kumtuks was founded as an alternative rehabilitation program to retain students during the crucial years between Grade 6 and Grade 9. The program was evaluated over the next three years and pronounced generally effective. It was recommended that the program be expanded. Kumtuks focuses on Native Studies and provides students with assistance in basic courses so that they may be able to re-enter the mainstream system. Britannia Outreach, another alternative rehabilitation program, opened in 1979 for students who had dropped out of school and, in some cases, had become street-entrenched. Although not initially designed as such, the program became an option used exclusively by Aboriginal students. The program accepts students between the ages of thirteen and nineteen. Also in 1979, three cultural enrichment workers were hired to work in five schools, funded jointly by the Ministry of Education and the federal secretary of state at the bidding of a community Native Indian Youth Advisory Committee.

A three-phase study, begun in 1980 by the Vancouver School District, led to the present organization of First Nations educational services. The first phase of this study found that:

(1) Native Indian students are more mobile than are the comparison students; that is, the number of changes both in home addresses and schools attended were significantly higher among Native Indian students.
(2) Native Indian students were absent from school more often than were the comparison students.
(3) Achievement levels among Native Indian students were lower than were those among the comparison students.
(4) There are fewer Native Indian students graduating from high school, and the drop-out rate among Native Indian students is much higher than it is among the comparison students.

Parents and students were surveyed in a follow-up study, and this revealed that the majority of parents and students wished to remain a part of the regular system and would consider segregated alternatives only as a last resort. Both parents and students felt that children were progressing at an average level and that programs should be geared to prevention rather than remediation. They stated that cultural education should be a high priority and that there should be more Native personnel in the school system.

The study recommended hiring a coordinator of Native Indian education and establishing an Indian education council. Other recommendations emphasized the need to recruit more First Nations teachers and assistant teachers as well as counsellors. The development of First Nations curriculum resources, cultural enrichment programs, cross-cultural sensitivity training for non-First Nations staff, First Nations parental involvement, and communications were all part of the recommendations. It was suggested that the establishment of a First Nations cultural survival school should be assessed. These recommendations would form the foundation for the Vancouver School District's efforts to meet the needs of First Nations students and families.

Current First Nations Programs in the Vancouver School District
As a result of the 1980 study, the First Nations education specialist and the First Nations Advisory Committee came into being in 1982. The First Nations Advisory Committee consists of representatives from urban First Nations organizations as well as the principals of two schools with high First Nations enrolments, school board consultants, district principals, senior officials, a trustee, a district parent representative, and representatives from First Nations programs and services. Its job is to advise the school district trustees and officials with regard to improving First Nations services and programs, to seek funding for special programming and curriculum, to encourage cultural enrichment, to promote equity for First Nations students, and to promote employment equity for First Nations staff. The First Nations education specialist provides leadership and direct services for a wide range of First Nations education initiatives, and acts as a liaison between the district and the First Nations community.

Support services are provided by a First Nations education itinerant who acts as a general resource person to schools and teachers and seventeen school support workers (formerly, cultural enrichment workers) who work in twenty elementary and secondary schools. Workers may be school-based or area-based, depending on First Nations student enrolments in the various schools. Workers provide tutorial and cultural enrichment activities both inside and outside the classroom, and they also help teachers to develop an awareness of First Nations cultures, serving as a cultural mediator between parents, staff, and students, and promoting parental involvement.

The district's First Nations programs span both elementary and secondary levels. Two all-day kindergartens focus on First Nations children and Grandview/?uuqinak'uuh Elementary School offers intensive cultural programming to First Nations students drawn from across the district. A primary resource room has been established at Grandview/?uuqinak'uuh to help prepare First Nations students for school entry. Three other elementary schools also have resource rooms to provide additional support to intermediate students of average cognitive potential who may be vulnerable because of their language skills and learning styles. In the resource rooms the mediated learning approaches developed by Israeli educator Reuven Feuerstein are central.

At the secondary school level, there are five programs that implement alternative and rehabilitative strategies in an attempt to reach out to First Nations youth, including some who are involved in street life. These programs are culturally based, incorporating core First Nations values such as respect, generosity, sharing, belonging, and caring. Their strength is their ability to provide holistic programs for their students, and their autonomy from the mainstream schools gives them the flexibility to address the needs of the student.

Significant numbers of First Nations students attend the nine schools that have been designated as inner-city schools by the Vancouver School District. These schools are multicultural and receive additional resources for strategic interventions, including staffing, programming, and support services. All of the schools have a First Nations school support worker, and those with the highest First Nations enrolments also have a First Nations resource teacher. All schools have active First Nations parent groups. First Nations students benefit directly from the additional staff and other resources of the inner-city program, and they have enriched the possibilities of student success. The First Nations education specialist contributed to the initial design of the inner-city school program, serves on the Inner City Schools Project Advisory Committee, and works with project teachers.

In addition to the elementary and secondary programs, the district followed the recommendations from the First Nations Education Advisory Committee to sponsor diverse activities whose goals are: to enhance the district's appreciation of First Nations in order to counteract the past devaluation of First Nations peoples' history, cultures, and traditions; to provide opportunities for school staff to learn more about First Nations (apart from the usual negative issues); to help urban Aboriginal community members to feel a sense of belonging at their school; to help the staff members assume their responsibility for working with First Nations students, despite the difficulties they face educationally and socially. Some of the activities developed in order to meet these goals are described below:

(1) *First Nations Leadership Camp.* Each spring forty First Nations students between Grades 8 and 10 attend a five-day leadership camp where they learn how to support one another in dealing with vital issues they face in their lives both inside and outside of school (e.g., AIDS, racism, family violence and abuse, feelings of isolation, and feelings of failure). The structure of the camp is based on First Nations leadership training: rigorous physical training; purification of body and spirit; emphasis on central values such as self-initiation, self-regulation, and self-directedness, creating and sharing, and mental and emotional focus. Students also learn their responsibility to

be good followers by supporting those who assume leadership roles. This helps them to be good leaders. The camp uses resources from the urban Aboriginal community, school personnel, First Nations school support workers, First Nations programs and district personnel.

(2) *Spring Salmon Festival.* Students from the alternative programs meet for a day to learn to express themselves through storytelling, singing, dancing, art, and games. By working in mixed age and First Nations culture groups, students have an opportunity to meet students from other programs and to deepen their peer support systems.

(3) *VanCity Savings Scholarships.* Each year two Grade 10 students are awarded $1,000 scholarships to be used for any post-secondary training, including apprenticeships. Two hundred dollars of the scholarship goes to a community charity or service organization of the student's choice in recognition of the First Nations' value of giving and receiving. With the scholarship comes a work experience opportunity in some aspect of banking service of interest to the student. Students are selected not only on the basis of grades, but also on their stories of how they meet life and school challenges. Throughout the years, many inspirational stories of perseverance and resilience have been collected from the student applications.

(4) *Inner City Schools First Nations Culture Celebration.* Each year four inner-city schools study First Nations culture. Aboriginal resource people from the school's community are hired to assist each school. This two-to-six-week study of culture culminates in a recognition feast attended by the whole school and community. Initially there was confusion because the way schools traditionally plan is to itemize and record every detail and to assign tasks, whereas in the Aboriginal community people are informed about the event and what is needed (e.g., volunteers, food), and people contribute what they can and do the work that needs to be done. Through these events people have learned to help each other understand their way of doing things and to compromise to accommodate one another's differences. Families have a greater feeling of control over, and acceptance of, school activities because they can contribute to the school community.

(5) *People of the Salmon.* To celebrate Vancouver's centennial, Indigenous songwriter and performer David Campbell was commissioned to write ten contemporary songs concerning the First Nations presence in the city and to perform them in every elementary school and First Nations program in the district. The idea was to bring to students and teachers an appreciation and awareness of the continued Aboriginal presence in Vancouver and to collect songs to add to school music programs. It is a joy to hear children of all ethnicities sing songs such as "The Oolichan Song."

(6) *Initiation Ceremony.* Each year one of the First Nations programs holds an initiation ceremony to honour and accept new Grade 8 students into the program. This ceremony is attended by school administration,

teachers, counsellors, district administration, Aboriginal community organizations, parents, and students. It is conducted by the Grade 9 and Grade
10 students under the supervision of staff and Elders. This is significant
because it helps Grade 8 students feel they have a place in the program,
and, at the same time, it helps Grade 9 and Grade 10 students feel their
responsibility towards others. The ceremony publicizes the students' commitment to their educational goals, an important part of traditional child
development practices. It also ensures a more informed and supportive
school staff, and it demonstrates to parents that the school and program
are committed to their children's success.

(7) *Resources.* First Nations educators and interested community members screened print and media resources to discard biased and aged
resources and to recommended replacements. The district supported the
development of materials appropriate to urban First Nations but targeted
to all schools and students. For example, *Sima7 – Come Join Me* (the intermediate student reader and teacher guide) is written to help people
become aware, and gain a deeper appreciation, of the cultural diversity of
First Nations; to deal with stereotypes and racism; and to help teachers
and students living in an urban environment to appreciate how students
feel when separated from their homelands and families.

(8) *First Nations: Circle Unbroken.* This collection of thirteen short video
programs introduces students, ages nine to adult, to a variety of contemporary First Nations perspectives on history, culture, spirituality, education, justice, the environment, racism, colonialism, and Aboriginal title.
We have chosen the best available documentaries and edited and revised
them for classroom use. These programs will provide students with rich
and complex images of the contemporary reality of the First Nations, their
sense of identity, and their relations with Canada. The video series is now
distributed throughout Canada by the National Film Board. In 1999, ten
programs were added to the series.

(9) *Professional and Staff Development Programs.* Programs have been
offered yearly to all district personnel – teachers, district and school administrators, area and school counsellors, psychologists, speech language
pathologists, alternative rehabilitation program staff, teacher librarians,
and special education staff. Some programs are custom designed to suit
the school staff or specialized areas, while others are advertised throughout the district. These programs are crucial for increasing knowledge and
understanding of First Nations cultures and issues, particularly since there
are no First Nations subjects required during the university training of
teachers and other school staff. A few of the programs are highlighted here
to give some idea of the scope of the offerings.

The Queen's Harbour Program was a four-and-a-half-day residential program that immersed participants in issues of social justice and equity, and it was held three times per year until 1996. It challenged participants to examine their own ideas and attitudes as well as policies, systems, structures, and biases in the organizations in which they work. Participants took on the roles of senior administrators in the fictitious, but realistic, Queen's Harbour School District. In a safe yet stimulating and challenging environment, they were involved in decision making regarding a large number of pressing issues. First Nations scenarios were specially constructed for the Queen's Harbour Program, all based on actual experiences. The history of Aboriginal education, presented with facts, legislation, and policies interwoven with personal stories made a profound impact on participants because, for the majority, it was the first time they had heard that history. Many commented, "I grew up near a reserve," or "I went to school with Natives, but I never knew any Natives." It was important for people to understand the effect of policies and policy interpretation on people's lives, and the participants in the program had to be willing to take a stand with regard to advocating for First Nations students and to demanding an appropriate, unbiased curriculum.

The Spirit of the Drum Workshop is conducted over a period of six weeks in four-hour sessions. The participants learn to construct a drum, to appreciate what the drum means to First Nations, and to understand the various drum beats belonging to a variety of First Nations. They compose their own songs, design their own symbols to paint on their drums, and teach drumming and singing in the classes. Participants in this workshop are profoundly touched by the experience. The workshop ensures that the participants leave with a deeper understanding of the philosophy and values of First Nations and that they understand the creative process of sharing one's inner story. Similar workshops cover cedar weaving (bark and root), Northwest Coast button blanket making, beading, food, and medicinal plants. For all of these topics, the values and beliefs of the people are shared with the participants.

The Multigenerational Family Systems Approach Training For First Nations School Support Workers Program is a three-year training program designed to give workers a strong theoretical framework as well as skills and greater self-understanding. The workers are faced with very complex and often overwhelming challenges related to helping parents and their children feel safe and connected to schools in Vancouver. The multigenerational family systems perspective is about honouring families and is particularly valuable in working with First Nations families. A family systems training program is being planned as a follow-up to professional development.

(10) *Personnel.* The Vancouver School District has made a commitment to be far more proactive in hiring First Nations personnel at all levels in the system and to make such hiring a priority for First Nations programs

and services. The district and the Vancouver Teachers Federation have joined together in the commitment to increase the hiring of First Nations teachers. The Human Resources Office and First Nations education specialists are in touch with training programs locally and nationally, and practicum placements are being encouraged. For example, we have worked with the First Nations House of Learning at the University of British Columbia to develop a First Nations teacher training program designed specifically for student teachers who plan to teach in large multicultural urban centres such as Vancouver.

These activities represent the diverse nature of our attempts to improve the quality of education for First Nations students. The range of these efforts demonstrates that it has been crucial to work on many fronts at the same time. Some initiatives are aimed at working directly with students, and others are aimed at increasing the professional capacities of teachers and support workers. Some help to create new resources that can be used in the classroom. Still others, by deepening the understanding of non-First Nations educators and administrators who make decisions that affect the well-being of First Nations children, are designed to change the whole context in which First Nations students are educated.

Feuerstein's Mediated Learning

In 1997, the video *Mind of the Child* won one of Canada's prestigious Gemini awards – the Canada Award – for its excellence. Distributed by the National Film Board, the video documents the Vancouver School District's use of the theories and intervention strategies of Reuven Feuerstein, an Israeli educator who believes that every child is capable of learning more efficient approaches to solving the problems presented in school and in everyday life. Feuerstein's instrumental enrichment program (FIE) was initiated in the district in 1986 in response to concerns about the responsiveness of First Nations children to educational programs.

In 1987 a First Nations resource room was opened for a pilot program at an inner-city school whose student population was 40 percent First Nations. A central component of the pilot was the FIE program. Initially, the curriculum was taught to selected First Nations students by pulling them out of their classes for 45 minutes a day. The five classes were from Grade 4 to Grade 7. At the end of the first year students scored higher in three cognitive abilities tests than they did at the beginning of the year (Vavrik 1986). The program had a positive impact on students' self esteem and confidence. According to the teacher, the students felt "special" in a positive way. Classroom teachers reported that the students initiated and led discussions in their regular classes on topics covered in the resource room. At the end of the year, students were requesting additional writing assignments or asking to have their spontaneous writing checked.

According to classroom teachers, First Nations learners in the FIE program improved their ability to grasp the lessons and completed tasks more successfully than did those who were not in the program.

Through the pilot project, we confirmed one of our suspicions: that teachers have to believe that the students are capable of learning demanding and abstract ideas. Without that belief, teachers are likely to give up on the students too quickly. The FIE curriculum gives teachers and students the opportunity to see that the latter can achieve and that their efforts will pay off.

The encouraging results of this pilot project led to a greatly expanded program. In subsequent years, the district supported the training of nine trainers in FIE methods and materials at different levels. By 1993, 1,000 practitioners had been trained in the theories, philosophy, and three applied systems. This movement began with teachers and has been driven by students. It is not an easy program to implement, and it requires a deep commitment from the teachers, school, and district administrators. While it consumes time, energy, and resources, it is worthwhile because it helps student learning.

By 1991 there was escalating demand from outside the district for training in all systems. Parents were wanting classes for their children, and advocacy groups (e.g., Down syndrome associations, Canadian and American fetal alcohol syndrome organizations) were interested in direct service programs dealing with assessment and tutoring as well as with training. This demand outstripped what the Vancouver School District could provide. A group of teachers, psychologists, speech language pathologists, parents, and community organizers proposed opening a centre to support the mediated learning program within the district, British Columbia, and the Yukon. The school district became a partner with the Variety Clubs International, supporting a non-profit Mediated Learning and Research Society to establish the Variety Learning Centre. The centre is dedicated to the assessment of children, intervention strategies, and the training of parents, educators, and other professionals in Feuerstein's mediated learning.

Why has Feuerstein's approach played such an important role in the classroom intervention strategies of the First Nations program? There is a remarkable parallel between the conditions that set the stage for the development of Feuerstein's instrumental enrichment and the context of First Nations peoples today. Feuerstein's work was formulated in the 1950s and 1960s, as he tried to work with survivors of the Holocaust who, as children, had suffered traumatic losses and emotional upsets due to separation and/or loss of parents as well as separation from culture and language communities. The parents and loved ones who normally "mediate" the experience of learning were unable to fulfill that crucial role, and many of the children survived precisely by not trusting adults. I could

see the same trauma and intergenerational interruption of cultural learning in the lives of First Nations children as a result of the residential school
experience and the devaluation of our heritage. This led me to study the
underlying dynamics of Feuerstein's approach and to grasp how children's learning is affected as trauma reverberates through succeeding
generations.

Feuerstein has developed a curriculum made up of different instruments
for different purposes. His criticism of traditional psychometric intelligence measures is echoed in current educational and psychological literature. Feuerstein's struggle with the problem of finding a more suitable
intelligence assessment instrument led to the development of a new,
dynamic tool, the learning potential assessment device (LPAD), which is
advanced as a more adequate measure of a child's cognitive abilities. This
achievement was followed by a comprehensive learning theory – structural cognitive modifiability (SCM) – that contains both diagnostic and
remedial implications and is built into the FIE curriculum.

Feuerstein's learning theory is elaborate, and it provides the rationale for
the instruments and curricula that flow out of his work: LPAD, FIE, Bright
Start: Cognitive Curriculum for Young Children (CCYC), Cognitive
Enrichment Advantage (formerly known as COGNET), and Mediating a
More Sensitive and Intelligent Child (MSIC). I will now provide a basic
description of his learning theory.

Feuerstein poses that we learn in two different ways: through direct
exposure to stimuli in our environment and through mediation by significant others. The mediator, usually a parent, relative, or caregiver, helps
the child to interpret and make sense of the world. This process is called
the mediated learning experience (MLE), and it is crucial to successful
learning. There are many reasons why mediation in the child's world may
be less than optimal. For example, insufficient mediation may result due
to the pressures of poverty, family disruption, or a dramatic cultural transition. Children also differ in their needs for mediation. Children with
specific learning difficulties may require more mediation than others.

Feuerstein also suggests that we "learn to learn" through the process
of cultural transmission. In a mediated learning experience, a culturally
initiated adult (parent, relative, caregiver) interposes herself between the
stimuli in the environment and the child. The child is prepared to become
a competent and functioning person within that cultural community.
When a mediated person with a clear sense of self is put into an unfamiliar environment, she/he can use her/his cultural knowledge to make sense
of the unknown without losing her/his sense of self.

Cognition and culture are interconnected. First Nations lifeways prepared the young to become full participating members of the family and
community. First Nations societies had elaborate and beautifully designed

systems for transmitting knowledge intergenerationally. Those leaders in our communities often share one thing in common: they are usually culturally competent adults who have been guides and mentors and have provided others with inspiration.

The FIE process is designed to replicate the mediational environment of the student's natural family and community. The teacher helps the learner to recognize the thinking processes that go into solving a problem. The learner is then challenged to consider more efficient ways of arriving at a solution. The teacher's questioning procedures help the learner become aware of the rules and structures that underlie effective problem solving. In addition, the teacher's mediations encourage the learner to identify other situations in life that require the same kinds of problem-solving strategies. This assists the learner to apply newly discovered skills to other areas of academic studies and everyday life through a system that Feuerstein refers to as "bridging." The strength of this process is that it enables students to connect their cultural knowledge to life in an urban setting, to academic subjects, to interpersonal relationships, and to career or vocational realms.

The core of the FIE program is a series of problem-solving tasks and exercises that are grouped into fourteen areas of cognitive development. They are called instruments rather than lessons because, in and of themselves, they are virtually free of specific subject matter. Their purpose is to serve as the means for cognitively oriented interactions between teacher and students. Since the curriculum content does not depend on prior cultural knowledge and world experience, students of many cultural backgrounds can succeed on an equal basis. The goal of each instrument is the development, refinement, and crystallization of functions that are prerequisites for effective thinking. FIE transforms the functions of learners by altering their passive and dependent cognitive styles so that they can become more active, self-motivated, reflective, and independent thinkers.

In June 1991, a short-term evaluation was conducted and valuable feedback was obtained, despite the fact that the students had been involved in the program for only six months (Kettle 1992). Teachers indicated that they saw improvements in the students' thinking and problem-solving abilities, and half the teachers also felt that the students' work habits had improved. The FIE tools helped teachers get a better sense of how to assist students who were experiencing difficulty in mastering a task (e.g., some students might require more repetition than others). An FIE teacher is apt to ask, "What do I need to change in my teaching to assist this child's learning of a task?"

In addition to this limited evaluation, there is considerable anecdotal evidence that suggests that FIE intervention has a transformative impact on the lives of students. Now that the FIE program has been operating for some time, further evaluative work is planned for the future. There is a large and growing body of research literature relating to the evaluation of FIE and mediated learning worldwide.

Reflections on Successes and Challenges

The school system has a history of assessing and labelling students for special placement. In the Vancouver School District 20 percent of the students in special remedial behaviour disorder classes are First Nations, and they make up 40 percent of the students in communications classes. In one inner-city school sixty-five students, out of a total First Nations population of seventy-two, are being assessed by the school-based team. Student transfers out of the home school continue to be regarded as an option for First Nations students, even when schools have increased resources.

In a 1986 study 500 Grade 5 teachers received a student profile of a ten-year-old boy that described him as being sometimes disruptive in class but not behaviour disordered. He was two to three years behind in language and mathematics, but he was not learning disabled. Attached to the profile was a questionnaire consisting of nine items. Samples of the questions are: "Do you, the teacher, have the resources you need to meet the needs of this child? Does your school have the necessary resources to meet the needs of the child? Will this student graduate? Would you have the support of the parents? Should this child be transferred to a special program?" Only the ethnicity of the child was changed: 25 percent of the 500 teachers received a profile describing the student as Caucasian, 25 percent as Asian, 25 percent as East Indian, and 25 percent as Native Indian. Of the returned questionnaires, the majority of the responses were positive when ethnicity was given as Caucasian or Asian, while the majority of responses were negative when ethnicity was given as Native Indian (Myles and Ratzlaff 1988).

One of our greatest challenges has been to help teachers and administrators to curb their first impulse to push First Nations students out of the school as quickly as possible and to direct them towards other resources. Part of our job is to help teachers realize that they have the expertise and resources to teach First Nations students. In the first LPAD training program, the majority of the evaluation forms filled out by the school psychologists and speech pathologists said something to the effect: "I realize now that I have given up on students far too quickly." These same professionals became strong advocates for First Nations students at school-based team meetings.

The evolution of the Native cultural enrichment worker position reveals many of the underlying tensions that are at play when one tries to work effectively in a public education school system. Initially, the purpose of the Native Indian Cultural Enrichment Program was to provide academic support to First Nations students through individual and small group tutoring and homework assistance. The name of the workers was changed from "First Nations tutors" to "Native Indian cultural enrichment workers" (NICEW) because, according to the teachers' collective agreement, tutors in Vancouver require a teaching certificate. The program evolved into small group pullout programs, with students engaging in craft-based cultural activities. Students often missed art, music, or physical education. The workers were not included in school-based professional teams and were left to work in isolation. They made home visits to discuss school concerns and provided small group academic support that they developed on their own.

Two of the workers were nearing completion of their teaching certificates, and one continued in a paraprofessional role after receiving his teaching credentials because, initially, he was not offered a teaching position. The workers were paid as paraprofessional support staff, but they performed some of the work of teachers and counsellors. During times of budget restraint and cutbacks, staff would make comments such as, "Why do we have a cultural worker for Natives and not one for Vietnamese, Chinese, Latin Americans, or Europeans?"; "Our school needs supervision aides and staff assistants, so why do we have workers who only work with Natives?"; "What are those workers supposed to be doing anyway?"

The tensions plaguing this marginalized position were addressed over a number of years. The district changed the name from "cultural enrichment worker" to "First Nations school worker," revised the job description, and raised the pay rate to reflect the unique traditional and cultural expertise that the First Nations staff bring to the service of First Nations students and that cannot be acquired through any mainstream post-secondary institution. Other changes were initiated in order to bring First Nations school workers into the teams of teachers and other professionals working with students. It was agreed that the worker, school administrator, and district supervisors would negotiate the assignment for each worker so that everyone would be supporting the school's goals for First Nations students. The workers received greater protection from the many competing demands from staff, and highly professional staff were encouraged to work with the school workers so that the students would benefit from all of this expertise. This program has become one of the district's most valuable services and serves as a model for other school districts. The workers not only serve First Nations students, but they also offer schoolwide programs to enhance the school community's knowledge and appreciation of First Nations histories and traditions.

As a result of these efforts, we are pleased to see that the staff involved in the programs and services has stabilized and that there is an increase in staff of First Nations ancestry as well as a greater willingness on the part of school administrators to hire First Nations staff. There is also a greater understanding of the need to be flexible and to negotiate with the Aboriginal community with regard to the design elements for programs.

At the same time, we continue to be faced with the reality that there is so much more to be done. Since 1984, it has been an ongoing yearly challenge to ensure that the provincially transferred Aboriginal education funds designated for Aboriginal students are spent appropriately and effectively. This has meant continually educating new district administrators and school board trustees and interpreting the funding guidelines for them. Each school district receives a basic amount for educating every student, including First Nations students. The designated funds provided to districts from the provincial government are intended to enhance and enrich services for Aboriginal students, not to bear the total costs of educating First Nations students.

Another funding challenge concerns the fact that additional funds for which First Nations students are eligible are usually based on disability, deficiency, and deprivation. Making a case for the funds means highlighting and amplifying the negative aspects of some First Nations students, thus further entrenching the negative stereotypes. The programs and services are vulnerable to changes in funding guidelines from the Ministry of Education, the mood and priorities of the school board leaders, and the shifts in political climate. For example, funds designated for Aboriginal people at the federal level are targeted to on-reserve communities, and urban populations have a very difficult time in gaining access to them.

Despite the fact that graduation classes are growing every year, the district still loses up to half of its incoming Grade 12 classes. The district hired a full-time youth and family worker to develop a tracking system for students so that they wouldn't so easily "fall through the cracks" and so that they could be placed in alternative programs as quickly as possible. In the past five years, this tracking program has allowed us to notice certain patterns. Students, even those who are successful, seem to be most vulnerable at exam and report card time. Other difficult times for retention are after holidays, especially Christmas and traditional functions in students' home communities.

The teaching of Aboriginal languages is a significant challenge in an environment such as Vancouver, where there are First Nations people from many linguistic and cultural traditions. Recently, at a board meeting during the question period for a proposal presented by the First Nations Education Advisory Committee, a trustee asked, "Why should we fund teaching First Nations languages when those languages are becoming extinct and they are not the language of business?" Another trustee asked, "How will we collect information on the educational aspirations of

First Nations parents if they won't even fill out the census data?" The provincial government has made a commitment to protect and to promote heritage languages, including First Nations languages, but we have not been successful in teaching any First Nations languages to children, although there is an adult evening class on the Cree language. It will be a challenge to offer language classes in the many First Nations languages spoken by families in Vancouver. We have explored offering courses to families and utilizing partnerships with neighbourhood houses and First Nations organizations rather than teaching only children.

We also face ongoing difficulties in making our presence felt in the classroom. The province developed a First Nations Studies 12 course three years ago, but, in 1997, there was not one class of First Nations 12 taught in Vancouver. A department head said that he would not teach First Nations Studies 12 because he couldn't teach about self-government or the treaty process due to the fact that he believes in "one law for all." In 1998, there will be two classes taught in alternate programs, where there will be more flexibility in the timetabling. During the summer, there will be a three-day course on the First Nations Studies 12 curriculum for teachers and parents, and we will try again to add the course to the school list of offerings for 1999. The integration of First Nations content into school subjects occurs with teachers who are willing to take the initiative on their own. Although there are provincial funds available to all school districts to modify curriculum and so to reflect a district's context and reality, none of our First Nations-focused proposals has been successful in getting funding.

Conclusion

I will continue to work towards a future in which Aboriginal children take pride in their heritage so that the beauty, joy, and peace that they feel in their homelands, with the eagles and salmon, the trees and the earth, will remain with them as they temporarily migrate into the cities. A firmly established First Nations identity will aid them in reaching out for the opportunities available in the city without having to feel that in order to belong in Canada, to participate as citizens in this country, they must divest themselves of their identity. I continue to work for the day when every Canadian, new immigrant or old, will be knowledgeable about First Nations and will accept the fact that First Nations history, values, and traditions are intricately woven into the fabric of Canadian identity. Education is the most powerful institution in any society, and teachers are its most powerful agents. As Aboriginal people we know this very intimately. Education has been a force for destruction. It is also a powerful force for construction, and it can produce citizens who are capable of determining their own future.

Acknowledgments
This chapter is based upon Lorna Williams, "Urban Aboriginal Education: The Vancouver Experience," Royal Commission on Aboriginal Peoples (Ottawa, 1994).

References
Feuerstein, R. 1993. *Don't Accept Me as I Am: Helping Retarded People to Excel*. New York: Plenum.
Kettle, H. 1992. *Evaluation of the Instrumental Enrichment Program: Student Assessment and Research*. Vancouver School District No. 39.
Myles, David W., and Harold C. Ratzlaff. 1988. "Teachers' Bias towards Visible Ethnic Minority Groups in Special Education Referrals." *BC Journal of Special Education* 12, 1: 19-27.
Vavrik, J. 1986. *Native Resource Room Project (Macdonald Elementary) Progress Report: Student Assessment and Research*. Vancouver School District No. 39.

8

The Information Legacy of the Royal Commission on Aboriginal Peoples

Marlene Brant Castellano

A Unique Resource

The Royal Commission on Aboriginal Peoples (RCAP) has created an information legacy in the CD-ROM *For Seven Generations* (RCAP 1997), which offers teachers, curriculum developers, and adult educators a unique resource. The CD-ROM is the result of a joint effort between RCAP (which made available its extensive document collection), Libraxus (a private-sector company that produced the CD-ROM), and the Government of Canada (which licensed and continues to market the publication). While royal commissions normally publish their research papers, RCAP was the first commission to release full transcripts of its public hearings and make them accessible in electronic form complete with search software.

The comprehensiveness of the information base mirrors RCAP's mandate, touching virtually every aspect of Aboriginal people's lives and their relations with non-Aboriginal people in Canada. The collection, which encompasses the equivalent of 100,000 pages of print text, was assembled and indexed electronically to support policy analysis and report writing by RCAP.[1] As the transcripts of each of four rounds of public hearings became available, they were distributed to libraries, stakeholder organizations, and government departments in order to stimulate reflection on issues raised in the hearings. The response from this select public was enthusiastic, and the idea of making the hearings available for ongoing public education was born. The CD-ROM subsequently became the principal vehicle for publishing research papers and republishing RCAP reports that originally appeared in print form.

This chapter introduces the content and capabilities of the CD-ROM and illustrates educational applications in existing curriculum and new approaches to Aboriginal studies. It concludes with a discussion of policy initiatives necessary to realizing the potential of the RCAP information legacy and thereby advancing public education.

Contents of *For Seven Generations*

The CD-ROM *For Seven Generations* includes an electronic version of all publications issued by RCAP, including the five-volume final report and special reports published during the life of the commission, over 200 research reports, and the equivalent of 60,000 pages of transcripts of oral presentations at public hearings and national round tables. Further detail on contents is summarized in Figure 1. All RCAP publications appear on the CD-ROM in both English and French, and research reports are presented in the language in which they were submitted. Approximately 30 percent of the oral testimony is in French.

For Seven Generations speaks in diverse voices. Commissioners present their collective wisdom in the five-volume report. They lay out the historical ground from which current issues spring. They examine thorny problems that have marred relations between Aboriginal and non-Aboriginal people. They propose solutions based on principles of mutual recognition, respect, sharing, and responsibility. They call on Aboriginal and non-Aboriginal people alike to make a renewed commitment to living together in harmony, and they propose practical and symbolic steps that might be taken to achieve a new relationship.

> Consideration of this history will surely persuade the thoughtful reader that the false assumptions and abuses of power that have pervaded Canada's treatment of Aboriginal people are inconsistent with the morality of an enlightened nation.
>
> – RCAP Report, *Looking Forward, Looking Back*, Vol. 1, 3

Aboriginal people speak on countless issues, through thousands of pages of transcripts that resound with the power of the spoken word. The realities of Aboriginal experience – pain and joy, frustration and energy, anger and hope – are told in Aboriginal people's own words without the mediating influence of another culture.

> I have no written speech. Everything that I said I have been carrying in my heart because I have seen it. I have experienced it.
>
> – Mary Lou Iahtail, RCAP public hearings

Organizations and communities, both Aboriginal and non-Aboriginal, offer analyses and recommendations in presentations made at public hearings.

RCAP commissioned research studies, to be completed by both Aboriginal and non-Aboriginal experts, on a wide variety of subjects. Reports reflect the insider perspectives of community-based researchers and the

Figure 1

Summary of contents of *For Seven Generations*

Report of the Royal Commission on Aboriginal Peoples

Volume 1: *Looking Forward, Looking Back*
Volume 2: *Restructuring the Relationship*
Volume 3: *Gathering Strength*
Volume 4: *Perspectives and Realities*
Volume 5: *Renewal: A Twenty-Year Commitment*

People to People: Nation to Nation – Highlights of the Final Report of RCAP

Commentaries on the Constitution and self-government, and special reports on Arctic relocation, treaties and land issues, suicide, and criminal justice

200 RCAP research reports

Transcripts of 2,000 oral presentations at RCAP public hearings and round tables, with finding aids created by RCAP staff to search testimony by subject, speaker, location, and policy area.

---

theoretical perspectives of academics. They assemble data from statistical reports, previous inquiries, and task forces. They analyze the implications for humane and informed policy making.

The diverse information base makes the contents of *For Seven Generations* relevant to students and teachers in secondary school, college, or university; to researchers or consultants dealing with Aboriginal issues; to practitioners in community services serving Aboriginal populations; and to members of the Canadian community who want to see the healing of relations between Aboriginal and non-Aboriginal peoples. Exploration of the information legacy can put readers in touch with current Aboriginal experience and can introduce new ideas about treaties and land reform, approaches to self-government, economic development, ways to revitalize Aboriginal cultures, holistic approaches to health and healing, the implications of Aboriginal control of Aboriginal education, and more.

Search Tools
Tools for searching the vast information base were embedded in the CD-ROM using FolioVIEWS, a full text retrieval software that gives instant access to any word, phrase, name, or organization on the CD-ROM every time it appears.

Commission publications and research reports contain detailed tables of contents that can be used to gain access to specific sections by clicking a mouse. Using "queries," the reader can locate key words, phrases, or presentations by particular speakers. Simple or complex searches can be constructed to find material on specific items or themes.

To help navigate tens of thousands of pages of public hearings, special consultations, and round table discussions, RCAP staff developed finding aids to enhance the basic search capacity of FolioVIEWS. The *wordfinder* is a customized thesaurus containing more than 600 entries that help to identify key words for searches. It is designed to facilitate communication across cultures. For example, if the reader is searching for information on "environment," then the Wordfinder suggests related words such as "pollution," "conservation," "ecology," "mega-projects," and "Mother Earth." A search can then be initiated using a string of related words to locate relevant paragraphs and to explore the presentations where they appear. *Group characteristics* such as gender, Elders, youth, and location of presentation can also be used as search criteria. The reader can query what youth had to say about education, for example, or the concerns of women in the Northwest Territories. *Source guides* assemble the results of searches already completed by commission staff on subject areas of major concern.

Selected passages can be printed directly from the CD, or a collection of search results can be saved to a computer directory for use with a DOS or MacIntosh wordprocessing program. The basic operations for using the software can be learned in less than an hour using the "Quick Start" instructions on the CD-ROM.

Education Guides

A small-scale market survey indicated that an information collection on Aboriginal issues would have a high degree of acceptance among educators. To explore educational applications RCAP contracted a team at the Ontario Institute for Studies in Education (OISE), University of Toronto, to develop applications of the proposed CD-ROM for adult and secondary school learners. Aboriginal and non-Aboriginal educators across Canada were provided with an early version of the CD-ROM and were invited to provide feedback on how the materials could be used in current learning contexts and what features would make the CD-ROM most accessible and useful. As a result of the OISE design effort and consultation with educators, an *Education Guide* for secondary school and adult learning was incorporated into the CD-ROM. "Quick Start" instructions take students, teachers, and librarians through the basic steps of searching, saving, and printing material. Teaching and study ideas on a variety of topics are suggested. For example, one unit focuses on communications media. Teachers and students are directed to the sections of the CD-ROM in which communications media, racism, and discrimination are discussed. A number of learning activities are suggested, illustrating the pervasive influence of communications media, emphasizing critical reading skills, and making connections to students' personal experience. Excerpts from the section

"The Media and Aboriginal People" in the *Education Guide* (RCAP 1997) are presented in Figure 2.

The Adult Learning Guide picks up related themes in sections entitled "Anti-Racist Education" and "The Justice System." Exercises provided for adult learners are suitable for self-directed study, workshops, or informal study circles.

The resource materials found in *For Seven Generations* can be used in a wide variety of subject areas, making the CD-ROM relevant to more than Aboriginal-specific courses. *The Secondary School Guide* presents curriculum units in use in different regions across Canada.[2] The units illustrate how material from *For Seven Generations* can be integrated into diverse courses of study, including language arts, history, geography, environmental studies and health, and Aboriginal Studies.

Claiming the Legacy

The information legacy of RCAP has been in the public domain since February 1997. Eighteen months later, between 400 and 500 copies of *For Seven Generations* had been sold. Anecdotal reports suggest that it has gained some currency in Native Studies and related programs in universities. The breakthrough sought by RCAP in secondary school and adult education has not yet been achieved. The limited use of the CD-ROM by educators can be attributed to a number of factors: the absence of promotional activity targeted to educational users; the purchase price of the CD-ROM relative to other curriculum resources; the exclusivity of provincial curriculum guidelines; and the investment of time and effort required to turn an information resource into a teaching tool.

Throughout the five years that it existed (1991-6) RCAP was talked about as a policy exercise designed to advise the Government of Canada on solutions to problems that troubled the nation. The commissioners believed that broad public education would be required to set the relationship between Aboriginal and non-Aboriginal peoples in Canada on a new course.

In their final report, submitted in November 1996, the commissioners recommended the creation of a task force (for at least the first year following publication) in order to promote wide public discussion of their findings and recommendations. The commission also recommended that the CD-ROM containing the final report, research studies, and public hearings be distributed by the Government of Canada free-of-charge to every Canadian high school, college, and university library. Neither of these recommendations was acknowledged in the official response by the federal government in January 1998 (Stewart 1998). While the statement of the Honourable Jane Stewart, minister of Indian Affairs and Northern Development, was encouraging in that it endorsed the broad principles of the

Figure 2

Excerpts from the Education Guide for secondary school

The Media and Aboriginal People

The main paths to information on this subject are: *Report of the Royal Commission on Aboriginal Peoples,* Volume 3: *Gathering Strength,* Chapter 6: "Arts and Heritage"; keyword search of hearings and round tables: "media, broadcasting, communication, publishing, stereotypes, racism, discrimination."

Topics for students to investigate:
- What is the role of media in the lives of Aboriginal People? Of non-Aboriginal people?
- What are the problems of Aboriginal media outlined in public hearings and *Report of the Royal Commission on Aboriginal Peoples,* Volume 3, "Arts and Heritage?" See the testimonies of Marie Mumford, Lynda Powless, Greg Young-Ing, Miles Morrisseau, and Ron Nadeau.

For class discussion:
- Collect newspaper articles about Aboriginal peoples. Ask students to read them critically and to analyze the points of view and language used. If possible, get copies of Aboriginal newspapers. Compare the way the same event is described in the mainstream and Aboriginal newspapers. Are the facts and tone of each article the same?
- Ask students what they think of when they hear the words "Indian" or "Métis." Discuss with them how stereotyping labels all members of a group, whether they fit into the mould or not. Examine RCAP testimony about racism, for example by Amber Flett and Phyllis Fishe.
- How do the experiences of visible minority students in your class compare with experiences revealed in the testimonies? (Note: Please consult your Ministry, Department, or Board of Education guidelines for teaching about sensitive issues).

Critical reading:
To develop critical reading skills, ask yourself some of the following questions:
- Whose point of view is being expressed in this testimony? Is it the view of the author, of her/his group or association, or of the community?
- Who appears to be silent (i.e., whose views are not heard?)?
- How do cultural values affect what people said in testimony? How do cultural values affect how they are heard?
- How do your own past experiences and expectations colour your reading of the testimonies?

report, its major substantive commitment was $350 million for healing the effects of physical and sexual abuse in residential schools. Facilitating awareness of RCAP's educational legacy among the Canadian public and successive generations of Canadian students was not on the agenda.

It's much easier to change structures, even to change legislation, than to change minds and attitudes, stereotypes and misunderstandings.

René Dussault, Co-Chair of RCAP
– Public Hearings, Big Cove, NB, 20 May 1992

Royal commissions are essentially ad hoc organizations. Once a commission delivers its report it is dissolved. In the absence of any apparatus to follow up its recommendations, the initiative is left to the government or the interested public. In the case of RCAP, the interested public has been made up primarily of Aboriginal organizations that have a stake in the implementation of recommendations and academics who have an interest in the Aboriginal dimension of Canadian issues.

Broad distribution of the commission's final report and the CD-ROM containing the information legacy has been inhibited by cost factors. With limited distribution of the CD-ROM in schools and little awareness among educators of its potential usefulness, pressure has not developed to move provincial and territorial ministries of education to incorporate *For Seven Generations* in the resource lists and curriculum guidelines that provide the frameworks for teaching. Leadership from provincial and territorial ministries is essential if the information legacy is to be introduced into schools, especially those where contact with Aboriginal students is minimal or where affirmation of the Aboriginal presence in Canadian life is non-existent.

Experience in field tests demonstrated that secondary school teachers already familiar with Aboriginal education and issues could quickly acquire the skills necessary to gain access to the content of the CD-ROM and to create learning exercises. Teachers and students who are new to both the content and the technology would require at least minimal orientation in order to discover its possibilities. More extensive work both on integrating Aboriginal material into existing courses of study and on designing integrated programs that adopt a more holistic approach to teaching and learning is also needed. While individual teachers and schools will continue to develop innovative teaching tools, resources should be committed on a province-wide basis for strategic and cost-effective curriculum planning.

If the barriers to its distribution and utilization are addressed, then *For Seven Generations* can make a major contribution to transforming teaching and learning by and about Aboriginal people in the next decade. This will require a joint effort on the part of government and interested members of the public to publicize the existence and to promote the study of RCAP's information legacy. The relatively high cost of obtaining the CD-ROM through the government publisher can be reduced by bulk purchases, government subsidies for educational use, or free distribution (as recommended by RCAP). Provincial and territorial ministries of education should examine how the CD-ROM can be used to enhance the appropriateness of curriculum for both Aboriginal and non-Aboriginal students. Aboriginal organizations can press for coordinated action to begin the grand task of public education aimed at changing the perceptions and attitudes that, in the past, have condoned assimilationist education and dehumanizing policies. Educators have a critical role to play in claiming, for the benefit of successive generations of students, the information legacy that RCAP has assembled.

We first need to understand that over and above hundreds of individual recommendations, the Commissioners directed us to examine the very core of how we have lived together in this country.

– Jane Stewart, Minister of Indian Affairs and
Northern Development, 7 January 1998

Notes
1 For a detailed discussion of how the electronic information base was developed and used in policy formation, see Mary Jane Commanda and Seymour Hamilton, "Qualitative Analysis of Oral Testimony," *Canadian Review of Social Policy* 36 (Winter 1995): 39-54. Also available in *For Seven Generations: An Information Legacy of the Royal Commission on Aboriginal Peoples*, CD-ROM (Ottawa: Libraxus, 1997).
2 Eight curriculum units are included in the CD, with permission of the authors:
   Emerging Aboriginal Voices was developed for intermediate students by Winnipeg School Division No. 1. This unit suggests activities to use with books by Aboriginal authors.
   Native Awareness: "Look, Listen, Ask" is an integrated unit developed for Grade 10 students by the teachers in Bellerose High School in St. Albert, Alberta. It includes sample lesson plans.
   First Nations: The Circle Unbroken contains excerpts from a teachers' guide to accompany a series of thirteen National Film Board videos that last approximately twenty minutes each. Sample titles are: "Cree Hunters," "Quebec Dams," "Education as We See It," and "Time Immemorial." The videos are suitable for most grades. The teachers' guide was developed in collaboration with the Vancouver School Board.
   Innuqatigiit is a curriculum for kindergarten to Grade 12 developed by the Northwest Territories Department of Education, Culture and Employment. Units include "Elders" and "Family/Kinship."
   The 1960s: A Time of Change develops the theme of Aboriginal peoples' relationship with the land and the different ways in which they perceive land. This unit was developed by the Kativik School Board of northern Quebec. The curriculum is published in French and English, and the sample unit is reproduced here in both languages, with notes added.

Societal Structures of Indian, Métis and Inuit People is a Grade 10 unit developed by Saskatchewan Education and Training.

Sustainable Development is a unit developed by the New Brunswick Department of Education, and it contains activities on sustainable development for Grade 11 or Grade 12.

Dene Kede. The kindergarten to Grade 6 portion of this curriculum developed by the Northwest Territories Department of Education is included as an example of how Aboriginal philosophy and worldview are incorporated into culturally appropriate curriculum. Curriculum for Grade 7 to Grade 12 was under development at the time the guide was published.

References

Commanda, Mary Jane, and Seymour Hamilton. 1995. "Qualitative Analysis of Oral Testimony." *Canadian Review of Social Policy* 36 (Winter): 39-54. Also available in *For Seven Generations: An Information Legacy of the Royal Commission on Aboriginal Peoples.* CD-ROM. Ottawa: Libraxus.

Royal Commission on Aboriginal Peoples (RCAP). 1996. *Report of the Royal Commission on Aboriginal Peoples.* Vol. 1: *Looking Forward, Looking Back;* Vol. 2: *Restructuring the Relationship;* Vol. 3: *Gathering Strength;* Vol. 4: *Perspectives and Realities;* Vol. 5: *Renewal: A Twenty-Year Commitment.* Ottawa: Canada Communications Group.

–. 1997. *For Seven Generations: An Information Legacy of the Royal Commission on Aboriginal Peoples.* CD-ROM. Ottawa: Libraxus.

Stewart, Jane, Minister of Indian Affairs and Northern Development. 1998. Notes for an address on the occasion of the unveiling of *Gathering Strength: Canada's Aboriginal Action Plan,* 7 January. http://www.inac.gc.ca

9
Issues of Pedagogy in Aboriginal Education
Kathy L. Hodgson-Smith

Prologue

I am an Aboriginal woman and I belong to a culture known by many as the Métis. I am a mother of three sons, now grown to be men. I come from a very large family whose history spans many centuries of living on this particular land, history made long before books were written or educational institutions built. Our family stories tell of Cree and Anishnabe roots, grandmothers from whom I am descended. Others of my family speak of earlier life in Red River. On quiet evenings, when I sit with my mother in her kitchen, she tells me such things.

If I walk back through my life and reflect on my education, I find I have always been in school. My family and the land from which I was born were my first teachers. Then walls were built that kept my family and the land away. Within these structures, I came to be schooled in a "formal" way, and, twenty-two years later, I have returned to my mother's kitchen and my father's armchair to learn again as a child. I have completed a master's degree in educational foundations, and I work as faculty in a Native teacher education program in Saskatchewan. In the pages that follow I will share some of what I have learned throughout both my formal and family education, knowing that my words are both an echo of those before me and an extension of my own being. All my relations.

Aboriginal Pedagogy

> We teach what we know as an act of love.
>
> – Annie

In June 1993, several Aboriginal women were asked to speak about Aboriginal pedagogy at the Learned Societies Conference in Montreal. As we organized our thoughts about the overriding themes of this workshop, one member of the group of four spoke with her grandmother in northern Saskatchewan. Out of her conversation, spoken in Cree, her grandmother, Annie, said: "We teach what we know as an act of love." This became our guiding thought and the title for the workshop, and it has stuck with me ever since.

Pedagogy has been defined by the *Concise Oxford Dictionary* as the science of teaching. For Annie, pedagogy is an act of love. These two definitions are, for me, different in fundamental ways, and yet I believe Annie might suggest they are one and the same. These two definitions frame two distinct epistemologies: one that seeks knowledge from an external source (science) and one that acknowledges the personal, internal nature of knowing (love). What we have come to understand about the scientific approach to knowledge does not allow us to comfortably consider how two such unique concepts might come together into one comprehensive definition of pedagogy. It might be suggested that Annie's definition is not valid because it is not found in the *Concise Oxford*, hence rendering unnecessary any reformulation of our understanding of the term "pedagogy." However, in light of the research presented here, I find her definition essential to highlighting the contradictions and limitations of previous research in this area and suggestive of future directions. Our definition of pedagogy is fundamental to the questions we ask about teaching and learning.

Pedagogy as science, for the purposes of definition, includes the knowledge of the nature of learning (partially gained through the field of psychology and often described as learning styles) and the instructional strategies developed around this knowledge (teaching styles and methods). Much of the research reported in this document has approached the study of pedagogy as scientific, extending and broadening our knowledge of teaching and learning within the framework established.

This approach to the study of pedagogy has come to find significance in the relationship between teacher/student and teacher/community. Beyond that, research has linked pedagogy with curriculum and content and, more recently, has included the importance of language and culture. In some ways, the previous research on pedagogy as science has moved steadily towards Annie's definition of pedagogy as an act of love, although the word "love" is never mentioned. Similar words, such as "caring," are sometimes referenced, but the scientific method requires that we maintain our objectivity in searching for knowledge. Love is too subjective, too emotional, too unprofessional; caring, on the other hand, might be an acceptable compromise. We sit on the floor at Annie's feet, but we do not hear her, it seems. To understand her, we must take her words inside and rethink the world from inside out. I suggest that previous research on pedagogy has not done this with the same vigour that it used to search from the outside in.

This document is entitled, "Issues of Pedagogy in Aboriginal Education." It is not entitled "Aboriginal Pedagogy." There is a fundamental difference between the two approaches to pedagogy, and herein lies the heart of this document. Pedagogy is not merely styles, methods, and strategies. It is also the epistemological/philosophical framework from which one approaches instruction. If I were to describe or define Aboriginal pedagogy, it would be imperative that I speak to the philosophical and epistemological beliefs that inform and guide cultural practice. The Medicine Wheel of the Plains Cree, for example, in its broadest interpretation, holds as a central teaching the importance of relations. What does this mean? What are the implications of its meaning? How does Annie's definition give us insight into possible meanings? How might these meanings affect how we approach teaching and learning? I suggest that previous research has not explored pedagogy in this way, even though it reflects an effort to address the issues of educating Aboriginal people.

Approaching the Research

This chapter is excerpted from the Royal Commission on Aboriginal Peoples (RCAP) research document of the same name. I wrote it under my former name: Vermette. The purpose of the research was to review the literature on pedagogy and Aboriginal education and to highlight the central debates, explicating key questions for future research. The first part of the research is based on a search of Educational Resources Information Center (ERIC) databases. Time was limited, however, so this body of literature was not examined as fully as I would have liked. Some of the materials proved to be very dated, reflecting the brief time in which we have known what little we do.

The second part of the project consisted of research conducted with individuals prominent in the field of Aboriginal education in Canada. Twenty telephone interviews were conducted using a series of questions to gather personal reflections on the nature of Aboriginal pedagogy. Final permission was granted by the interviewees for the drafting of the RCAP research report. The selection of individuals for the research began as a tentative list compiled on a province-by-province basis. As individuals were canvassed, more names were mentioned – a snowball sampling approach. Many of the individuals so identified were not available. A list of those interviewed appears in my original paper (Vermette 1997).

Although the original document reviews a wide range of subjects related to pedagogy, teaching, and curriculum, this chapter focuses primarily on the debates around learning styles. Through the years, learning style has been a focal point of research, and it is useful to be aware of both its contribution to our understanding of Aboriginal pedagogy and of its limitations.

Issues of Pedagogy in Aboriginal Education 159

Learning Styles

Learning style (LS) has been defined as an individual's characteristic strategies of acquiring knowledge, skills, and understanding (More 1984). The study of LS originated in the study of individual differences. As educators and researchers tried to understand the tremendous range of individual differences between children, they began to look for the sources of these differences (More 1984). Research began at the level of cognitive processing and, over time, has come to acknowledge the influence of various internal and external forces. Cultural differences and affective responses to the learning environment are two examples of such factors.

Learning styles research has been conducted in a wide variety of contexts. Researchers have investigated the learning styles of various age and cultural groups across the continent and have employed a variety of methods and tools with which to do so. A large portion of the learning styles research has been conducted with middle and upper year students or adults. Few of the studies identified gender, nationality (i.e., Swampy Cree, Métis, Wyandot), or region (urban/rural). Few primary studies have been undertaken in the last decade, and those that have been conducted in the last twenty years support the findings of earlier studies. Furthermore, the research assesses a variety of modalities, making comparison very difficult. Despite these limitations, the research is summarized below.

Many researchers suggest that Aboriginal children bring with them their own LS. Traditional culture and traditional child-rearing practices are targeted as influential in the development of LS among Aboriginal students (Kaulback 1984). The concept of hemisphericity ("right-brain, left-brain") is also considered influential, and some suggest that Aboriginal students are "right-brain learners" (Browne 1990).

Scaldwell, Frame, and Cookson (1984) have shown that Aboriginal students prefer to learn through observation and the manipulation of real examples. Their learning is best supported by the visual interpretation of presented materials. Navajo and Hopi high school students were identified as right-brained, and they functioned most effectively through the manipulation of concrete examples (More 1984). According to Wauters et al. (1989), Alaskan students overwhelmingly rate kinesthetic learning highest, followed by visual and tactile learning (see also Kaulback 1984). They note that traditional styles of learning emphasize the transfer of skills by observing and imitating the actions of Elders (Kaulback 1984). These ideas are supported through the work of Garber (1968), who found Grade 1 Navajo and Pueblo students to be adept at processing visual information.

Papago children, Grades 1 to 3, were identified as weak on auditory tests (Lombardi 1969). Sioux children of the same age level achieved similar ratings on tests (Kuske 1969; Downey 1977). Studies have shown that high school students scored lower than average on tests of verbal agility and above average in tests of perceptual analysis (Kleinfeld 1970), motor skills, and visual discrimination (John 1972). Kaulback (1984), Berry (1966), and Kleinfeld (1970) concluded that spatial skills were supported by cultural factors and that students of all ages held strong image memory.

Child-rearing practices are believed to strongly influence LS (Hilger 1951; Cazden and John 1971; Kleinfeld 1970; Rohner 1965). A watch-then-do preference is believed to reflect traditional learning methods (Cazden and John 1971). Piaget believed that if the interaction between parent and child makes much use of language (left hemisphere), and if the parent emphasizes such activities as counting, memorizing of nursery rhymes, and so on, then children will develop that type of cognitive functioning. Cognitive functioning develops as children interact with their environments. Piaget's idea then supports the research of Berry (1966), who believes that skills are supported by the nature of the learning environment and by such cultural factors as imitation (watch-then-do). Use of imagery when processing information, possibly reinforced by cultural conditioning, is identified as a much preferred LS of Aboriginal students (Tofoya 1982; John 1972; Bryant 1986; Karlebach 1986; More 1984; Greenbaum and Greenbaum 1983).

Drawing on the field dependency literature, More (1984) explains that field-independence is the degree to which an individual can separate a figure from its background, a part from the whole, or her/himself from the environment and other people. A field-independent person is more able to impose an organizational structure on an unorganized set of facts or observations than is a field-dependent person. Aboriginal students are identified as field-independent (MacArthur 1978), a probable result of their living style and child-rearing practices (Weitz 1971; More 1984).

Wauters et al. (1989) have found evidence that American Indian students: (1) possess low self-esteem and lack confidence in their academic abilities; (2) show a strong preference for precise guided assignments; (3) indicate a need for a variety of different classroom interaction patterns; (4) are significantly above non-Aboriginal students in their desire for frequent student/teacher interactions; (5) are more peer-oriented than non-Aboriginal students; and (6) are positively oriented to collaborative learning and small-group tasks (see also Phillips 1972).

Farrell-Racette (interview cited below) used the Group Imbedded Figures Test, Dunn and Dunn Assessment Test, and Herbert Kohl's personal interview method to gather information on the LS of adult students in the Saskatchewan Urban Native Teacher Education Program. She has assessed, informally, that there is a significant preference for visual aids (diagrams, encoded symbols, imagery). Also, students prefer to follow a model or to learn by observation rather than to receive verbal instruction. She also identified a preference for hands-on experience and for being oriented to the whole before moving on to the parts. Using aspects of the oral tradition in the classroom, storytelling, and extensive examples seemed to be the most effective learning strategies.

LS research is not without its contradictions, however. In some cases, the weaknesses in LS research are articulated by the researchers themselves; in other cases, further research has raised inconsistencies. For example, Wauters et al. (1989) note that both Aboriginal and non-Aboriginal students vary from the established norms of their research instrument, the Productivity Environmental Preference Survey (PEPS). Brent Kaulback (1984), who uses the Illinois Test of Psycholinguistic Abilities (ITPA), says that it is verbally loaded and demands a good command of the English language. In order to obtain accurate results, testing on Aboriginal students needs to be conducted in their own language. If it is not, then the results may not be representative of their true abilities. The research supports the contention of Aboriginal people that many of the standardized tests used in the education system are not accurate indicators or measures of ability.

The results obtained by Weitz (1971), MacArthur (1978), and More (1984), who found Aboriginal students to be field independent, are contradicted by the research by Cullinane (1985). Cullinane found non-Aboriginal students to be more field independent than were their Aboriginal counterparts.

More (1987a, 1987b) concludes that an overemphasis on LS differences may lead to a new form of inaccurate labelling and stereotyping; preferences in LS are identified frequently but not with sufficient consistency to suggest a uniquely Aboriginal LS. Chrisjohn and Peters (1986) are frankly critical of the research identifying "right-brain" tendencies in Aboriginal students. They argue that not only have study results not been replicated, the tests themselves as applied to Aboriginal students are invalid.

Perhaps what is needed is a fuller consideration of the research findings to date. What are the implications of suggesting a uniquely Indian LS? What brings us to ask about Aboriginal LS in the first place? I suggest that this line of inquiry is assimilationist in nature. The question is part of addressing the larger issue of how Aboriginal students might find success in non-Aboriginal systems of education. The proposal that there is a unique learning style might suggest genetic differences between Aboriginal and non-Aboriginal students. The consequences of such a suggestion are both alarming and profound. The research findings could lead us to believe that Aboriginal students are not as able as their non-Aboriginal counterparts. In considering the research findings, it might be advanced that Aboriginal students are working from a deficit, since right-brained learners are postulated as being disinclined towards logical sequential learning. If teachers tended to teach to the right-hemisphericity of their

Aboriginal students, then this could have serious implications for literacy, since reading and writing are predominantly left-brain activities. At the present time, there is no such thing as a right-brain curriculum, so this leaves educators in a quandary. There is the potential for a right-brained industry to crop up in the interest of supporting LS research findings, and Aboriginal students would be directly affected by such an industry. The most important criticism, however, is that the research on the LS of Aboriginal students does not yield results that are significantly different from what is found in non-Aboriginal students.

I will now outline some of what was shared by educators in the telephone interviews reported in Vermette (1997). In that document, I drew upon interviews with Del Anaquod (director of education, Federation of Saskatchewan Indian Nations), Rita Bouvier (administrator, Saskatchewan Teachers' Federation), Jim Cummins (Ontario Institute for Studies in Education), Sherry Farrell-Racette (College of Education, University of Regina), Brian Menton (director of education, GNWT, Yellowknife), Lynn McAlpine (associate director, Native and Northern Education Program at McGill University), Don Robertson (director of Teacher Education Program, Brandon University), Verna St. Denis (University of Saskatchewan Indian Teacher Education Program), and Lorna Williams (First Nations consultant, Vancouver School Board).

What one can observe in the comments that follow is the sense that the application of LS research is likely to limit the options available for meeting the diverse needs of Aboriginal learners. According to Bouvier, to say that Aboriginal people have one unique LS that is static over time and place is to suggest that Aboriginal people do not have full range capacity as individuals and human beings. An analysis of LS research often reflects pathological constructions of Aboriginal peoples' cognitive capacities, child-rearing practices, and so on (Bouvier interview). The question of a unique Aboriginal LS puts "white folks on one side and minorities on the other" (Farrell-Racette interview).

According to Williams, LS research to date closes more doors than it opens. The research has focused on the difference between, rather than the differences within, groups. It has the power to influence how society perceives Aboriginal learners and how Aboriginal learners perceive themselves. Such perceptions influence practice. Again, difference can be perceived as a disadvantage. However, LS findings do not suggest significant differences. The research question might lead us to discover the LS of Aboriginal students in oppressive environments. The results of LS research may be no more than a response to a learning environment (which would extend to the methodology and instruments used in the research) that is foreign and antagonistic (Bouvier interview). LS research, at best, describes who Aboriginal people are as learners in unfamiliar contexts (St. Denis interview).

St. Denis suggests that Aboriginal students need to be taught the rules of the game. In counselling First Nation students at the post-secondary level, she considers it her responsibility to identify the rules of interacting in the university classroom. She tries to identify for the students the culture of the university and the relations of power within that culture. For example, they must sit at the front of the classroom, ask questions, look people in the eye, and that sort of thing. She believes that LS research is a way of stereotyping, or pigeon-holing, students. In alternative and supportive environments we may observe a range of styles for individuals, with place and time being seen as relevant factors (Bouvier interview). Bouvier suggests that LS research on Aboriginal students is probably representative of the LS of all learners who enter a new culture, a foreign environment, and/or an antagonistic environment. Williams agrees that there are consequences to there being cultural-linguistic differences between the culture of the school and the culture of the student, but she insists that these need not be considered disadvantages.

Farrell-Racette points out that, in traditional Aboriginal communities, learning is an intimate process. Traditionally, teachers loved their students dearly. Teachers were moms, dads, grandparents, and other loved ones. Student motivation was most often not individually oriented but, rather, family- and community-oriented. First Nations and Métis children are very autonomous. According to Anaquod, the parenting process is important, as education starts in the home. The traditional beliefs of the child, and the relationship between those beliefs and how children learn, must be considered in LS research (Farrell-Racette interview). The epistemological/philosophical beliefs of respective Aboriginal cultures have traditionally guided educational practice. The full implications of such a statement are as yet unknown, for the question of cultural knowledge and beliefs has not been applied to the question of Aboriginal LS.

What motivates Aboriginal children and how is their motivation tied to the aspirations of their families and communities? Is this a relevant question for LS research? More research needs to be conducted in order to uncover the relationship between Aboriginal children and their respective community aspirations and modes of instruction. McAlpine believes that children are influenced by their culture and the modes of interaction fostered in the community. She says that teaching styles are small-c cultural styles (i.e., ways of interacting) and that if there is a cultural match between student LS and teacher teaching styles, then there is less interference in the learning process.

Robertson notes that there must be more opportunity for northern and First Nations people to conduct research from a community perspective, which includes parents, communities, and Elders. We need to delve deeper into different perspectives on LS. Aboriginally controlled programs and organizations need to be supported financially in order to carry on such research (Robertson interview). To date, not enough is known about how children learn and about the neurological processes of either Aboriginal or non-Aboriginal students (Anaquod interview).

In conclusion, LS research does not suggest that there is a unique Aboriginal learning style. Moreover, LS research to date poses many problems for educators. Few of the research instruments are culturally sensitive, and, therefore, they have the potential to produce biased research results. Generalizations and stereotyping have serious implications for race relations. The idea of universal attributes lends itself to ghettoization and should therefore be approached with caution (Menton interview). Any argument based on anatomical or biological differences lends itself to racism. The application and interpretation of LS research is often negative, with Aboriginal people being perceived as deficient in relation to their non-Aboriginal counterparts.

LS research should not be considered in isolation from other elements of pedagogy. The failure to acknowledge the oppressive impact of school environments and to see LS within that context is a likely result of a fragmented approach to investigating Aboriginal learning. It is not surprising that many Aboriginal educators have turned their attention to creating whole learning environments that are infused with Aboriginal values both in terms of curriculum and in terms of pedagogical processes.

LS research must be understood in the broad context of relations between Aboriginal people and state-sanctioned schools. Cummins, a faculty member at the Ontario Institute for Studies in Education, believes that historical patterns in the relationship between schools and Aboriginal students must be reversed. Instructional approaches must activate, respect, and amplify students' prior experience, and we must develop assessment methods that do not see the problem in the child. Fundamentally, pedagogy is political. Minority groups are always problematized, and we must begin to problematize the way dominant groups see themselves.

In educational institutions in Canada, a variety of teaching styles and strategies have been developed. Much of this has taken place in tandem with the increasing body of research on LS. Arthur More (1987b) suggests that teachers must identify the LS of the individual student and match their teaching styles to that of the learner. Teachers must seek to improve weaker LS by using strong or preferred ones; then they must teach students to select those teaching styles that are appropriate to the task at hand.

If the contradictions and generalizations within LS research are not acknowledged and fully considered, then where have we come in terms of the development of appropriate and culturally sensitive teaching methods and styles? In considering Annie's statement, that we teach what we know as an act of love, what are the implications for teaching methods? The old people always grant individuals the dignity of speaking what they know. We need to seek the knowledge of the Elders in order to find our way through the maze of the future. Aboriginal children deserve to grow in their understanding of themselves as Aboriginal people. They deserve to live and learn in the knowledge of their ancestors.

Many researchers undertook to understand learning styles as a way to improve the learning environment for Aboriginal students. To date, these efforts have not unravelled the complex processes of learning and teaching, nor have they been guided by the diverse and dynamic understandings held and practised within Aboriginal communities. The journey into understanding the LS of Aboriginal students has just begun, and the answers will come from deeply considered questions about ourselves as researchers and educators.

Epilogue

Two years ago I attended a strategic planning workshop at a local high school. This particular day was set aside for the Aboriginal community to voice its opinions regarding future organization of secondary education in Saskatchewan. About thirty-five Aboriginal people attended, including Elders, parents, teachers, students, and concerned community members. By the afternoon session, there were only about fifteen people remaining. Elders and parents were the first to leave.

Upon arriving at the meeting, participants were given a folder that contained the pre-set agenda; forms to gather information regarding the history and background of the participants; questionnaires; and sheets on which to write down their concerns and ideas. Desks were arranged in a circle, and participants were asked to complete the first sheet, which contained questions like: What schools have you attended? What grade did you complete? What is your highest level of education? How have you been involved in the educational system prior to today's meeting? Participants read over the sheet, and some took pens from their handbags or pockets. Those of us who had pens immediately began to help the Elders to fill out their sheets. The room remained virtually silent, and the air became thick with frustration and concern. Many of the participants had not received more than Grade 3 or Grade 4 and were hesitant to place this on their sheet. Elders felt this data collection was wasting their time, and they wished to speak to the issues at hand. Finally, one woman stood up and suggested that this sheet was too difficult for many people to complete and that we should get on with a discussion about current educational issues. She questioned the purpose of filling out forms when so much of importance needed to be said. The workshop organizers became

quite defensive about the validity of the forms but, after some consideration, agreed to move on with the agenda.

The next thing on the agenda was a getting-to-know-one-another game.
It was like a bingo card with all kinds of little anecdotes. You were to go
around the room and find participants who could say they had travelled
to the United States in the last year or who knew the words to a Beatles
song. Again, the same woman stood up and suggested that we go around
the circle and introduce ourselves instead of playing the game. The organizers again regrouped, after some words of support for the game, and we
moved on down the agenda.

The next item on the agenda was a question that was something like
this: What do you see as the relevant issues in secondary education? Workshop organizers had two flipcharts set up at the front, and they asked that
we share our opinions so that they could organize and record our
responses on the flipchart sheets. The first speaker spoke about her grandson who was having such a hard time at the school. She told of her observations of him and the concerns he had expressed to her. It was a very
moving account of her grandson's struggles, and she was obviously struggling to find the words to express herself. The workshop organizers questioned her in order to clarify a few items, and then, when she was done,
they began the task of rewording and shortening her story into point form
for the flipchart sheets. The paraphrasing was difficult and, in the end,
did not at all summarize what she had said. The whole undertaking took
about half an hour. Finally, I stood up and suggested that we forego the
flipcharts and just have a discussion in which the organizers could contribute. I asked that they stop writing and just listen to the speakers. There
would be plenty of time to record responses later, but for now it was
important to allow discussion to flow. Many of the words that followed
were adults' stories of their children's experience or of their experience
as teachers of Aboriginal students. Suggestions were made regarding the
handling of student issues, but little of the discussion fell under the head-
ings I have suggested in this research document. Much of the discussion
was in the form of narrative, and I daresay that the organizers felt that the
participants had not stuck to the agenda or addressed the questions for
which they sought answers. And so the day unfolded. It was a very frus-
trating day for all of us, and I wonder what was really achieved.

The Aboriginal people who spoke that morning told of their personal
experiences and their children's personal experiences in the educational
system. They could not/did not speak of corporate agendas or of learning
styles or of pedagogy, as such. They spoke, instead, of alienation and lone-
liness and frustration. They spoke of the pride they felt for their children's
accomplishments and of their inability to help their children with algebra

and physics. They spoke of the dreams they had for Aboriginal youth and the need for them to get an education. They spoke of love.

When we broke for lunch, many of the participants spoke privately about their dissatisfaction and suggested that nothing of importance would happen here. It was just a waste of time, they said. So they went home. When the final report on the strategic planning meetings came out, it was clear than none of their concerns had significantly influenced the direction of the school. There was one small section on the concerns of the Aboriginal community that nominally reflected what had taken place that day, but, for the most part, the report reflected other concerns much more clearly.

Drop-out rates of Aboriginal students in Canadian schools have remained high despite the vast amount of research conducted in an effort to alleviate this problem. Aboriginal parents are still on the periphery of educational decision making regarding their children's education. Communities continue to battle over local control of educational policy and the language of instruction, and they have limited resources with which to put their visions into practice. Pedagogical issues remain at the heart of the matter because students make the final judgment and students themselves remain voiceless. The hegemonic point of view continues to control the questions, and the answers seem to leave us with nowhere else to go.

Where does research go from here? Can research advance the needs and perspectives of Aboriginal people better than this local school board? Are the agendas already established, or is there room to accommodate and further the vision of Aboriginal people? Are we really listening, and are we prepared to act on what we hear? Do our current educational research methodologies allow us to listen and to advance creative approaches and to invent new practices? Is there room in the system to make the necessary change? If we answer any of the foregoing questions in the negative, then perhaps no more research needs to be done. Unless there is a paradigm shift, concerned individuals will continue to be frustrated and confused, and the possibilities will remain clouded and hidden.

Acknowledgments
This chapter is based upon Kathy L. Vermette (present author under previous name), "Issues of Pedagogy in Aboriginal Education," Royal Commission on Aboriginal Peoples (Ottawa, 1996).

References
Berry, J.W. 1966. "Temne and Eskimo Perceptual Skills." *International Journal of Psychology* 1: 207-29.
Browne, Dauna Bell. 1990. "Learning Styles and Native Americans." *Canadian Journal of Native Education* 17 (1): 23-35.

Bryant, H. 1986. "An Investigation into the Effectiveness of Two Strategy Training Approaches on the Reading Achievement of Grade One Native Indian Students." PhD diss., University of British Columbia.

Cazden, C.B., and V.P. John. 1971. "Learning in American Indian Children." In *Anthropological Perspectives on Education*, ed. M.L. Wax, S. Diamond, and F. Gearing, 253-72. New York: Basic.

Chrisjohn, R.D., and M. Peters. 1986. "The Right-brained Indian: Fact or Fiction?" *Journal of American Indian Education* 25 (2): 1-7.

Cullinane, D. 1985. "A Cognitive Style Study of Native Indian Children." MA thesis, University of British Columbia.

Downey, M. 1977. "A Profile of Psycholinguistic Abilities of Grades One, Two and Three Students of the Flathead Reservation." PhD diss., University of Montana.

Garber, M. 1968. "Ethnicity and Measures of Educability." PhD diss., University of Southern California.

Greenbaum, F., and S. Greenbaum. 1983. "Cultural Differences, Non-verbal Regulation and Classroom Interaction: Sociolinguistic Interference in American Indian Education." *Peabody Journal of Education* 61 (1): 16-33.

Hilger, M.I. 1951. *Chippewa Child Life and Its Cultural Background*. Washington, DC: Government Printing Services.

John, Vera. 1972. "Styles of Learning and Styles of Teaching: Reflections of the Education of Navajo Children." In *Functions of Language in the Classroom*, ed. C.B. Cazden, V.P. John, and D. Hymes, 331-43. New York: Teachers College Press.

Karlebach, D. 1986. "A Cognitive Framework for Deriving and Interpreting Learning Styles Differences among a Group of Intermediate Grade Native and Non-Native Pupils." PhD diss., University of British Columbia.

Kaulback, Brent. 1984. "Styles of Learning among Native Children: A Review of the Research." *Canadian Journal of Native Education* 11 (3): 27-37.

Kleinfeld, J. 1970. "Cognitive Strength of Eskimos and Implications for Education." Institute of Social Economic and Government Research, University of Alaska.

Kuske, I. 1969. "Psycholinguistic Abilities of Sioux Indian Children." PhD diss., University of South Dakota.

Lombardi, T. 1969. "Psycholinguistic Abilities of Papago Indian School Children." PhD diss., University of South Dakota.

MacArthur, R. 1978. "Ecology, Culture and Cognitive Development: Canadian Native Youth." In *The Canadian Ethnic Mosaic*, ed. L. Driedger, 187-211. Toronto: McClelland and Stewart.

More, A.J. 1984. "Indian Students and Their Learning Styles: Research and Results, and Classroom Applications." Prepublication draft, Department of Educational Psychology and Special Education, University of British Columbia.

–. 1987a. "Native Indian Learning Styles: A Review for Researchers and Teachers." *Journal of American Indian Education* 27 (1): 17-29.

–. 1987b. "Native Indian Students and Their Learning Styles: Research Results and Classroom Applications." *BC Journal of Special Education* 11 (1): 23-7.

Phillips, S.U. 1972. "Participant Structures and Communicative Competence: Warm Springs Children in Community and Classroom." In *Functions of Language in the Classroom*, ed. D. Cazden, D. Hymes, and V. John, 370-94. New York: Teachers College Press.

Rohner, E.P. 1965. "Factors Influencing the Academic Performance of Kwakiutl Children of Canada." *Comparative Education Review* 9: 331-40.

Scaldwell, W.A., J.E. Frame, and D.G. Cookson. 1984. "Individual Intellectual Assessment of Chippewa, Muncey and Oneida Children Using the WISC-R." Paper presented at the MOKAKIT conference, University of Western Ontario, London, Ontario.

Tofoya, Terry. 1982. "Coyote's Eyes: Native Cognitive Styles." *Journal of American Indian Education* 21 (2): 21-33.

Vermette, Kathy L. 1997. "Issues of Pedagogy in Aboriginal Education." In *For Seven Generations: An Information Legacy of the Royal Commission on Aboriginal Peoples*. CD-ROM. Ottawa: Libraxus.

Wauters, J., J.Bruce, D. Black, and P. Hocker. 1989. "Learning Styles: A Study of Alaska Native and Non-Native Students." *Journal of American Indian Education*. Special Issue, 53-62.

Weitz, Jacqueline. 1971. "Cultural Change and Field Dependence in Two Native Canadian Linguistic Families." PhD diss., University of Ottawa.

Part 4
Post-Secondary Education: Negotiating the Promise

Post-secondary education provides entry into the vocational and professional roles valued and rewarded in Canadian society. For Aboriginal peoples, post-secondary education has held out the hope of nurturing individual talents and providing escape from grinding poverty. This promise of a better life has been embraced by many Aboriginal people, not only for personal gain but in order to help whole families and communities to attain a higher quality of life.

But, historically, post-secondary education has come with a price, as it does today. An 1876 amendment to the Indian Act forced Indians who attained higher education to relinquish their Indian status – to become "enfranchised." Even when enfranchisement was no longer a legal consequence of attending university, the intensity of the socialization experienced by Aboriginal individuals tended to alienate them from their communities and their origins (Castellano 1970). For many Aboriginal students, strong assimilative forces are still a prominent feature of the post-secondary education experience.

Aboriginal people are now asserting that the pursuit of higher education should not mean a forced choice between Aboriginal identity and educational attainment. In contemporary post-secondary education, the challenge is to negotiate the conditions within which Aboriginal values, culture, and identity can thrive. The chapters in this section take up this theme.

There is no doubt that there are more Aboriginal individuals in post-secondary programs than has been the case in previous generations. Today,

Table 1

Aboriginal and non-Aboriginal populations aged 15+ showing highest level of schooling, Canada, 1981 and 1996

Education	1981 Aboriginal (%)	1981 Non-Aboriginal (%)	1996 Aboriginal (%)	1996 Non-Aboriginal (%)
Less than high school graduation	71.2	47.5	53.6	34.8
High school graduation only	6.1	13.1	8.6	14.3
Some post-secondary/no diploma	7.7	9.7	20.8	10.8
Non-university w/ diploma	12.4	19.8	12.5	24.5
University w/ diploma	2.6	9.9	4.5	15.6

Note: Includes those attending and not attending school.
Source: Statistics Canada, 1981 and 1996 Census.

many youth go on to college and university programs after high school. Adults who left school early or who interrupted their education to care for families often return to school as mature learners and go on to professional careers. The increasing number of Aboriginal graduates gives the impression that education outcomes are fast improving. However, statistical profiles show quite a different picture, as the summary table above indicates.

Using census data from 1981 and 1996, it can be seen that Aboriginal university completions have increased from 2.6 percent to 4.5 percent in this period. But in the same span of time, non-Aboriginal university completion rates have increased from 9.9 percent to 15.6 percent. The gap between Aboriginal and non-Aboriginal university completions has grown from just over 7 percent to 11 percent.

The increased disparity is repeated in completions of technical and college programs. While the Aboriginal completion rate has remained steady (12.4 percent in 1981 and 12.5 percent in 1996), non-Aboriginal completion rates have increased from 19.8 percent in 1981 to 24.5 percent in 1996.

It is apparent that completion rates for Aboriginal people in post-secondary education have edged upward over the fifteen-year timespan. However, the relatively lower levels of program completion are particularly troubling in a global economy that demands increasingly higher levels of formal education. It is important to understand the conditions that contribute to the persistence of inequitable education outcomes and to define strategies that support Aboriginal students' success and continuing on until graduation.

Post-secondary education is not simply about transmitting information and skills. It is a cultural and political terrain structured by power relations.

As Eber Hampton discusses in Chapter 12, the gains in Aboriginal control seen in elementary and secondary education have not been replicated at the post-secondary level. Most education, as it is practised, remains assimilative. Aboriginal people have been well aware of the implicit agenda of post-secondary education and have clearly identified colleges and universities as sites of cultural struggle and negotiation.

Hampton's analysis draws on Barnhardt's (1991) typology of Aboriginal post-secondary education, which identifies the assimilation model, the special program or department model, the federated or affiliated model, and the autonomous institution model. A fuller assessment of the typology is published elsewhere (Hampton and Wolfson 1994). A significant development in autonomous institutions has been the emergence of Aboriginally controlled post-secondary colleges, technical institutes, and learning centres at the community or regional levels. Their programs are often accredited through partnerships with provincial colleges and universities. As detailed in the education chapter of the RCAP report, such institutions have come to play a crucial role in helping students to complete academic programs. The only Métis-controlled post-secondary institution in Canada, the Gabriel Dumont Institute (GDI) in Saskatchewan, is discussed in Chapter 10 by John Dorion and Kwan Yang. Like tribal colleges in the United States, Aboriginally controlled post-secondary institutions in Canada represent some measure of self-governance in higher education.

More commonly, programs have developed within Canadian mainstream institutions, creating niches of Aboriginal innovation, like the First Nations House of Learning (FNHL) at the University of British Columbia, described by Ethel Gardner in Chapter 11. The institutional arrangements for such programs vary from place to place, with different degrees of involvement by Aboriginal constituencies in governance of the program and institution. Participation may be quite limited or may involve full and active partnership.

What motivates Aboriginal people to establish their own education systems or to find a way to work within the strictures of the status quo? The desire to put Aboriginal knowledge and core values at the centre of learning has led to the creation of many Aboriginal programs. Drawing on work by Kirkness and Barnhardt (1991), Gardner argues that the four *R*s – respect, relevance, reciprocity, and responsibility – should characterize the experiences of students regarding what they learn, how they learn, and the larger environment in which they learn. Her interviews with students at the University of British Columbia illustrate that there is much yet to be accomplished with regard to putting these values into practice in day-to-day relationships within the university.

Hampton outlines key features of these different institutional arrangements, identifying governance structures of post-secondary institutions as highly influential in determining whether post-secondary education serves Aboriginal goals of self-determination or whether it perpetuates the assimilationist agenda of our colonial past. He argues for a post-secondary institution that is not only controlled by Aboriginal people, but that also takes Aboriginal knowledge and values as its focus. The establishment of an Aboriginal Peoples' International University, as recommended by RCAP, would provide a means of achieving Aboriginal self-government and would serve as a visible expression of self-determination. Such an institution could utilize electronic communications to link Aboriginally controlled initiatives within Canada and beyond its borders through a network of decentralized campuses and centres of excellence.

The groundwork for electronically linked Aboriginal institutions has already been laid. In addition to geographically specific institutional development, Aboriginal communities have also been experimenting for nearly three decades with distance education as a way to permit students to study close to home. In Chapter 13, Lynne Davis gives examples of instances in which distance education is the primary or secondary delivery method used to instruct youth and adults. Davis's research was conducted at the brink of the explosion of Internet communications. Courses that one may access through World Wide Web-based sites have subsequently multiplied the opportunities for developing virtual learning environments. As Aboriginal education leaders contemplate alternatives for the future, emerging communication technologies will provide new design options for strengthening the bonds between Indigenous-centred institutions both in Canada and internationally.

The case studies on GDI and FNHL, together with Hampton's discussion of the Aboriginal Peoples' International University in Chapter 12, address, in rich detail, the difficulties and triumphs involved in defining unique spaces for Aboriginal education at the post-secondary level. Whether in an Aboriginally controlled or a mainstream institution, it is important to build a learning environment that will help students succeed. This must include programs with Aboriginal content, a critical mass of Aboriginal learners, appropriate support services, and Aboriginal instructors. The contribution of such program infrastructure is emphasized further in communities where distance education is being implemented.

One of the features that distinguishes Aboriginal post-secondary education from mainstream programming is the strong grounding of Aboriginal programs and institutions in Aboriginal communities. Many programs, like that described by Dorion and Yang at GDI, are designed specifically to address needs put forward by Aboriginal communities. The First Nations House of Learning responds to a variety of community advisory committees that participate in institutional planning and program implementation. This notion of being accountable to an external constituency is uncommon in the Canadian university environment, where the ethic of academic freedom is considered sacrosanct. Community colleges are accustomed to responding to market-driven concerns, and increasingly, cash-strapped universities are being coaxed to follow suit.

The effectiveness of institutions with regard to delivering the benefits of post-secondary education will be tested in the new millennium as a youthful population creates a robust demand for higher learning and credentials. Will accommodations to Aboriginal needs within mainstream universities be sufficient to achieve the educational outcomes that Aboriginal people desire? Or will Aboriginally controlled post-secondary institutions assume a dominant position in educating the next generation of Aboriginal learners? New ways of matching institutional services with Aboriginal learning needs may be required as an increasing number of Aboriginal students graduate from high school with varied career goals. While the last three decades have resulted in a strong base of diverse achievements upon which to build, Aboriginal educators will continue to be challenged to nurture the spirit and values of Aboriginal knowledge while negotiating the complex terrain of post-secondary education.

References

Barnhardt, R. 1991. "Higher Education in the Fourth World: Indigenous People Take Control." *Canadian Journal of Native Education* 18 (2): 199-231.

Castellano, Marlene. 1970. "Vocation or Identity? The Dilemma of Indian Youth." In *The Only Good Indian*, ed. Waubageshig, 52-60. Don Mills: Ontario New Press.

Hampton, E., and S. Wolfson. 1994. "Education for Self-Determination." In *Aboriginal Self-Government in Canada: Current Trends and Issues*, ed. J. Hylton, 90-107. Saskatoon: Purich.

Kirkness, V., and R. Barnhardt. 1991. "First Nations and Higher Education: The Four R's: Respect, Relevance, Reciprocity, Responsibility." *Journal of American Indian Education* 30 (3): 1-15.

Statistics Canada. 1981, 1996. Census Data.

10

Métis Post-Secondary Education: A Case Study of the Gabriel Dumont Institute

John Dorion and Kwan R. Yang

Métis Education in Saskatchewan

Post-secondary education is a priority concern of Métis people and their organizations. High rates of population growth and the limits of employment in Métis communities cause Métis people to look to the broader Canadian labour market for employment. Competition there requires the Métis to be equipped with the right education and skills to compete for jobs. In the struggle for political and economic rights Métis people pursue two major goals: (1) maintaining a distinct Métis identity and culture and (2) achieving self-identification and self-government.

Post-secondary education has a critical role to play in opening employment opportunities, reinforcing Métis identity, and establishing self-government. This chapter outlines the contemporary employment and education situation of Métis people and documents the approach of the Gabriel Dumont Institute, a Métis-controlled institution established to respond specifically to the needs of Métis communities and off-reserve Aboriginal people.

Despite the importance of post-secondary education to any discussion of Métis self-government, self-determination, and human resource issues, Métis education is under-researched and under-documented. There are few studies that address the historical evolution of Métis education, and even fewer that analyze the specific circumstances of Métis students in public schools or post-secondary institutions. Although "Indian control of Indian education" has evolved since the 1970s, there has been much less attention paid to the Métis educational context. In fact, generalizations are often transferred from First Nations education to Métis education without any critical analyses of parallels and divergences.

The following statistics concerning the Saskatchewan Métis people's educational attainments are taken from the 1991 Census of Canada (see Table 1).

Table 1

Métis population 15 years and over by highest level of schooling in comparison with other groups, 1991, Saskatchewan

Schooling	Métis	Indian	Inuit	Total
Total population	15,955	39,280	230	739,680
Less than grade 9	3,485	12,260	—	116,780
	(21.8%)	(31.2%)	—	(15.8%)
Grades 9-13	6,885	14,560	85	303,210
	(43.2%)	(37.1%)	(37%)	(41.0%)
Some post-secondary	5,145	11,350	95	254,980
	(32.2%)	(28.9%)	(41.3%)	(34.5%)
University	440	1,105	25	63,710
	(2.8%)	(2.8%)	(10%)	(8.6%)

Notes: Grades 9 to 13 includes certificate and non-certificate. Some post-secondary includes trades certificate or diploma and other non-university with and without certificate. University includes university with and without degree.
Source: All the data in this table are compiled from the 1991 Census Survey of Canada.

As is shown in Table 1, 21.8 percent of the Métis population of Saskatchewan, age fifteen and over, had less than Grade 9 education (compared to 15.8 percent of the same age group in the total population). Sixty-five percent of the Métis population had not received any post-secondary education and training (compared to 56.8 percent of the total population). Furthermore, 2.8 percent of Métis people had received some level of university education (compared to 8.6 percent of the total population).

Summing up, the largest pool of employable Métis, 65 percent in 1991, lacked the higher education necessary to compete for employment in a technology- and· information-based economy. By recognized standards of literacy, 21.8 percent of Métis were functionally illiterate. For this category, the most immediate need was literacy training and basic education. Although 43.2 percent had some level of secondary education, they would still have trouble competing in the labour market. The need for post-secondary vocational training and university education is evident.

Accurate data regarding participation and achievement of Métis people in the area of post-secondary education are scarce, and data sources are limited. However, some useful sources are available for the total Aboriginal student population at the University of Saskatchewan's College of Arts and Science and at Palliser Campus of the Saskatchewan Institute of Applied Sciences and Technology (SIAST).

The *Affirmative Action Monitoring Report* from the College of Arts and Science of the University of Saskatchewan provides some revealing data. Students of Aboriginal ancestry comprised 4.2 percent and 2.8 percent, respectively, of first-year and upper-year enrolments in 1991-2. In combination they represented slightly over 3 percent of the total enrolment in the College of Arts and Science, while Aboriginal people comprised 9.5 percent of the total population of Saskatchewan (University of Saskatchewan 1992; RCAP 1996, 1:22)

First- and upper-year Aboriginal students were admitted to the college with averages below those of the general arts and science first-year admissions in 1991-2. This reflects the failure of elementary and secondary education in Saskatchewan to prepare Aboriginal students for post-secondary education. Student drop-out rates continue to be exceptionally high, and those who survive to graduation often have lower levels of academic achievement than do their non-Aboriginal counterparts.

Once students are in the university system, one measure of success relative to all arts and science students is the cumulative percentage average of upper-year students (GPA). According to the *Affirmative Action Monitoring Report*, the GPA distribution indicates that a negligible number of Aboriginal students received grades of 80 percent or more (compared with 35.1 percent of all upper-year arts and science students). At the same time, 6.9 percent of Aboriginal students obtained marks of 50 percent or below, whereas 1.6 percent of all upper-year arts and sciences received failing grades.

To sum up, Aboriginal students participated in the college at a lower rate than would be expected from their proportion of the general provincial population. Admission averages for Aboriginal students were lower than those of the total student population, and Aboriginal students' academic achievement was, on average, relatively lower.

What is happening with Aboriginal participation at the college level? The *Comprehensive Student Affirmative Action Plan* from the Palliser Campus of the Saskatchewan Institute of Applied Sciences and Technology provides some interesting data (SIAST 1992). The report claims that, considering that approximately 9.6 percent of the provincial working-age population is Aboriginal, Aboriginal students are fairly well represented at Palliser Campus, having an overall participation rate of 8.3 percent in the period between 1 July and 31 December 1988 (SIAST 1992, 10). It points out, however, that Aboriginal students are under-represented in the business, technology, and industrial programs on campus. Most of the Aboriginal students of Palliser Campus were enrolled in the programs offered by the Extension Division, making up 29 percent of its total student population. In contrast, Aboriginal students were substantially under-represented in all the on-campus programs, having participation rates ranging from 3.9 percent to 6.9 percent.

The data from these two Saskatchewan institutions suggest that Aboriginal peoples are substantially under-represented in the university system and in those college programs that are closely linked with economic and

employment growth. Special measures are evidently required to better prepare Aboriginal students to enter and succeed in post-secondary education
and training. The Royal Commission on Aboriginal Peoples reported that
"the proportion of the provincial population that is Aboriginal in origin is
expected to increase from 9.5 per cent in 1991 to 13.9 per cent in the year
2016 ... The share of the Saskatchewan population made up of Aboriginal persons under 25 years of age is projected to be 20.5 per cent by the
year 2016" (RCAP 1996, 1: 23). The success of Aboriginal post-secondary
institutions in Saskatchewan provides models for responding effectively to
what is likely to become a deepening crisis in Aboriginal education. We
turn our attention now to the Gabriel Dumont Institute, the only Métis-
specific post-secondary institution in Canada.

Gabriel Dumont Institute: A Métis Post-Secondary Institution

The Gabriel Dumont Institute of Native Studies and Applied Research
(GDI) is the educational arm of the Métis Society of Saskatchewan. It offers
a wide range of educational and training programs to the Métis people
across the province. With its main office in Regina and sub-offices in Saskatoon and Prince Albert, GDI's programs are delivered to Métis communities on a needs basis.

In 1992, GDI articulated its mission statement as follows: "To promote
the renewal and development of Métis culture through appropriate
research activities, material development, collection and distribution of
those materials and the design, development and delivery of specific educational and cultural programs and services. Sufficient Métis people will
be trained with the required skills, commitment and confidence to make
the MSS [Métis Society of Saskatchewan] goal of Métis self-government a
reality" (GDI 1992a).

GDI is governed by a board of governors comprised of six members,
with four alternative members and an additional representative from the
Métis Nation of Saskatchewan. The board members are identified by
region, with two each representing the southern, central, and northern
areas of the province. Members of the board are jointly appointed by the
Métis Nation of Saskatchewan and the government of Saskatchewan.

GDI's day-to-day operations are overseen by the executive director, the
director of university programs, and the director of finance and administration. A research and development unit reports to the executive director. GDI is funded by a variety of agency sources, primarily the Core grant
to cover operational costs and a SUNTEP (Saskatchewan Urban Native
Teacher Education Program) grant from the province of Saskatchewan as
well as from such sources as the Métis Pathways to Success Secretariat of
the federal government, Métis regional management boards (RMBs,) and
local management boards (LMBs).

GDI was formally incorporated as a non-profit corporation in 1980 to serve the educational needs of the Saskatchewan Métis and non-status Indian peoples. With more than a decade of experience in education and research, the institute has been instrumental in the development of technical infrastructure and the education of professional personnel for the Métis Nation.

As a completely Métis-directed educational and cultural establishment, GDI is unique in Canada.[1] At its inception, the institute focused on education through cultural research as way of renewing and strengthening the heritage and achievement of Métis and non-status Indian peoples in Saskatchewan. It soon became apparent, however, that the institute would need to become more directly involved in education to fully serve the multifaceted needs, including the employment needs, of Métis communities.

As a result, GDI established a curriculum unit in order to pursue the development of curriculum and historical educational materials. The curriculum unit primarily focused on the development of teaching materials in Métis history and culture as well as other materials intended to increase awareness of Métis history and culture, including books, videos, CD-ROMs, audiotapes, and posters.

The institute's efforts to strengthen Métis education evolved into the establishment of the well-known SUNTEP program – a four-year teacher education program leading to a bachelor of education degree designed specifically for Métis students. In essence, SUNTEP trains Native teachers to meet the needs of Native students, and it has served as a model for Native adult education programs across Canada. In addition, GDI has succeeded in developing and delivering culturally relevant training and education programs in Métis communities all across Saskatchewan. The programs are accredited and cover a wide range of areas, including business administration, law enforcement, human justice, health care, resource technology and management, recreation and early childhood education, and housing administration.

GDI programs have been designed with a number of special features. First, almost all GDI programs are community-based. This means that courses leading to diplomas are offered in towns and urban centres across Saskatchewan. Students can take the courses and complete their education in their own communities instead of having to leave home to take courses on the campuses of universities and colleges. In this way, students can maintain their cultural and political awareness within a bicultural and sometimes bilingual context. Second, most of the GDI programs offer a sixteen-week preparatory phase that includes academic upgrading related to specific programs. This enables students whose schooling has been interrupted or whose academic standing does not meet program admission requirements to gain access to diverse post-secondary studies. Third,

GDI programs offer a strong Native studies component to enable students to grow in the knowledge and pride of their heritage and cultural identity. Fourth, GDI provides a comprehensive system of supports that gives students full access to individual and family counselling. Last, each of GDI's programs includes, if at all possible, an applied practicum phase.

The development and support functions of GDI are carried out by three units: curriculum development, research and development, and library information services. Unfortunately, it has been very difficult to secure funding to carry out the very important tasks of research and development. When monies have been available, the research unit has been instrumental to the GDI and its membership in that it provides a wide range of services in the following areas: research and policy analysis, community needs surveying and assessment, program development and implementation, funding acquisition, short- and long-term strategic planning, and liaison and advisory services. Post-secondary educational programs that were developed and implemented by the research and development unit in past years have included Native human justice, Métis business administration, integrated resource management, health care administration, and Métis housing administration cooperative education programs. In recent years, the research and development unit has been greatly reduced due to funding limitations.

GDI has sought funding in order to undertake a wide spectrum of research issues that are important in Aboriginal communities and contemporary Canadian society. Notable projects accomplished in past years include a research project on literacy contracted by the federal department secretary of state (now Heritage Canada) entitled "Literacy for Métis and Non-Status Indian Peoples: National Strategy" (GDI 1991); a social economic assessment of uranium mining projects in northern Saskatchewan entitled "Positions and Concerns for the Proposed Uranium Mining Projects in Saskatchewan: A Position Paper" (GDI 1992b); and a major province-wide study for the Royal Commission on Aboriginal Peoples (RCAP) on the topic of Saskatchewan Métis family literacy and youth education (Yang 1993). Again, like its development function, GDI's research services depend upon securing external funding.

The GDI library was established in May 1980 in Regina, and it contains a remarkable collection of uncatalogued materials on Aboriginal rights and Métis history as well as published books and journals. The collection covers a wide variety of materials, including the political, social, and economic history of Indian and Métis peoples documented from British colonial records, Hudson's Bay Company records, the Selkirk Papers, and Canadian government records and transcripts. The GDI library information services have been instrumental in fulfilling the institute's goal of providing resource services for students, staff, and community. The GDI library information services are provided through two major locations – Regina and Prince Albert – to support the institute's educational, training, curriculum, research, and other program initiatives in various program delivery locations.

GDI serves 800 to 1,000 adult students each year and also oversees the Dumont Technical Institute, which is federated with the Saskatchewan Institute of Applied Sciences and Technology (SIAST). Gabriel Dumont College, affiliated with the University of Saskatchewan, was established in 1995. The majority of the GDI student population is of Métis origin. In 1992, 126 students successfully completed their course requirements and graduated with SUNTEP degrees (or certificates or diplomas in the case of other programs). Between 1980, when it was initiated, and 1990, SUNTEP graduated 370 students, 80 percent of whom were female.

The profile of academic and vocational programs offered by GDI changes annually, so any one year provides only a snapshot of GDI programs at a fixed point in time. In its 1995 and 1996 annual report, GDI reported SUNTEP and a Métis social work program in Cumberland House as its university programs. In addition, it delivered Métis management and entrepreneurship programs at a number of locations. The same year, the Dumont Technical Institute offered programs in adult basic education, youth care worker training, General Equivalency Diploma preparation, introduction to office management, business administration, micro computer repairs, computer applications, truck driver training, heavy equipment operator training, and a gambling addiction workshop.

Saskatchewan Urban Native Teacher Education Program (SUNTEP)
SUNTEP is a four-year program offered by GDI, designed specifically for Métis students, and leading to a bachelor of education degree. It is one of the family of Indian Teacher Education Programs (ITEPs) dedicated to preparing Aboriginal teachers to meet the unique needs of Aboriginal communities. Since its inception, its special educational purpose and unique features have drawn substantial attention from the research community. Some research has gone into exploring a number of issues related to SUNTEP education, including special requirements of SUNTEP programming, factors influencing students' persistence in the SUNTEP program, elements of peer support among SUNTEP students, and comparison of the differences and similarities between SUNTEP and other Aboriginal teacher education programs. The research on SUNTEP constitutes one of the few research collections focused on Métis education, and it makes a very important contribution to our knowledge of Métis education.

Shortly after its inception in 1980, Bouvier (1984) conducted a case study on GDI's SUNTEP. After examining the historical development and the outcomes of this specialized training, Bouvier claimed that for teachers to be effective in helping children to succeed, they need more than their "Nativeness." They must achieve a sense of self-fulfillment, develop skills that will meet the needs of the communities they serve, and acquire certain knowledge that they must pass on to students. In order to prepare teachers appropriately, educators who provide this training must understand the stresses of this particular group and their special requirements, acknowledge the aspirations of the communities served by this endeavour, and provide the knowledge and skills that Native teachers will require in order to do their work. In addition, the educational organizations and systems involved must support Native teachers beyond pre-service training so that they can create an environment in which Native children will succeed.

In order to clarify the factors influencing students' persistence in the Regina SUNTEP, Barber (1986) surveyed thirty-five SUNTEP students. Demographic findings showed that the majority of the SUNTEP students had been out of school for a number of years. Barber also found that a number of factors contributed to student persistence, including passing grades, experiencing satisfaction with being a SUNTEP student, and positive relationships with peers and faculty. In addition, having adequate study skills and habits was seen to contribute to academic success, and self-confidence was seen as an indicator that the student would complete the program. Moreover, the SUNTEP students selected family support, personal motivation, and the desire to become a professional person as major factors in their decision to stay in the program. Last, the respondents also pointed out that lack of financial support, lack of study skills, and lack of preparation in high school were major obstacles to them staying with SUNTEP.

Scarfe (1990) furthered the research on SUNTEP by analyzing how senior SUNTEP students and graduates in Regina perceived the importance of program elements that contributed to peer support. Scarfe found that the following factors were believed to contribute to the development of a supportive group: elements of program structure and delivery, opportunities for interaction, emphasis on Indian/Métis identity, and components intended to build interpersonal and group skills. Among these factors, emphasis on Indian/Métis identity (i.e., the cultural components of the program) and elements of program structure and delivery received significantly higher ratings than did the others.

Based on the analysis of a number of factors, McBeath (1985) provided a comparative study of teacher education for Indian and Métis peoples in the province of Saskatchewan. There are three such programs: GDI's SUNTEP, NORTEP in northern Saskatchewan, and a program run by the

Saskatchewan Indian Federated College. McBeath pointed out that the three teacher education programs shared some similarities and also had their unique features, depending upon the needs they were trying to fulfill (e.g., those of status Indians; Métis; non-status Indians on reserves, in remote communities, or in urban areas).

The most notable similarity among the three programs is that they all involve a considerable amount of power-sharing among Native authorities, community agencies, and universities. Quantitatively, the three programs have been most successful in preparing Native teachers to meet the demands in the province. Qualitatively, they appear to be successful in providing quality education to Native students, especially in the areas of cross-cultural education and Native content. To conclude, McBeath pointed out that the post-secondary education systems have been attempting to graduate Indian students for years without being able to achieve much success. But Native-specific teacher education in Saskatchewan seems to have what is needed for change; that is, innovative and hard-working faculty; Native involvement; extra finances; the provision of a shielded, supported, and somewhat isolated group of dedicated students; and supportive schools in which to work and learn.

Qualitative Study: The Voices of GDI's Faculty and Students
As a part of the research for RCAP (Yang 1993), a study was conducted to elicit the views of faculty and students concerning the strengths and weaknesses of GDI programming and the appropriateness of GDI's program elements vis-à-vis being a model for Métis post-secondary education. In total twenty-five people participated in the project, completing in-depth interviews. Respondents were from three post-secondary programs (SUNTEP, the Native Human Justice Program, and the Métis Housing Management Program) and two divisions (research and development, and curriculum). The study findings are summarized as follows:

Overall
The study confirmed that GDI's programs greatly increase the employability and income of graduates. The following is indicative of student responses: "Before I enrolled in the SUNTEP program, I was working at Burger Baron as a short order cook. When I finished SUNTEP, I got a job right away as a teacher at Queen Mary School. The comparison in salary is a big change, a lot better for a teacher of eight years than a short order cook. I feel a lot more satisfied with my career" (a thirty-one-year-old female graduate from the SUNTEP program in Prince Albert).

Respondents spoke about the importance of GDI graduates as role models for youth and for current students. GDI's emphasis on vocational training was highly respected, since its education programs are providing excellent preparation for jobs. Moreover, students recognized the significance of GDI's programs in non-economic terms, particularly in helping students to develop self-esteem and a strong identity as Métis people. As described by one student: "Métis post-secondary education should create an awareness and an interest in Métis culture. It is important because it is the fundamental thing to maintain a collective identity as a group: the Métis."

Institution Mission

Respondents were asked to read GDI's mission statement and to present their perspectives on its strengths and shortcomings. Responses to the mission statement were very positive, but there were a number of suggestions recommending that the mission statement be expanded to include a stronger statement of GDI's links to the Métis Nation's goal of self-government and self-determination. These suggestions are very revealing in that the Métis people who were interviewed demonstrated a much stronger sense of Métis nationhood and Métis nation building than they had before. They expressed their strong determination to re-establish Métis self-government through education and culture. Correspondingly, they demanded that GDI play a major role in the Métis Nation building process.

Educational Programs

As described earlier in this chapter, GDI offers a wide range of programs to the Métis students of the province of Saskatchewan. Basically, almost all GDI programs are vocationally oriented and prepare students for jobs in a wide range of professions. Based on their own experience, participants generally evaluated GDI programs as sound, well-prepared, and credible. Among the areas of improvement were better inclusion of Métis content in the curriculum and better representation of Métis people among the GDI staff.

> The standards of the Gabriel Dumont Institute are very high; the instructors must meet the requirement standards. The graduates and students learn better with the close relationships they have with their instructors. The student/teacher ratio is a lot smaller than other institutions. (Student in Métis Housing Management Program)

> I think the curriculum is somewhat Native studies-oriented, not Métis studies-oriented. I think the program should try to focus more on the Métis aspect instead of the Native aspect. Despite this, I found the curriculum is very good, well prepared, and competent to prepare students to meet the academic standards of other educational institutions as well as in the labour market. (Fourth year SUNTEP student)

Some instructors of mine were Métis. I think there should be as many Aboriginal instructors as there possibly can [be]. The Métis instructors are well prepared, informative, and knowledgeable. Our Métis students looked up to them as one of us. (SUNTEP graduate)

Student Performance

Faculty and students expressed the view that GDI graduates and students are highly regarded in their workplaces. Most of the participants pointed out that the GDI graduates and students are competent and can match the academic standards set by mainstream educational systems. Some participants further indicated that GDI graduates and students have better qualifications in the area of cross-cultural training than do those from mainstream schools.

The GDI students can match the academic standards of the mainstream educational institutions. At Queen Mary School [where the participant works] there are eight SUNTEP graduates employed. They teach all through the three divisions of the school. I believe the school is still looking for more SUNTEP students. (SUNTEP graduate)

The students in the Native Human Justice Program are energetic and committed to the program. The previous graduates have been able to locate jobs, and more are in the places where they were doing their practicum. (Student in Native Human Justice Program)

The participants also raised two serious problems faced by GDI graduates and students. The first is the lack of post-secondary education assistance for Métis students, as this generates a lot of financial stress and debt loads.

The debt I will have to repay to both the Canada and Saskatchewan Student Loans will keep me in debt for a very long time. Over my four-year SUNTEP program, my student loans had grown to a total of $48,000. When I entered the program, I never knew I would be left with such a large debt upon completion of the program. I strongly believe that the governments should, instead of offering student loans, reinstate the bursary program. If there is no significant financial assistance available to the Métis students, most of them will end up with $30[,000] to 50,000 loan debts and will be unable to pay the debts back. The students will soon start to default on their student loan payments and even declare bankruptcy. I almost took this route. (SUNTEP graduate)

The second problem is that, when students are looking for jobs after their graduation, many of them face discrimination. A notable claim is that many employers, especially government organizations and agencies, think Métis people are different from Indians and should not be included in employment equity hiring. A SUNTEP graduate reported: "Some of my fellow students applied for jobs in Saskatchewan. But they were discriminated against by the educational system because they are Métis. The ones who were lucky enough to get hired on by the affirmative action clause were mostly treaty Indians."

Discrimination is also encountered in the form of unfairly negative evaluations of GDI programs and students: "I was granted an interview with one of the school divisions. During the interview, the gentleman in charge told me that the SUNTEP degree is a farce. He also told me that my degree meant nothing to regular schools because I was specialized in Native Studies."

Community Delivery Model

The most distinctive features of GDI's program delivery are community-based programming and community delivery. These two elements were believed by the participants to be the most crucial with regard to the relationship between community and institutions. Recommendations were made to improve the delivery model of Métis post-secondary education in three respects. First, community programming should emphasize Métis self-government, community ownership, and better communication with the communities guided by a Métis Education Act. Second, high quality Métis post-secondary education can be accomplished through maintaining academic standards, better inclusion of Métis studies, provision of orientation and preparatory training, and federation with universities. Third, vocational orientation should be improved through labour market analysis, the installation of job-oriented programs and cooperative education programs, the provision of career counselling services, and the expansion of professional training fields.

GDI's model for delivering post-secondary education to Métis people is highly regarded by the participants as highly effective. Repeatedly, participants pointed out the essential importance of three elements that are integral to GDI's vision: community-based programming, the retention of Métis languages and culture, and vocational education.

Elements in a Métis Model of Post-Secondary Education

The sum of experiences in GDI program delivery, research on factors promoting student retention and achievement, and qualitative studies on student and community expectations provide the basis for defining the essential elements of future Métis post-secondary programs and institutions.

(1) Métis post-secondary education should be community-based. In order to accomplish this, the following steps should be taken: educational institutions should be Métis self-governed and community owned; institutions should be governed by a Métis education board and guided by a Métis education act; institutions should promote better communication with their Métis constituencies; and the educational institutions should promote more involvement of Métis parents and Elders.

(2) Métis post-secondary education should provide the highest quality education to the Métis people. This should be accomplished in the following ways: academic standards should be high in order to compete with and match those of the mainstream educational systems; substantial components of Métis studies should be included in the curriculum whether delivered in Métis-controlled or mainstream post-secondary institutions; orientation and preparatory training should be made available to Métis students; and federation or affiliation of Métis post-secondary institutions should be explored.

(3) Métis post-secondary education should be vocationally oriented so as to prepare students for the job market. In order to ensure this, the following strategies should be adopted: vocational orientation of programs should be achieved through analysis of the labour market, cooperation with industries, and assessment of Métis people's employment needs; job-oriented programs and cooperative education programs should be designed to meet the needs of both students and industries; personal and career counselling should be made available to all Métis students; and training and education should cover a broad spectrum of professions, particularly those that show potential for growth in a changing economy.

Conclusion

Aboriginal post-secondary education plays a vital role in the fostering of Aboriginal leadership, which, in turn, promotes Aboriginal self-determination and self-government (Bad-Wound 1991). Similarly, any discussion of Métis self-government and policy making in Métis affairs cannot proceed far without information about Métis people, especially information regarding post-secondary education.

In the areas of Métis and non-status Aboriginal education policy, government agencies have not been guided by an equivalent to the position paper *Indian Control of Indian Education* (National Indian Brotherhood 1972). Métis submissions to governments and to RCAP have called for a coherent, integrated plan for Métis self-determination, beginning with an act of Parliament establishing principles of Aboriginal self-government in all education programming.

The present chapter has attempted to expand the discussion about Métis post-secondary education by bringing together a variety of information sources and studies that can inform debate about the direction and future of education for Métis people. By undertaking primary research on the programming and delivering mechanism of GDI, we have been able to provide a basis for articulating a model for Métis post-secondary education. We hope that Métis authorities, government policy makers, and the general public will find that this work furthers the process of providing programs and services that will guarantee Métis people a secure economic and culturally based future.

Acknowledgments
This chapter is based upon John Dorion and Kwan R. Yang, "Métis Post-Secondary Education: A Case Study of the Gabriel Dumont Institute," Royal Commission on Aboriginal Peoples (Ottawa, 1993).

Note
1 The Louis Riel Institute in Manitoba is also becoming active as a result of current encouragement of Métis participation in education.

References
Bad-Wound, E. 1991. "Teaching to Empower: Tribal Colleges Must Promote Leadership and Self-determination in Their Reservations." *Journal of American Indian Higher Education* 3 (1):15-9.

Barber, C.A. 1986. "A Study of Factors Influencing Persistence in the Regina SUNTEP Program." MA thesis, University of Regina.

Bouvier, R.E. 1984. "Specialized Training in the Saskatchewan Urban Native Teacher Education Program: A Case Study." MA thesis, University of Regina.

Gabriel Dumont Institute. 1991. *Literacy for Métis and Non-Status Indian Peoples: A National Strategy*. Regina: Gabriel Dumont Institute.

–. 1992a, 1995, 1996. *Annual Reports*. Regina: Gabriel Dumont Institute.

–. 1992b. *Positions and Concerns for the Proposed Uranium Mining Projects in Saskatchewan: A Position Paper*. Regina: Gabriel Dumont Institute.

McBeath, A. 1985. *Teacher Education for Indian and Métis People in the Province of Saskatchewan, Canada*. Research report. University of Regina.

National Indian Brotherhood. 1972. *Indian Control of Indian Education*. Ottawa: National Indian Brotherhood.

Royal Commission on Aboriginal Peoples (RCAP). 1996. *Report of the Royal Commission on Aboriginal Peoples*. Volume 1: *Looking Forward, Looking Back*. Ottawa: Canada Communications Group.

Scarfe, D.R. 1990. "Student Perceptions of Elements of Peer Group Support in the Saskatchewan Urban Native Teacher Education Program." MA thesis, University of Regina.

SIAST, Palliser Campus. 1992. *Comprehensive Student Affirmative Action Plan*. Moose Jaw.

Statistics Canada. 1993. Custom Tables of the 1991 Census. Ottawa.

University of Saskatchewan, College of Arts and Science. 1992. *Affirmative Action Monitoring Report*. Saskatoon: University of Saskatchewan.

Yang, K. 1993. *Saskatchewan Métis Family Literacy and Youth Education Strategy*. A report for the Royal Commission on Aboriginal Peoples. Regina: Gabriel Dumont Institute.

11
First Nations House of Learning: A Continuity of Transformation
Ethel Gardner

> I renounced finally my bow and arrow for the spade and pen. I took off my soft moccasins and put on the heavy and clumsy but durable shoes. Every day of my life I put into use every English word that I knew, and for the first time permitted myself to think and act as a white man.
>
> – Ohiyesa, a Sioux (Wright 1991, 3)

Charles Eastman (Ohiyesa's English name) believed that it was in the interest of himself and his people, the Sioux, to relinquish his Sioux ways and to assimilate into the imported settler society. Ohiyesa, sans "soft moccasins," graduated from Dartmouth College in 1887 and later received a degree in medicine from Boston University, a rare accomplishment, even by today's standards of education, for Indians in North America (Wright 1991, 3). In 1993, 120 years later, the University of British Columbia graduated its first First Nations doctor from its School of Medicine, again, a rare accomplishment for an Aboriginal person of this continent.

The distinctions between "thinking and acting like a white man" and being a Sioux would have been clearer in Ohiyesa's day than today. In Canada, there was a time when gaining a university education meant being enfranchised automatically into Canadian society and being stripped of one's Indian identity. Being Indian and being civilized was considered somewhat of an oxymoron. Most of us bypassed the spade, but many of us are choosing to take up the pen, and yet we did not "renounce the bow and arrow" willingly, as did Ohiyesa. Government legislation and assimilationist policies served either to eradicate, or to push underground, much of our traditional knowledge and many of our traditional practices. Most of our languages are now in danger of becoming extinct as a result of the imposed education that was forced on our peoples through the residential school system. We are still reeling from the effects of the dark and not so distant painful past. Our "soft moccasins" have a different meaning for us today, and the "durable shoes" are still "heavy and clumsy." Our First Nations ways are not always obvious in the tangible relics with which we are often stereotyped today, and we struggle to make sense of how we fit in this modern technological and knowledge-driven society.

In May 1993 the First Nations House of Learning celebrated the opening of the First Nations Longhouse on the University of British Columbia (UBC) campus. The longhouse is to serve as a "home away from home," where First Nations students, staff, and the community at large can celebrate together the philosophies, values, and cultures represented by the diverse First Nations population on campus. Ohiyesa would be amazed by the events that transpired during an entire week of ceremonies and feasts celebrating First Nations ways – at a university.

However, when it comes to delivering higher education to First Nations, the state of affairs at UBC is not all roses and sunshine. It is important to applaud all the milestones that have been reached to date, and this chapter will try to do justice to them. Although there are many successes to boast of, there are still many challenges with regard to "access and relevance" issues as these relate to First Nations in higher education.

In 1992-3 it was estimated that there were 250 First Nations students enrolled in degree programs at UBC and that, if their numbers were proportionate to their numbers in the general population, then there should have been closer to 1,500 First Nations students enrolled. With the advent of the new longhouse, bringing First Nations issues at UBC into higher profile than ever before, enrolments are expected to increase. The House of Learning wants to have 1,000 First Nations students enrolled at UBC by the year 2000 – an ambitious but not impossible goal. The question remains, How can we soften the "heavy and clumsy but durable shoes" so that they fit more comfortably?

First Nations House of Learning: An Overview of Programs at UBC
The establishment of the First Nations House of Learning in 1987 provided a mechanism for expanding the delivery of education to First Nations at UBC. The university went from providing a limited focus on education and law to providing higher education to First Nations on a university-wide scale and establishing new initiatives. The House of Learning has made a conscious effort to build upon the successful components of UBC's earliest First Nations programs – the Native Indian Teacher Education Program (NITEP), the Native Law Program, and the Ts' 'kel Graduate Program in education. The historical development of these three programs, from which evolved the basic model for the First Nations House of Learning, is described below.

NITEP Model
In 1969, a small group of Indian educators, called the British Columbia Native Indian Teachers' Association (BCNITA), submitted a funding proposal for a Native teacher training program to the BC provincial government. After five years of discussions with various university and government

representatives, NITEP was established at UBC in 1974 (Archibald 1986, 34). As NITEP matured, it became evident that six factors were key elements in its success:

(1) *An advisory committee.* Initially, this committee was composed of people from the British Columbia Native Indian Teachers' Association (BCNITA) and the Faculty of Education; later, students were included. The committee drove NITEP's objectives to increase the number of Native Indian teachers who would be certified to teach in BC schools and respond to the educational background, heritage, needs, and desires of First Nations peoples in the province (Archibald 1986, 34).

(2) *Relevant studies.* Indian studies courses were included in NITEP's design to strengthen NITEP students' identities and to increase their awareness and understanding of First Nations cultures and issues.

(3) *Staff.* Although not initially stated, having Native Indian staff for NITEP became a goal in 1980. Since then, NITEP has been staffed almost entirely by First Nations personnel, including field centre coordinators and on-campus staff.

(4) *Field centres.* Students attend classes for the first two years at a field centre. As of 1992-3, there were four full-time centres in operation, that number remaining constant to date. The field centres permit the students to complete their studies close to home, maintaining contact with their own people. Group cohesiveness develops in the centres and continues when the students transfer to the UBC campus (Kirkness 1992).

(5) *Support function.* An extremely important component of NITEP is the support service provided at field centres. The key person at each centre is the coordinator – a master teacher who administers the centre, conducts student seminars, organizes student teaching placements, coordinates itinerant instructors, and counsels and tutors students. The support component continues when students move to campus (Kirkness 1992). The House of Learning now houses the central administration for NITEP and is a place where students can visit, study, and hold social get-togethers.

(6) *Evaluation.* Several external evaluations have been conducted on NITEP. An evaluation conducted by the Rudolph Dreikurs Institute in 1988 determined that NITEP was continuing to meet its objective to increase the number of Native teachers in British Columbia and that NITEP graduates were equipped to work wherever they chose (Pepper 1988, cited in Kirkness 1992). An external evaluation conducted in 1997 recommended the establishment of a Department of First Nations Education, effecting a transition from special program to departmental status. All of the key elements of NITEP, except for the

field centre concept, would later be replicated in the First Nations House of Learning and incorporated into new initiatives.

Native Law Program

The interest in Native law began as early as 1973 because a number of prominent law faculty members at UBC were involved with the "Indian question." These faculty members included Professors Lysyk, Jackson, Sanders, and Thompson (Kirkness 1992). In 1975, the Justice Development Commission Task Force on the delivery of Legal Services to Native Peoples submitted a brief to the Faculty of Law at UBC that emphasized the total absence of Native lawyers in British Columbia. In 1976, the faculty initiated an affirmative action program to facilitate the admission of First Nations applicants to the law school. Since then, the Faculty of Law at UBC has played a leading role, not only in graduating First Nations lawyers (almost as many as all other Canadian law schools combined), but also in teaching, researching, and writing about First Nations issues. Today the level of representation of First Nations students at UBC's law school is among the highest in Canada.

In 1984, a Native UBC law graduate was appointed director of the Native Law Program. It was his responsibility to promote law as a field of study among Native people; to ensure that the academic and personal needs of the students were met; and to organize special speakers, courses, and programs. An advisory committee was formed that included Native law students and members of the law faculty (appointed by the dean). The committee has monitored the program and conducted internal evaluations of a formative nature.

The director's responsibilities have evolved to include administration of the program, teaching, and research. The director is also in charge of student services and arranges tutorials for all first-year students. Students are generally given help with everything from housing to funding. The First Nations Law Program strives to make the law school experience relevant to the needs and objectives of First Nations students, and it offers six courses related to pertinent issues and rights of First Nations (Borrows and Wood 1993, 17).

Two key elements that were helpful in increasing participation of First Nations students in both the Native Law Program and in NITEP were interest among prominent faculty members and affirmative action mechanisms (which ensured reserved spaces for enrolment).

Ts' 'kel Graduate Program

The Ts' 'kel Administration Program (MEd) began in 1984 under the leadership of Verna Kirkness in response to a need for advanced educational leadership training for Native Indian people. By that time NITEP had been in operation for a decade and had fifty graduates with BEd degrees. Several had already moved into leadership positions; others aspired to do so (Downey 1987, 9). The NITEP Advisory Committee provided guidance and support for the development of the Ts' 'kel Program. To reflect the committee's expanded role, it became known as the Native Indian Education Advisory Committee. The first group of students helped the faculty to develop some of the First Nations courses and also named the program "Ts' 'kel" – a Halq'emeylem word meaning "golden eagle." To many First Nations, the eagle symbolizes great achievement and accomplishments.

Initially, the Ts' 'kel Administration Program provided an opportunity, through a master's degree in educational administration, for interested and qualified First Nations people to develop expertise and leadership abilities that would be of benefit to First Nations schools and other educational programs. Eventually, the Ts' 'kel Program evolved to include master's and doctoral options in educational studies, educational psychology and special education, curriculum and instruction, counselling psychology, and language education. The program, now called Ts' 'kel Graduate Studies, is headed by two Aboriginal co-directors who are both graduates of the program.

In 1987, the final year of the three-year experiment, a summative evaluation concluded that "Ts' 'kel has been most successful and has the ingredients necessary for a continuation of that success" (Downey 1987, 105-6). As of May 1993, there were twenty-three Ts' 'kel graduates employed in key leadership roles in band and public schools, colleges, First Nations post-secondary institutions, and universities (Archibald 1993, 38). Ts' 'kel's reach was extended into the international realm through a memorandum of agreement with the University of Alaska, Fairbanks, to facilitate the exchange of students and faculty, collaborative research and publication, and information exchanges through conferences, symposia, and congresses. Ts' 'kel formed the first gateway into UBC for First Nations graduate students and, through the memorandum of understanding, paved the way for the House of Learning's long-term goal of founding an international component.

First Nations House of Learning: Building on Success
The origins of the House of Learning go back to 1983, when UBC president Dr. K. George Pedersen asked Verna J. Kirkness and Thomas Berger to co-chair a committee to advise the President's Office on ways the university could better serve First Nations peoples and their communities. In 1984 the committee recommended making the university accessible to more Native students; increasing enrolment in all faculties; and helping the university's departments, schools, and institutes to make their course offerings more relevant to Indian people.

British Columbia's 1984 education cutbacks could have meant the end of the project. However, when Dr. David Strangway assumed the presidency from Dr. Pedersen in 1985, one of the things he did during his first week in office was to meet with Kirkness concerning the state of Indian programs and participation at UBC and the recommendations of the 1984 report. With crucial support at top levels of the university, the Donner Canadian Foundation was approached and donated start-up funds for a three-year period. The grant arrangement stipulated the gradual decrease in funding, with the understanding that UBC would fully fund the program if it proved successful after its three-year developmental stage. A summative evaluation in 1990 concluded that the House of Learning was achieving its mandate, mission, and goals, and its operations were duly incorporated into UBC's budget.

In 1987 the First Nations House of Learning opened its doors with a mandate to make UBC resources more accessible to British Columbia's First Peoples and with a mission to provide quality education that was determined by its relevance to the philosophy and values of First Nations. To carry out this mandate and mission, the following objectives were set: (1) to facilitate the participation of First Nations people in a wide range of study areas by providing information on post-secondary opportunities and support services; (2) to expand the range and depth of program and course offerings within the faculties, schools, and institutes at UBC related to those needs identified by First Nations people and communities in British Columbia; (3) to identify and promote research that would extend the frontiers of knowledge for the benefit of First Nations; (4) to increase First Nations leadership on campus; (5) to establish a physical facility (longhouse) on campus to enhance access and support services for First Nations students; and (6) to establish a long-range plan that included the possibility of founding an international component for the advancement of Indigenous peoples around the world (FNHL Brochure 1988).

The First Nations House of Learning was made directly responsible to the President's Office, and it was to be guided by a president's advisory committee. This committee included representatives from the First Nations community, heads of First Nations initiatives, and UBC faculty and students. Members were appointed by the vice-president (academic) and provost for a three-year term. Students were chosen by their peers as representatives for one-year terms. The strategic positioning of the House of Learning at the higher administration level meant a break from being linked to any single faculty, enabling it to pursue its mandate, mission, and objectives across all faculties, university administrative and service units.

Verna J. Kirkness was appointed the founding director of the House of Learning in September 1987. By November 1987 Ethel Gardner was hired as assistant director and Kathy Morven was hired as secretary. The tiny staff of three set out to implement the mandate, mission, and goals of the newly established First Nations House of Learning.

By then, a model of organization and operation had already evolved from the successful programs of the past. The crucial components of this model had emerged from the evolution of NITEP, the Native Law Program, and Ts' 'kel: (1) the direct involvement of First Nations people in the design and delivery of programs; (2) the development of courses and programs that reflect the philosophies and values of First Nations; (3) the provision of a "home-away-from-home" support function for students, staff, their families, and friends; and (4) the ongoing assessment of programs.

One of the first tasks of the House of Learning was to determine community-identified priorities for post-secondary education. After a series of ten consultation meetings and workshops conducted throughout the province in 1988, the professional needs most often identified by communities were in the areas of education, health care, natural resource sciences, commerce and business administration, and First Nations languages (Gardner 1989). The First Nations House of Learning began addressing how these expressed needs could be fulfilled, and discussions began with the appropriate departments. In developing new initiatives focus groups, workshops, and advisory committees were established to incorporate First Nations input and perspectives into the new programming.

The House of Learning also serves a coordinating, or umbrella, function in that it integrates the activities of the First Nations program staff with services for all First Nations students (outside those provided by respective First Nations programs). For example, each year the House of Learning prepares: (1) a *First Nations Studies Calendar*, which includes information on First Nations programs, courses with First Nations content, services for students, and financial information (including bursaries and scholarships for students); (2) the *First Nations House of Learning Newsletter*, which incorporates campus-wide news and information; (3) the *First Nations House of Learning Annual Report*, which includes updates on campus-wide activities and new initiatives based on a workplan established for that year; and (4) an issue of the *Canadian Journal of Native Education*. A promotional video on the building of the longhouse has also been produced.

Other umbrella activities of the House of Learning include organizing conferences and the President's Speaker Series on First Nations Issues, conducting student career awareness workshops upon being invited to do so by First Nations communities; liaising with UBC faculty, departments, schools, and institutes; liaising with other BC universities and First Nations post-secondary institutes; distributing materials; promoting opportunities for First Nations involvement in UBC; hosting First Nations guest speakers; hosting international visiting professors; seeking funding for such projects as videos and publications, and library materials; and developing new program initiatives.

Three initiatives of First Nations House of Learning are discussed below as illustrations of the way in which the House of Learning has fostered linkages between the needs of First Nations communities and the potential of the university community to respond with expertise and resources.

First Nations Health Careers (FNHC)
The first initiative established under the auspices of the First Nations House of Learning was First Nations Health Careers. Since 1988 it has been co-administered with the Office of the Coordinator, Health Sciences. The program was designed to encourage First Nations people to enter health professions. Goals and objectives of the Health Careers Program were congruent with those of the House of Learning but were targeted to a group of ten health professions that cross several different faculties. Goals and objectives included creating access to health care studies and providing support services, consulting with First Nations communities for identifying priorities, collaborating with faculties to develop relevant courses and seminars, and identifying First Nations research needs. The advisory committee structure was replicated and includes First Nations community people who have a particular interest or expertise in medicine and the health sciences plus members of the UBC faculty. First Nations Health Careers has created courses that incorporate First Nations concerns and examine First Nations health issues, and it has also created a non-credit Summer Health Institute for First Nations community health care workers.

Youth Programs
Under the auspices of First Nations Health Careers a new youth element was added to the range of opportunities for First Nations students at UBC. First, a Synala Honours Program was established, a six-week intensive summer program for Grade 11 students that aims to help prepare students for university. Second, the Summer Science Program is a one-week course offered twice in the summer for students from Grades 8 to 9 in the first week and Grades 10 to 11 in the second week. The program introduces students to the campus and exposes them to science-related educational and professional opportunities for which they can begin to prepare. In each of these youth programs students are exposed to First Nations role models in science- and health-related fields and are exposed to First Nations perspectives on science. Third, an early access program allows students to get a head start in becoming acquainted with UBC by beginning the first year of their degree program in the summer instead of in September.

In 1993, an evaluation of First Nations Health Careers gave it a very positive review, acknowledging that "the number of students enrolled in health/science faculties provides testimony to communities that health and science careers are within reach of all First Nations" (FNHC Evaluation Report 1993).

The Longhouse: "Home Away From Home"

With successful precedents set from prior programs, with clear goals for "access" and "relevance," with an infrastructure designed to create stronger links between UBC and First Nations communities, the building of the longhouse on campus served as a visible and undeniable statement that First Nations people had moved into UBC.

The House of Learning's goal for a longhouse-style building became realizable when philanthropist Jack Bell donated a million dollars to UBC – a donation the Bell family wanted specifically designated for First Nations priorities. After consultations with staff, students, First Nations, and UBC community members, the longhouse idea became part of UBC's World of Opportunity Capital Fundraising Campaign, in which dollars raised would be matched by the provincial government. First Nations House of Learning director, Verna J. Kirkness; Squamish Elder Chief Simon Baker; Musqueam Elder Vince Stogan; Haida Elder Minnie Croft; and former judge Alfred Scow headed up the Longhouse Committee, which was established to oversee the building of the longhouse and to ensure that community input was incorporated at all stages of its development.

The longhouse officially opened its doors in May 1993 and now includes: offices and meeting places for First Nations programs and new initiatives; counselling services; X̱wi7x̱wa Library services; S-Takya Childcare Centre; an Elders' lounge; a fully equipped computer laboratory; full kitchen facilities; a student/staff lounge; student office space; and a sacred circle structure for quiet time, meditation, and simple ceremonies. The most prominent place in the longhouse is the magnificent Great Hall called Sty-Wet-Tan, which houses carved representations from different First Nations across British Columbia. "Sty-Wet-Tan" is a Musqueam name that means "Spirit Power of the Western Wind."

In 1994 the community liaison coordinator's position, which had been created earlier in the First Nations House of Learning's development and was held by Madeleine MacIvor, was changed to coordinator, student services. MacIvor's new role was to develop and coordinate the on-campus student services component and to establish a database of First Nations student participation in the university. Among the many activities generated through this role was liaising with on-campus student organizations, including the Native Indian Student Union, the First Nations Law Students Association, the American Indian Sciences and Engineering Society, and the Association of Graduate Aboriginal Students. With growing First Nations enrolments in increasingly diverse areas of study, particularly areas not necessarily associated with specific First Nations initiatives, a sense of community was needed. And MacIvor, the longhouse staff, and students set out to nurture this at the longhouse.

The House of Learning staff burgeoned from three in 1987 to include a director; an associate director; a coordinator, student services; a building manager; two librarians; three childcare staff; counsellors; part-time Elders-in-residence; a part-time computer technician; and two secretaries.

Four *Rs*: Respect, Relevance, Reciprocity, and Responsibility

An assessment of the philosophy underlying the First Nations House of Learning and the impact of its activities is facilitated by application of the four-*Rs* framework developed by Kirkness and Barnhardt (Kirkness and Barnhardt 1991). This framework was used to gather reflections from staff and current and previous students on issues faced when attempting to deliver innovative post-secondary education to First Nations students. The eight staff members who were interviewed were from the House of Learning (3), the Native Indian Teacher Education Program (3), the First Nations Health Care Professions Program (1), and Ts' 'kel (1). The six students interviewed were from the Native Indian Teacher Education Program (3), forestry (1), nursing (1), and Ts' 'kel (1). The interviews took place in the summer of 1993 at the newly built longhouse complex, where the staff had relocated only a few months before. The interviews were guided by a set of questions related to the four *R*s, drawing on the participants' experiences in post-secondary education and on their visions for an ideal post-secondary education at UBC. None of the fourteen participants felt there was any need for anonymity and, therefore, they are all named. Only a small portion of their testimony is used here, and only some of the participants are quoted. It must be stated that what is presented in this section could never do justice to the rich, thoughtful, often philosophical and reflective discussions that actually took place in the interviews, which ranged from forty-five minutes to an hour and a half.

Respect

Kirkness and Barnhardt say that respect is "the most compelling problem that students face when they go to university," and this study confirmed that assertion. What became evident is that First Nations staff and students are demanding to have a dialogue with the "producers of knowledge," demanding to be heard, to have the issues of misrepresentation of First Nations addressed. They are demanding to have First Nations knowledge recognized, respected, and valued. This demand is causing tensions for both First Nations and the "producers of knowledge," and it is causing a lot of pain and agony for the First Nations students who seem to be caught in the tangle. Consider the following statement from a First Nations student:

In my psychology classes, two of them [professors] for sure made comments about Native people. They both said First Nations people have no
business living in the city, that they should all live on the reserve, because
when they go to the city they all end up on skid row, and that First
Nations people are a tragedy because they are all poor and drunk and
have high suicide and death rates, and that most cannot make it in the
city, or at college level, and that their traditional beliefs of the shamans
and medicine people, that those were people who were schizophrenics
because they heard voices. (Deina Jules interview, summer 1993)

Obviously, gross long-standing negative stereotypes of First Nations are
being perpetuated here. Who is responsible for setting the record straight?
How are students to respond to blatant racist perspectives? What effect do
these incidents and attitudes have on the students' educational experience? What reactions can students expect from their professors if they
challenge them?

What seems to be missing in the discussions, and what probably needs
to be addressed, is the construction of a mechanism to enhance students'
ability to establish ways of diffusing the pain and to provide them with
opportunities for developing a constructive dialogue. The pain is not created so much by any one isolated incident as it is from the cumulative
effect of being constantly exposed to a barrage of mini-aggressions, both
subtle and blatant. In addition to the need for equipping students with
coping and empowering mechanisms, it is apparent from the interviewees' comments that faculty need to be sensitized to First Nations
issues and that they would benefit from learning how to "listen." An
insight from Jo-ann Archibald can illuminate the need for this: "It's the
outsiders or the experts who have learned from the Native people who
have forgotten that the people they have learned from are people, and
they treat them as objects, as artifacts" (Archibald interview, summer
1993). The interviews provided a forum for discussing the nature of
respect – a topic about which all the interviewees showed great awareness.
Documenting how the issue of respect is manifested allows for the possibility of gaining greater understanding of the issue and devising positive
ways of responding to it.

Relevance
The discussion of relevance focuses on the ability "to help students to
appreciate and build upon their customary forms of consciousness and
representations as they expand their understanding of the world in which
they live" (Kirkness and Barnhardt 1991). The House of Learning and the
First Nations programs at UBC utilize the NITEP model – "Raven's Way of
Expanding the Circle" – as a basic philosophy for creating an environment

that reflects the cultures and values of First Nations. This model places the student at its centre and expands its focus to include family, community, and national and international spheres. It incorporates the holistic perspective of attending to the four dimensions of the human being: the physical, the mental, the emotional, and the spiritual. Aspects of this model were discussed by the respondents. Concepts such as identity, family, community, and sense of place, engendered particularly by the longhouse, are significant components in the discussion of relevance, as they relate to the student in his/her position at the centre. A student reflects on what the longhouse meant for him:

> I think this place has been important in letting me feel just as good as anybody else here. Even just coming here when I am feeling down, when no one is around, I just come and sit down and have a cup of coffee or whatever. It is refuge for a while. Having this place, the First Nations House of Learning, is a very important step – you have a place that is safe when things get tough on the outside. Coming here is like going to a reserve. I feel like I'm going home in a sense. It is, I don't know, it's hard to explain how I feel being here. It is nice to be here. It is an inner sanity. (Angus Dickie interview, summer 1993)

First Nations programs have, thanks to activities, ceremonies, and curriculum, been largely successful in instilling in students a sense of pride in being First Nations people. First Nations involvement in the development and design of the curriculum was identified as a very important factor in obtaining successful results. However, the growing numbers of students enrolling at UBC are comprised of a very diversified population that comes from First Nations communities across the continent. The House of Learning and the First Nations programs will have to consider the challenge of attending to the needs of the multinational First Nations community that is evolving at UBC.

Staff members are aware that providing a holistic experience for students at UBC that attends to the four dimensions of the human being needs to be expanded. They recognize that gaining a university education relies heavily on the mental dimension, often at the expense of the other dimensions. Expanding the focus on the mental to include the physical, emotional, and spiritual dimensions is a goal that the staff is working towards.

Reciprocity
Reciprocity, Kirkness and Barnhardt write, "means moving away from the role dichotomy between the producers and the consumers of knowledge in university settings. Education which emphasizes teaching and learning

as two-way processes, in which the give-and-take between faculty and students opens up new levels of understanding for everyone, is more likely to validate First Nations students' experiences and knowledge bases" (Kirkness and Barnhardt 1991, 12).

Respondents identified many opportunities for establishing collaborative efforts that can create an environment that is respectful of First Nations. What the respondents suggest is a give-and-take process, promoting a sense of "we-ness" rather than a "them-and-us" atmosphere. Madeleine MacIvor affirms the requirements for a two-way process: "if you get back to that whole notion of respect and reciprocity, it can't be a one-way thing. It can't be just the university community learning from us. We have to learn from them, and not necessarily change who we are, but understand where they're coming from and what their reservations are, and why their reservations are there" (Madeleine MacIvor interview, summer 1993).

That kind of reciprocal process requires collaboration and the ability to learn from the tensions inherent in bringing differing approaches and contents together. Roland Chrisjohn discusses the disparities in the value typically assigned by academic institutions to different kinds of knowledge:

> If I am a White Anglo-Saxon Protestant who can't speak Oneida, and I go talk to a second grade educated Oneida on my home reserve of Oneida of the Thames, and write out the grammar and publish a dictionary, I get my PhD. But quite frankly, as an anthropologist, I wouldn't know the language one-tenth as well as that little uneducated Oneida man or woman sitting on the reserve. And yet, that person, well, that's just an Indian – a smelly, old, dirty person with a grade two education, [who] is quite dismissible. But who has the knowledge there? It's that smelly, old dismissible Oneida that has knowledge there. So, it's the attempt to commodify the knowledge that puts the university in the position of power, not the knowledge itself. So, I don't know. I wish I could tell the university – you don't produce knowledge, acknowledge that. (Personal communication, summer 1993)

The collaborative approaches already in place include establishing respectful dialogue and sharing between faculty and students through forums and conferences; and between faculty, administration, and First Nations staff and community members through advisory bodies. Successful collaborative efforts, however, are only beginnings, and much more is desired (e.g., including First Nations at all levels of the university structure, such as the board of governors and senate). Research was identified as an area in which more collaborative efforts could be established.

Responsibility

Responsibility through participation is best illustrated in Kirkness and Barnhardt's citation of Tierney's (1991) critical analysis of the role of colleges with regard to Native American students:

> All organizational participants will be encouraged to come to terms with how they may reconstruct and transform the organization's culture. As opposed to a rhetoric of what mainstream organizations will do for Native Americans – a top-down managerial approach – the struggle is to develop strategies and policies that emerge from a vision of working with Native Americans toward a participatory goal of emancipation and empowerment. (Tierney in Kirkness and Barnhardt 1991, 11)

In discussing responsibility, respondents focused on what they felt was needed to achieve the goal of providing a post-secondary education that responds to the needs of First Nations. Respondents identified the need for housing, counselling, daycare, operational dollars, and the expansion of programs and courses. They also discussed the importance, as Angus Dickie stated, of "maintaining the roots of where we came from."

Respondents suggested that First Nations ought to be included in all aspects of the university, including the senate, board of governors, and the dean's advisory committees. Creative affirmative action policies for increasing First Nations faculty could fill a glaring gap in First Nations participation: "In the US universities you can become a full professor without a doctorate if you are First Nations because they recognize the need to encourage more First Nations people, but I can't see UBC doing that. If they are worried about standards, why don't they just use the qualifying student category. They could use that for every faculty on campus. If you don't make it, then try something else. What do they have to lose? They could do that with faculty as well" (Rod McCormick, interview 1993). Respondents identified a role for Elders as adjunct professors: "My ideal. I think part of what I was saying, is that they should have an Elder taking a meaningful active part in teaching courses because they lived the life, they know the history more than the professors. An Elder would have the inside perspective" (Deina Jules, interview 1993). Increasing First Nations student participation in competitive areas through a quota system was also suggested as a viable option: "They could certainly allocate spaces over and above their quota for First Nations students. That could make it more user-friendly. For instance, in the high competitive area like we have in medicine, where there are only forty new spaces per year, and we've got two pre-meds this year. In the area of dentistry, which doesn't take many students, I think we could get a couple. It would be more user-friendly to have ... I hate to call it a quota system" (Angie Todd-Dennis, interview 1993).

On the part of the university administration, an overall vision in the form of a mission or policy statement on First Nations education might facilitate the implementation of the goals and objectives that the House of Learning and First Nations program staff and students are already striving towards.

First Nations House of Learning Model:
Strengths and Weaknesses

The university structure, and the relationships within that structure, offer opportunities for, as well as barriers to, promoting the mission and objectives of the First Nations House of Learning. The House of Learning's mission is clear in that its aim is not only to improve university access for First Nations, but also to provide a quality education that reflects the philosophies, values, and cultures of a diverse population. Thus, creating greater access and relevance are the challenges to which the House of Learning must respond. Its clear mandate, mission, and objectives provide the agenda that the House of Learning is attempting to fulfill. The House of Learning, being strategically located at the higher administrative level, is able to reach UBC's upper echelons in its attempt to induce changes relevant to its mandate. The advisory committee structure effectively influences change by providing direction, guidance, and expertise from a variety of stakeholders, the most important of whom are its First Nations members.

The greatest challenge to influencing the kind of change the House of Learning is aiming for is convincing the various units to mobilize the financial and human resources required to implement them. The establishment of the House of Learning was definitely a step in the right direction. UBC has acknowledged that "Native people need greater opportunities for advanced education," and it has pledged in its mission statement that it "will provide them" (Strangway 1989, 41). How UBC will provide greater opportunities for First Nations peoples has been left largely to the House of Learning. Further commitment, in the form of a university-wide strategic plan and a commitment to finding the financial resources, is needed in order to provide those greater opportunities.

Change is slow and is constrained by the inflexibility of a huge bureaucracy. However impatient we may become for the arrival of those greater opportunities, the gains must be kept in focus. The longhouse, one of those gains, and a very significant one, has been built since Dr. Strangway's 1989 report, *Second to None,* was developed in 1989. Further to the important initiatives of establishing the House of Learning and building the longhouse, it is important to continue the momentum by continuing the dialogue between the House of Learning staff and First Nations communities.

The strength of the UBC model is in its history. It was established through trial and error, beginning with NITEP and refining and expanding that model in later initiatives. With the establishment of the First Nations House of Learning in 1987, a structure was put in place to further expand First Nations initiatives university-wide and to facilitate coordination among those already in place. The UBC model also includes a philosophy that consolidates UBC First Nations initiatives around a collective vision based on the NITEP model. UBC's commitment to First Nations is included in its mission statement. However, specific policies and mechanisms for identifying First Nations enrolment are yet to be negotiated. The First Nations longhouse on campus provides a physical First Nations presence at UBC and is evidence of the university's recognition of First Nations issues and concerns.

First Nations community involvement through the advisory committees and through community consultations has been useful in ensuring that the UBC initiatives respond to First Nations priorities and needs. Internal and external evaluations of the First Nations initiatives have been, and continue to be, beneficial with regard to the continued improvement and refinement of programs and services.

Prior to the establishment of the First Nations House of Learning, opportunities specifically designed for First Nations existed primarily in the Faculty of Education and the Faculty of Law. Since then, opportunities have expanded to health careers, forestry, engineering, sciences, agricultural sciences, graduate studies, commerce, and arts. A modest program that offers First Nations languages has begun. The Department of Linguistics has declared First Nations languages a priority concern. The First Nations Professional Sciences Access Program has been established in order to prepare students for enrolment in the professional sciences. First Nations enrolments in master's and doctoral programs outside of Ts' 'kel is increasing, and support for this needs some strengthening.

The focus of most of the First Nations initiatives at UBC has been to attract First Nations students to the campus and to strengthen on-campus support services. The limitations of UBC's model are evident in its reticence to respond to regional concerns, to offer community-based programs, and to enter into affiliation agreements with First Nations post-secondary institutes. All three of the province's other universities – Simon Fraser, the University of Victoria, and the University of Northern British Columbia – offer community-based programs, programs with flexible structures, and affiliations with Aboriginal post-secondary institutes. Over the years, of course, NITEP has been consistent in offering a community-based component.

Overall, the House of Learning has been a useful model for a comprehensive university such as UBC, particularly in attracting and accommodating First Nations students drawn from local, provincial, national, and international locations to a vast array of programs at both the undergraduate and graduate levels. We have four universities in the province competing to meet the demands of First Nations higher education, each with its own agenda for doing so. Although each university can respond to a variety of needs based on its respective strengths, it must also seek creative and innovative strategies to attain its goals with regard to First Nations. Each university has a moral and ethical responsibility to make accessible to all sectors of society the educational opportunities they afford. In this sense, UBC must compete creatively in order to respond to a sector of society that, historically, has not enjoyed the benefits of Western higher learning.

1998 Update

A 1998 evaluation of the First Nations House of Learning sums up accomplishments to date and the challenges that lie ahead:

> We have argued throughout this report that knowledge of Aboriginal issues and appreciation of Aboriginal perspectives is central to the modern mission of the University. Attention to Aboriginal education continues to be a matter of justice, correcting inequities that spring from oppressive policies of the past. But even more compelling is the growing evidence that in Aboriginal cultures knowledge with intrinsic value for human survival can be found. Relations between Aboriginal and non-Aboriginal peoples in Canada are at the heart of troubling questions about the future of the Canadian federation. And negotiating means through which peoples with disparate histories, traditions and loyalties can live together respectfully and harmoniously poses challenges of global proportions.
>
> In its ten years of existence the FNHL has had an extraordinary impact on the University community's awareness of First Nations issues and goals. The University has moved to open the door to full participation of First Nations people in university studies through program development in departments, schools and faculties and through the introduction of an admissions policy which goes some way toward compensating for deficits in past education practices. In December 1997, as a demonstration of institutional commitment to Aboriginal education, the Senate and Board of Governors formally approved a goal statement to enroll 1000 First Nation students by the year 2000.
>
> In some quarters of the University goal statements have added another layer, seeking to foster appreciation of the cultures and histories of Aboriginal people and their place in contemporary Canadian society. This is expressed most cogently in the Faculty of Forestry strategy which asserts that all forestry graduates require at least a minimum understanding of relations with First Nations to practice their profession effectively in B.C.

In our view, the task of transforming the University has been well begun, but it is not yet done. Inviting First Nations people into the house is the first step. Accepting them as partners in the work of knowledge creation is the next step. (Castellano and Hampton 1998, 23-4)

Acknowledgments
This chapter is based upon Ethel Gardner, "First Nations House of Learning: A Continuity of Transformation," Royal Commission on Aboriginal Peoples (Ottawa, 1993).

References
Archibald, Jo-ann. 1986. "Completing a Vision: The Native Indian Teacher Education Program at the University of British Columbia." *Canadian Journal of Native Education* 13 (1): 33-45.
–. 1993. "'Ts' 'kel Golden Eagle' and 'Ts' 'kel Talents.'" In *A Commemorative Issue of the First Nations House of Learning Newsletter*.
Borrows, John, and Robin Wood. 1993. "First Nations Law Program." In *A Commemorative Issue of the First Nations House of Learning Newsletter*.
Castellano, Marlene Brant, and Eber Hampton. 1998. "Review of the First Nations House of Learning." Unpublished manuscript, University of British Columbia.
Downey, L.W. 1987. *The Story of Ts' 'kel: A Program in Educational Administration for Native Indian Education*. Vancouver: University of British Columbia.
First Nations Health Care Professionals Program Evaluation Report (FNHC). 1993. Vancouver: First Nations House of Learning, University of British Columbia.
First Nations House of Learning Brochure. 1988. Vancouver: First Nations House of Learning, University of British Columbia.
Gardner, Ethel. 1989. *First Nations House of Learning Community Consultation Report*. Vancouver: First Nations House of Learning, UBC.
Kirkness, Verna J. 1992. "First Nations House of Learning: A Case of Successful Transformation." In *Beyond Multi-Cultural Education: International Perspectives*, ed. Kogila A. Moodley. Calgary: Detselig Enterprises.
Kirkness, Verna J., and Ray Barnhardt. 1991. First Nations and Higher Education: The Four R's – Respect, Relevance, Reciprocity, Responsibility." *Journal of American Indian Education* 30 (3): 1-15.
Pepper, Floy. 1988. *Summative Evaluation Findings of the Native Indian Teacher Education Program* (UBC). Portland: Rudolph Dreikurs Institute.
Strangway, David. 1989. *Second to None: Service through Excellence*. Vancouver: University of British Columbia President's Office.
Wright, Bobby. 1991. *American Indian and Alaska Native Higher Education: Toward a New Century of Academic Achievement and Cultural Integrity*. Washington, DC: Indian Nations at Risk Task Force.

12
First Nations-Controlled University Education in Canada

Eber Hampton

Challenging Assumptions about Education

The Royal Commission on Aboriginal Peoples (RCAP) recommended the establishment of an Aboriginal Peoples' International University: "The Commission recommends that a university under Aboriginal control, which could be called the Aboriginal Peoples' International University, with the capacity to function in all provinces and territories, be established to promote traditional knowledge, to pursue applied research in support of Aboriginal self-government, and to disseminate information essential to achieving broad Aboriginal development goals" (RCAP 1996, 3:533). This recommendation is a challenge that grew out of our people's testimony. I believe it is the most difficult and perhaps the most important educational challenge for First Nations, Inuit, and Métis people of this generation. To explain why, I must start with a story.

In many of the old stories the hero is forced to gamble with a giant. In some ways education is like gambling. We bet our children's lives. Some win, but too many lose. The goals of education are like wonderful prizes for the lucky few. The results of the education gamble are usually much worse. Trying to understand the mismatch between the wonderful goals and the terrible results of education for most of our people made me think of a story. It is too new to be much good, but it does help me think about education and social policy.

Once upon a time twin giants were born. One was evil and one was good. Because they both had the same name people had trouble telling them apart. The evil twin tricked people by saying he was the good giant. He tried to change people so that they would be just like him. He always pretended to know what was right and told children they were stupid and bad. He ate most of the children who met him, but he kept a few favourites and made them fat and arrogant.

The good giant tried to help people. He made children happy and helped them find answers to their questions. The children who met this giant grew strong and wise. As the children grew older and became adults, the good giant remained their friend and they were always welcome at his house.

Of course both giants were named education. We must know the difference between these two giants if we are to stop gambling with our children's lives. And of course reality is more complex. Experience, conversation, and research have shown that we use the word "education" in at least five very different ways (Hampton 1995). In Figure 1, I summarize these five definitions of education.

We have made some progress, but still, the kind of education about which we know the most is education for assimilation. In January 1998 the Honourable Jane Stewart, minister of Indian Affairs and Northern Development, on behalf of the Government of Canada, expressed "profound regret for past actions of the federal government which contributed to difficult pages in the history of our relationship together." With regard to those who suffered sexual and physical abuse at residential schools the minister expressed deep sorrow (Stewart 1998). The formal Statement of Reconciliation that was widely disseminated was an important first step in recognizing that devastating wrongs have been done in the name of education. The residential schools were education as assimilation in its purest, but not its only, form.

In a paper written for RCAP, I told how my grandfather helped me understand my own educational experience:

Figure 1

Five definitions of First Nations education

Traditional education	The forms of education practised by First Nations before non-First Nations schools were introduced
Education for assimilation	Non-First Nations education applied to First Nations with the goal of assimilation
Education by First Nations	Education administered and/or delivered by First Nations using non-First Nations curriculum, methods, and structures
Education for self-determination	First Nations-controlled education with the goal of self-determination
First Nations education sui generis	First Nations education as a thing of its own kind: based on the cultures and spirit of First Nations, designed and implemented by First Nations

I didn't understand my own education until grandpa helped me put it in perspective. In college I took a course in the psychology of human motivation. I was talking to grandpa about the stuff we were studying, concentration camps, brainwashing and prisoners of war when he said: "We are prisoners of peace." When he said that, my own educational experience fell into place. I suddenly understood the love-hate relationship I have with education. Education has hurt us and education has helped us. It is part of the problem and part of the solution. Fire that cooks our food and the fire of napalm are both called fire. In the same way, not everything we call education is the same. (Hampton and Wolfson 1994, 90-1)

It is painful to realize that the First Nations of Canada have been prisoners of peace for generations. When we look at the record of residential schools it is relatively easy to see how they functioned as instruments of captivity (Chrisjohn and Young 1997; Newbauer-Hampton 1995; Churchill 1994; Wolcott 1987). All of them had as their goal the destruction of the identities, languages, and cultures of First Nations children. The United Nations Convention on Genocide defines genocide as the attempt to destroy a people as a people. Education with the goal of assimilation is a tool of genocide. It attempts to replace the language, culture, values, worldview, institutions, and economics of First Nations with those of another people. While the abuses perpetrated in residential schools have had grievous and long-lasting effects, it is important to recognize that the destructive program of education for assimilation was not confined to those institutions.

Most, but not all, university education in Canada today is education for assimilation. Universities typically operate on the assumption that Eurocentric content, structure, and process constitute the only legitimate approach to knowledge. First Nations history, culture, knowledge, and language are largely ignored, and even when they are subjects of study, the perspective is almost always Eurocentric. TeHennepe (1993), for example, documents the experience of First Nations students in some anthropology classes that denigrate First Nations knowledge and experience. Happily, there are exceptions to this rule, as some professors recognize the cultural foundations of their views and acknowledge the existence of other perspectives.

It is essential that we face the fact that current Canadian universities are products of the traditions, cultures, and languages of European immigrants. In general, the institutions, policies, and practices of English and French immigrants to Canada have been based on the assumption that their way is universal, comprehensive, true, and right. Sincere efforts to practise multiculturalism and inclusiveness as well as moves towards just treatment of Aboriginal peoples take place within a Eurocentric legal, institutional, and societal context.

Universities are expressions of, as well as contributors to, that context. In the Canadian university context we have been prisoners of peace to the extent that we have allowed Eurocentric universities to monopolize higher education for our people. We are slowly changing that reality. We repeatedly tell our young people how important it is to get an education. We have not paid enough attention to why so few of them do. We need to see the way in which universities continue to implement the assimilationist agenda that applied in residential schools. We need to strengthen our people's effort to transform university education into an expression of self-government as well as a tool for achieving it.

From a Weapon of Captivity to a Tool of Self-Determination

One clear indication of the hopes that First Nations have placed in education as a tool for self-determination is the presence of three key provisions regarding education in the numbered treaties. The failure to implement education in accordance with an Aboriginal understanding of the commitments undertaken has distorted education, transforming it from a tool of self-determination into a weapon of captivity. In treaty negotiations First Nations agreed to share an immense and rich land with European immigrants. In return, the Crown committed itself to major responsibilities in the areas of health, economic development, and education.

With respect to education, the Crown's responsibility included three key provisions: (1) establishment of schools, (2) equal educational outcomes, and (3) choice. These three provisions are not small things. Understanding and implementing them will be less expensive than keeping Indians captive in the prison, welfare, and assimilative school systems of Canada. But of far greater importance than the financial benefits are the human benefits. The economic and social health and the integrity of the Canadian people require that we understand and implement these three provisions.

First Nations Institutions

First, the Crown committed itself to the establishment of First Nations schools. In treaty language it assumed the responsibility of establishing a school on each reserve that requested one. Historically, instead of carrying out this responsibility, the Canadian government used the churches to establish residential schools both on and off reserve. The government later paid schools, under provincial jurisdiction, to accept First Nations students.

In the treaties Canada had obligated itself to fund First Nations institutions. Instead, it funded church and provincial institutions. It was not until the 1970s and the move towards Indian control of Indian education that Canada began to reap benefits accruing from First Nations institutions.

Regardless of its political popularity or lack thereof, the fact remains that Canada has a moral and legal obligation to fund First Nations educational institutions.

Equal Educational Outcomes

Second, the Crown committed itself to equal educational outcomes. The testimony of Elders is corroborated by Alexander Morris, the Queen's representative: "Your children will be taught, and then they will be as able to take care of themselves as the whites around them" (Morris 1982, 213). In terms of self-sufficiency it is clear that equal outcomes have not been achieved. The equal outcome standard is higher than that of equal access or equal resources for education. Achieving it requires not only access to resources for education, but institutions, structures, curriculum, and pedagogy that are educationally effective. First Nations schools are a necessary component for achieving equal outcomes. Based on results over the past few hundred years, it is unreasonable to expect that provincial schools and universities alone will be able to produce equal educational outcomes.

Equal educational outcomes require that the proportion of First Nations university graduates match that of the general population. We are a long way from reaching that goal. In fact we are slipping behind, as the increasing enrolment of First Nations university students is less than the growth rate of university education in the non-First Nations population. In spite of significant commitments by some universities to First Nations education, the proportion of First Nations students that they enrol is far less than the proportion of First Nations people in the whole population. First Nations schools at the elementary and secondary level have been essential to significantly improving elementary and secondary outcomes for First Nations students. The same requirement applies at the university level. The impact of First Nations control of a post-secondary institution can be seen in Saskatchewan. The University of Regina has an Aboriginal enrolment of approximately 15 percent, while the Aboriginal population of Saskatchewan is 14 percent. This equal enrolment of Aboriginal students is due to the University of Regina's federation with the Saskatchewan Indian Federated College (SIFC), a First Nations-controlled university college. Without SIFC, the University of Regina's Aboriginal enrolment, like that of other universities, would be far less than proportionate.

Provision of Choice

Fundamental to education for self-determination is a third treaty provision, that of choice. Choice is by definition a key ingredient in self-determination, and First Nations have made clear from the beginning that they reserve the right to adopt and adapt education on their own terms. While concluding a treaty implies a meeting of minds between parties, it is now clear that the vision of First Nations and that of the Crown were based on different assumptions. Underlying the Canadian government's interpretation of treaty obligations was an assumption that education was a tool for assimilation. For the Europeans, the expectation was that Indians would assimilate into a non-Indian way of life. The goal was for the student to take on the culture, language, and values of teachers who were emissaries of colonial society. First Nations had, and have maintained, a different vision. We see education as a tool of self-determination for our people.

Education as self-determination succeeds. A self-determination approach to education is not only the right thing morally and socially: it works. In the area of secondary schooling, for example, as Indian and Northern Affairs Canada (INAC) has devolved control of schools to the bands, the percentage of fourteen- to seventeen-year-old students in school has increased from 46 percent to 88 percent (INAC data cited in SIFC 1993).

This massive increase in one measure of educational success has been brought about by an important but limited change in social policy. First Nations control of band schools is still limited by the imposition of provincial jurisdiction. As First Nations exercise increasing jurisdiction over curriculum and other operations, First Nations students will not just stay in school and graduate; they will gain the tools to live wisely on the Earth.

Functions of Universities in Society

University education is an instrument of self-determination in two senses: it is a tool for implementing self-government, and it is an expression of self-government. Education is one of our ways of preparing our young people and ourselves to exercise self-determination as skilfully, competently, wisely, and knowledgeably as possible. It enhances our ability to be self-determining. Realistically, Canadian universities are ill equipped to fulfill this role. Our students and communities should have the choice of benefitting from what provincial universities have to offer, but Indian control of Indian education is not just for elementary and secondary education. It is even more important that we seize our responsibility for university education as an expression of self-government. We have the responsibility to articulate the knowledge, the philosophies, and the ideals of our living cultures. We have the responsibility to give the best that we have to our youth, both in terms of our own knowledge and experience and in terms of support for their own learning.

Universities do more than teach students. Universities define their responsibilities in terms of three roles: teaching, research, and service. A fourth role, certification, could be thought of as part of the teaching role but is important enough in its effect on First Nations to examine separately (Chrisjohn et al. 1997).

In its teaching role the university transmits knowledge, skills, and culture. It does this by selectively organizing and conveying information as well as by setting up learning environments and experiences. The curriculum is composed of organized and selected objectives, content, and methods for helping students learn. All of this is based on cultural assumptions, beliefs, and values. Much of this cultural foundation is unstated and has been called the hidden curriculum. Included in the hidden curriculum are: beliefs about what is important to learn; the place of First Nations in history and contemporary society; the roles of teacher, students, parents, and community; and values of individual and group learning, along with many other factors.

Universities teach about First Nations in their hidden curriculum as well as in their stated curriculum. They transmit attitudes, values, and beliefs about what is important, who is credible, the "right" way to do things, and the place of Aboriginal peoples in Canada. Social policy makers, bureaucrats, administrators, and teachers at all levels, from kindergarten to graduate school, go through an educational process designed both consciously and unconsciously to teach them certain attitudes, facts, and values. Social science as shaped by the university forms a major part of elementary, secondary, and post-secondary curricula and exerts a powerful influence on public thinking and debate about First Nations issues.

The research function of the university may be even more important than the teaching function. Certainly, universities act as if research is more important than teaching (Smith 1991). Research is the foundation for teaching as well as often being the basis for government, legal, and social decision making. Research is usually described as a search for truth aimed at producing and communicating organized knowledge. Researchers are required to be knowledgeable about, and to refer to, past research. In practice, research produces a massive body of more or less organized knowledge, opinion, fact, concept, and theory concerning topics of interest to researchers and funding sources. Education trains and acculturates researchers (Reinharz 1984), and then researchers shape education. Curriculum and textbooks are based on research. Social policy is based on the facts, concepts, and theories of researchers. Research is a culturally based activity supported by the universities and outside funding sources.

An examination of any university's research budget will show that very little is spent on issues of direct interest to Aboriginal peoples, and almost none is conducted by Aboriginal people. Research topics are chosen on the basis of the interests of researchers and funding sources and are based on non-Aboriginal worldviews, concepts, theories, and methodologies. They advance the personal and professional interests of researchers and are rarely used to advance Aboriginal objectives. There are important exceptions to this rule (e.g., in court cases in which research by experts has helped establish facts). However, for the most part, we are both researched to death and neglected. As the research directors for RCAP wrote: "Aboriginal people are not represented within their own context or on their own terms" (Castellano and Hawkes 1993, 44).

Through its research function the university provides the conceptual foundation for bureaucrats, administrators, consultants, and experts who design and sell the ideas and analyses underpinning government decision making. Universities encourage their researchers and teachers to serve as paid and unpaid experts for governments, recognizing such services as consistent with employment contracts and as a factor in evaluating professional accomplishments.

It is this service function of education that provides an army of university experts with the time, incentive, and rationale to serve as consultants and technicians. Some university faculty members make as much (or more) through their consulting businesses as they do through their full-time university salaries. Other academic experts, socialized in the same mould, are the primary judges of the quality of the university expert's work.

Through their certifying function universities control access to jobs, salary levels, credibility, status, and the attention of influential audiences. At a recent conference on Aboriginal employment, the representative of a major construction company explained that his company would always choose the job applicant who had a diploma or degree before the one who did not. He was not convinced by participants who argued that this educational criterion had nothing to do with the person's ability to do the job. Armstrong, Kennedy, and Oberle, in a study documenting the relationship between university education and employment, point out that the relationship between education and employment shows up most clearly across four levels of education. The labour force participation rate for Indians with less than a high school diploma is only 37.9 percent. This figure rises to 86.9 percent for Indians with a university degree. Unemployment rates among Indians with less than a high school diploma is 38.9 percent compared to 11.8 percent for those with a degree (Armstrong et al. 1990). These are significant differences, and they clearly indicate the important impact of education's certifying function on the economic well-being of First Nations individuals.

Economic well-being among Indians increases with education, and the differences in labour force activity between Indians and non-Indians decreases as education level increases. Labour force participation rates for Indians with a university degree are almost identical to that for non-Indians. The gap between Indian and non-Indian employment and unemployment rates is also much less for the university-educated population than it is for those with less education. Higher education is now a requirement for many jobs, and it has been estimated that 48 percent of the new jobs created between 1986 and 2000 will require seventeen or more years of education (Holmlund 1993).

Universities qualify teachers for certification and prepare doctors, lawyers, nurses, public health inspectors, and most other professionals for licensing. The university prepares speechwriters for politicians and qualifies the lawyers who draft legislation and the experts who are quoted in the mass media. Most government leaders and their bureaucrats and technicians are shaped and trained by the university. Increasingly, the next generation of Aboriginal leaders will be university-trained. No other institution has such a pervasive effect on our lives.

Extending Aboriginal Control

"If you talk to any Aboriginal leader in this country, you will not get an argument about the value post-secondary education has brought to our communities. We have had all these other things in our communities – welfare programs, make-work jobs, and all those other things – but real changes are happening because our people are going to university and taking their skills and using them, with the knowledge of our old people, to start to make meaningful changes in our community" (Watts 1989).

Unfortunately, it is in university education that we have made the least progress in terms of First Nations control. Almost all First Nations education dollars are still spent on universities and programs that are not under First Nations control. In terms of First Nations control, First Nations university education is where elementary and secondary education was twenty years ago. Saskatchewan Indian Federated College, with an enrolment of 1,600 students, is the only First Nations institution recognized by the Association of Universities and Colleges of Canada (AUCC) as offering university-level education. It is not only the sole First Nations member of AUCC, it is the most poorly funded member and the only member without proper facilities. There are many other First Nations post-secondary institutions that are making steady progress in spite of under-funding and hostile policies. The good news is that we can expect massive progress as First Nations assume greater control over their own university education. The Report of the Royal Commission on Aboriginal Peoples (RCAP) documents the variety of Aboriginal post-secondary institutions and the success they have achieved (RCAP 1996, 3:517-22).

Even without First Nations control over university education, clear benefits have grown out of First Nations programs. In its preparation for the treaty commissioner's work, the Department of Education of the Federation of Saskatchewan Indian Nations commissioned two papers examining the economic costs and benefits of First Nations education (Ross and Usher 1992; Federation of Saskatchewan Indian Nations 1990). Working with the same data in different ways, both of these documents conclude that the benefit of major increases in First Nations educational spending would outweigh the costs by more than two to one. In dollar terms alone, welfare is more than twenty times as expensive as university education.

We have made progress. School retention rates are one concrete measure of gains made. The increasing number of First Nations students entering and completing university is another. It is clear that if we are to continue making progress even more changes in curriculum, jurisdiction, personnel, and funding are required.

Securing funding for programs targeted to Aboriginal priorities is difficult enough. Financing Aboriginal institutions has proven even more problematic. It can be argued that if the First Nations population received proportionate benefit from educational allocations by governments, then the level of funding available to First Nations would be more than three times the funding levels of standard post-secondary programs. To illustrate, the federal government assigns tax points and cash transfers to the provinces for health, education, and social services based on the total population of the province (including First Nations). In that sense university education of First Nations students is funded once on the same basis as everyone else. However, First Nations people are about half as likely to attend university as are other people. So long as First Nations peoples are grossly under-represented in university populations it makes sense for the provinces to allocate enriched funding in order to progressively erase the disparity. This would mean providing funding at twice the basic rate in order to support First Nations programs. However, because the provinces have consistently maintained that, under the Constitution, First Nations education is a federal responsibility, most provincially supported colleges and universities decline to assume responsibility for providing adapted programs. They introduce specific First Nations programs only when they receive earmarked funds from the Department of Indian and Northern Affairs or other sources. At this point First Nations participation in university education has been financed three times, but funding actually applied to First Nations needs and priorities remains limited and precarious.

What is the quality of this education that is paid for three times over? In a few cases it is excellent. There are some very good programs and some very good First Nations and non-First Nations professors. However, we could reasonably expect that extra funding would lead to extra effort and good results. The facts show the opposite. Most of our students drop out before the second year of university. First Nations students face university courses that systematically discount their presence and their identity (TeHennepe 1993). Universities spend much less on first-year students than on advanced students, and even the students who continue are mostly in the so-called "low-cost programs" rather than in the "high-cost programs" like medical school, science, and engineering. Accountability to First Nations communities even for targeted programs varies from low to non-existent (Fiddler 1995). Some have advisory boards, some do not. The only vestige of real First Nations control in university education exists in some First Nations-controlled post-secondary institutions. Even there, non-First Nations institutions often control the courses and the faculty approvals.

First Nations social policy is rightfully a First Nations responsibility. Education based on the cultures and spiritual values of First Nations can be a tool for fulfilling that responsibility. It is true that an educational system that works costs fewer dollars than welfare and prisons. It is true that it makes more sense to purchase educational success than to purchase educational failure. But there is a higher truth than money. Jurisdiction is just another name for responsibility. First Nations education is our responsibility. The big problem in education is not reinventing the wheel. We must reinvent education to meet our peoples' standards.

In treaty negotiations, the queen's representative committed the Crown to equal educational outcomes leading to equal economic and social well-being. The Crown's failure to perform this obligation is often attributed to a lack of will or funding. Even though these problems have been significant, the Crown's essential failure has been in its adoption of an assimilation model of education. The assimilation model is most clearly seen in the residential school experiment. However almost all of our university students are in institutions whose primary goal is to assimilate them into non-Aboriginal society. Education as assimilation has not succeeded in the past and it will not succeed in the future. It is only in partnership with First Nations-controlled institutions that Canada can fulfill its obligation (and need) for equal educational attainment for First Nations students.

Creating an Aboriginal Peoples' International University
There are four models of First Nations university education currently in use:

(1) the assimilation model
(2) the special program or department model
(3) the federated or affiliated model
(4) the autonomous institution model (RCAP 1996, 3: 513-22; Hampton and Wolfson 1994, 92-103; Barnhardt 1991).

Each of these models exhibits inherent strengths and weaknesses, some of which are summarized in Figure 2.

The strengths and weakness listed in Figure 2 are suggestive rather than definitive. Important individual and, in some cases, institutional successes have been achieved by all of the models. The weaknesses suggest the

Figure 2

Models of indigenous higher education

Model	Strengths	Weaknesses
Assimilation model	A few strong and lucky individuals succeed. Cheap.	Students are expected to attend and assimilate into non-indigenous university. Most students are damaged, most leave before graduation, labelled as failures. Protects university from beneficial change.
Special program model	Special programs or departments are set up as part of, and under the control of, non-indigenous universities. More students succeed. Some First Nations staff are hired. May create some legitimate place at university.	Often no accountability to Aboriginal community people. Frequently seen as second class. Usually relies on soft funding. Depends on extraordinary student, staff, and administrative commitment to succeed. Does not create equal enrolment and success.
Federated model	Creates a partnership between an indigenous-controlled institution and a non-indigenous university. Can create equal enrolment and increased success. Has real indigenous control and creates partnership between indigenous peoples and university. Place at the table with other universities (AUCC).	Partnership requires continual work and negotiation. Equal partnership difficult. Aboriginal institution often seen as junior partner. Funding inequities.
Autonomous model	Creates a stand-alone indigenous institution. Fosters individual student success and enhances capacity in the Aboriginal community. At the table with colleges (AUCC). Responsive and accountable to communities. Great potential.	Does not yet have a place at the table with other universities. Small population base for most. Usually underfunded. Often must buy courses and faculty from non-indigenous universities.

challenges we face in placing Indigenous knowledge and priorities at the centre of a university agenda. Important progress has been made, but non-Indigenous universities still control most, though not all, of the teaching, research, and service agenda. Alone, none of the existing models can meet the need. A fifth approach recommended by RCAP, the creation of an Aboriginal Peoples' International University (APIU), offers a way to link and build on existing and emerging institutional initiatives (RCAP 1997, 530-9).

Building on Strength

The mission of an Aboriginally controlled university would centre around the articulation and dissemination of Aboriginal knowledge and advancement of the self-determined priorities of Aboriginal communities. The philosophy underpinning such an institution is as old as Aboriginal cultures themselves, but the form it might assume is still evolving. Workable models are foreshadowed in the Saskatchewan Indian Federated College (SIFC), which has operated under Aboriginal governance for over twenty years, establishing precedents for like-minded organizations of more recent origin.

The record of achievement of Aboriginal institutions is impressive (RCAP 1996, 3: 517-22). They regularly report retention and graduation rates of more than 75 percent. They set program priorities in response to direction from the communities they serve and adapt delivery modes and schedules in order to make education accessible. They assign a place of honour and influence to Aboriginal Elders and their knowledge. They provide support services, Aboriginal role models, and mentors to assist students in navigating new cultural terrain. They broaden the options of their alumni by negotiating the ground rules by which students can continue their education in colleges and universities under provincial jurisdiction. Whether affiliated with provincial institutions or operating autonomously, Aboriginally controlled institutions have carved out a niche for themselves in post-secondary education.

The next step in the evolution of Aboriginal control of Aboriginal education is the chartering of an Aboriginal university or universities that would assume the full range of university functions: teaching, research, community service, and certification.

Implementing the Concept of an Aboriginal University

RCAP recommended the establishment of an APIU that would serve as a "network of coordinated regional institutions and programs representing diverse cultural and linguistic traditions – those of First Nations, Inuit and Métis peoples" (RCAP 1996, 3: 530). It is not intended to replace or compete with existing programs and institutions; rather, it would facilitate partnerships and joint programs. Instead of existing as a single campus, the APIU would be a network of institutions working together to pool educational resources. It would assist in the use of technology to share courses, curriculum, research, and mutual support. It would support advanced research needed by our institutions and communities. It would link with other indigenous university initiatives around the world.

Success or failure in implementing the APIU concept will depend predominantly on leadership from Aboriginal people. Support from federal and provincial governments will be needed, but these institutions cannot lead the way. Only Aboriginal people, including our educators, leaders, and institutions, can transform education from a weapon of captivity into a tool for self-determination.

Based on our people's testimony, RCAP recommended that we start with a steering group:

> The commission recommends that First Nations, Inuit and Métis leaders in collaboration with the federal government establish a steering group funded by the federal government, with a three year mandate (a) to explore options, conduct consultations and prepare a plan to implement an Aboriginal Peoples' International University by the year 2000; and (b) to collaborate with other working groups in determining the appropriate location of a documentation centre and archive, an electronic information clearing house, and statistical data bases. (RCAP 1996, (3), 534)

Whether along the lines recommended by RCAP or on some other model, Aboriginal people can design a university system that works for our students and our communities. There is wide consensus among Aboriginal people that Aboriginal control offers the best hope of significant educational improvement and development. This is as true for university education as it is for elementary and secondary education. In order to implement an APIU we will have to exercise political and educational will. We will have to move away from seeing ourselves as separate communities competing against one another for scarce resources controlled by government agencies and join in active collaboration as communities and nations pursuing shared goals. We can pool financial and human resources to make it happen if we have the commitment. Joint action makes sense to the extent that together we can accomplish things for our students and our collective future that we could not accomplish alone.

Our oral histories are rich with stories of how our grandparents and their grandparents lived on this land, harvesting its wealth, trading to enrich their lives, defending their territories, making treaties for peace and mutual benefit. Many of our people are now turning their efforts to remembering and conserving our languages and traditions. It is time to recall also our capacity for collaborative action – action that reaches across territorial and national boundaries. The institutions of higher learning that we create to express and enhance our human right to self-determination will not be captive to the forms and functions of conventional Canadian universities. Nor will they operate in isolation from mainstream institutions. Aboriginal peoples' universities, if such they are called, will take their place in the array of options accessible to Aboriginal people, demonstrating that education can be transformed from a weapon of assimilation into a tool of self-determination.

References

Armstrong, R., J. Kennedy, and P. Oberle. 1990. *University Education and Economic Well-being: Indian Achievement and Prospects*. Ottawa: Quantitative Analysis and Socio-Demographic Research, Finance and Professional Services, Indian and Northern Affairs Canada.

Barnhardt, R. 1991. "Higher Education in the Fourth World: Indigenous People Take Control." *Canadian Journal of Native Education* 18 (2): 199-231.

Castellano, M.B., and D. Hawkes. 1993. "An Overview of the State of Research in the Field of Aboriginal Affairs." In *Integrated Research Plan*, 41-58. Ottawa: Royal Commission on Aboriginal Peoples.

Chrisjohn, R. and S. Young. 1997. *The Circle Game: Shadows and Substance in the Indian Residential School Experience in Canada*. Penticton: Theytus. Also available in *For Seven Generations: An Information Legacy of the Royal Commission on Aboriginal Peoples*. CD-ROM. Ottawa: Libraxus.

Chrisjohn, R., V. Ayoungman, and S. Young. 1997. Their analysis of the function of education in society is contained in two papers available on the Treaty 7 website: <www.treaty7.org>.

Churchill, W., ed. 1994. *Indians Are Us: Culture and Genocide in Native North America*. Toronto: Between the Lines.

Federation of Saskatchewan Indian Nations (FSIN), Post-Secondary Education Centre. 1990. *Post-secondary Education Programs: A Cost/Benefit Assessment of Saskatchewan Indian Student Participation*. Saskatoon: Federation of Saskatchewan Indian Nations.

Fiddler, C. 1995. Accountability of ISSP Programs. Saskatoon: Federation of Saskatchewan Indian Nations.

Hampton, E. 1995. "Towards a Redefinition of Indian Education." In *First Nations Education in Canada: The Circle Unfolds*, ed. M. Battiste and J. Barman, 5-46. Vancouver: UBC Press.

Hampton, E., and S. Wolfson. 1994. "Education for Self-determination." In *Aboriginal Self-Government in Canada*, ed. John H. Hylton, 90-107. Saskatoon: Purich.

Holmlund, B. 1993. *A Strategic and Operational Plan to Increase the Number of First Nations People in the Science-based Professions*. Regina: Federation of Saskatchewan Indian Nations, Office of Education.

Morris, A. 1982. *The Treaties of Canada with the Indians*, ed. P.R. Randall. Toronto: Coles.

Newbauer-Hampton, T. 1995. "Education and Genocide." Unpublished honours paper available from author.

Reinharz, S. 1984. *On Becoming a Social Scientist*. New Brunswick, NJ: Transaction.

Ross, D., and P. Usher. 1992. *Education as an Investment for Treaty Indians in Saskatchewan: The Economic Costs and Benefits*. Regina: Federation of Saskatchewan Indian Nations, Department of Education.

Royal Commission on Aboriginal Peoples. 1996. *Report of the Royal Commission on Aboriginal Peoples*. Vol. 3: *Gathering Strength*. Ottawa: Canada Communications Group.

Saskatchewan Indian Federated College (SIFC). 1993. *Brief to the Royal Commission on Aboriginal Peoples.* Regina: Saskatchewan Indian Federated College.

Smith, S. 1991. *Report: Commission of Inquiry on Canadian University Education.* Ottawa: Association of Universities and Colleges of Canada.

Stewart, Jane. 1998. Notes for an address by the Honourable Jane Stewart, Minister of Indian Affairs and Northern Development. Ottawa. Indian and Northern Affairs Canada. 7 January.

TeHennepe, S. 1993. "Issues of Respect: Reflections of First Nations Students' Experiences in Post-secondary Anthropology Classrooms." *Canadian Journal of Native Education* 2 (20): 193-260.

Watts, G., President, Nuu-Chah-Nulth Tribal Council. 1989. Testimony before the House of Commons Standing Committee on Aboriginal Affairs.

Wolcott, H. 1987. "The Teacher as an Enemy." In *Education and Cultural Process: Anthropological Approaches*, ed. G. Spindler. Prospect Heights, IL: Waveland.

13
Electronic Highways, Electronic Classrooms: Distance Education in Canada

Lynne Davis

> The technology is available to provide high quality education services and specialized programming via satellite to remote locations to supplement the local curriculum and resources and to link other communities with the unique resources of the remote sites. Interactive programs will allow the students to actively participate in instruction and courses presented through distance education.
>
> – Assembly of First Nations (1988)

> Since it is not feasible to provide full, traditional educational services to isolated northern communities, equivalent upgraded services could be provided by use of two-way satellite and/or microwave communications to link such students with master teachers at learning centers.
>
> – Nielsen Task Force Report (1985)

> All the situations we are talking about involve distance and scattered populations. Distance education has used technology to gather these people together and put them in learning environments which they would not otherwise have access to because of location – no resources exist.
>
> – Saskatchewan Indian Institute of Technologies (1990)

Distance education has captured the imagination of educators and policy makers alike. For some, distance education offers new possibilities to open up access to learning opportunities that have been beyond the reach of remote communities. Learners could enjoy expanded educational choices and, at the same time, remain in their home communities with their families and escape the cultural disruption of moving to a distant urban institutional setting. For policy makers, distance education is a potentially cost-effective delivery system that can provide equitable access to services while limiting instructional costs.

The promise of distance education is particularly relevant to the needs and circumstances of Aboriginal learners. The proportion of Aboriginal people achieving post-secondary graduation is much smaller than that of the general population. To reduce this disparity, post-secondary institutions have introduced a number of strategies to improve access and retention of Aboriginal students. Some institutions have developed off-campus or field programs where instructors deliver courses directly in Aboriginal communities. Admissions have become more open as students are admitted with mature student status. Increasingly, institutions have initiated access programs that facilitate entry into specific programs (like law or health professions) or transition programs that help students become accustomed to the demands of post-secondary studies. Many institutions hire Aboriginal counsellors and/or coordinators. Today, more Aboriginal people are involved in the governance of post-secondary institutions, which results in the offering of programs and services more attuned to the needs of Aboriginal communities. At the same time, Aboriginal communities and tribal groups have established their own post-secondary institutions, where cultural values can be built into the curriculum and activities of institutional life.

Where does distance education fit into these attempts to broaden educational opportunities for Aboriginal people? For nearly two decades, the promises of distance education have loomed on the horizon. The purpose of this research is to explore how institutions and communities have begun to realize this vision of a more accessible and cost-effective educational future. In contrast with moving the instructor to the learner, this study takes as its focus educational arrangements in which the instructor and the learner are physically separated. Self-study packages with telephone tutoring, radio, audio-teleconferencing, audiographics, and video-conferencing are some of the formats that have been used to bring together instructors and learners.

The research on which this chapter draws (Davis 1997) was designed to develop a current profile of distance education in Aboriginal communities. One of the challenges is drawing the line between what is and what is not distance education. For example, does distance education include those instances in which an instructor travels from a central site and has face-to-face contact with students? Some researchers would consider this distance education, while others would call it open learning. Open learning includes all attempts by institutions to assist learners in pursuing their studies at the time, place, and pace of their choosing, using a variety of instructional approaches (Canada 1989). For the purposes of this paper, distance education has been defined as efforts in which technology is used to serve as a bridge between teachers and students. Despite this definition, in several of the examples discussed, there is also face-to-face contact between the teacher and the students, and in one project profile the instruction is entirely face-to-face.

This chapter assumes that readers are familiar with the traditional barriers to formal education encountered by Aboriginal people. The problems of achieving excellence in educational services have been well documented in studies such as *Tradition and Education* (Assembly of First Nations 1988) and *First Nations and Schools: Triumphs and Struggles* (Kirkness and Bowman 1992). The study has included a number of initiatives that span high school and post-secondary education because many adults are completing their high school education using distance learning.

This chapter is written for three overlapping audiences. First, some readers may be new to the distance education literature. The general introduction to distance education is intended to provide background material in a Canadian context. Second, there are distance education practitioners who may wish to know about projects that relate to their own work. Third, there are Aboriginal educators and policy makers who want to assess the state of the field in ways that illuminate the role distance education might play in meeting the future goals of Aboriginal education.

General Introduction to Distance Education in Canada

Canada has a long history of trying to overcome the barriers of distance in providing education. Correspondence courses were first offered at Queen's University in 1869. Through the decades, educators have made good use of the technology of the day. More recently, following the lead of Britain's Open University, post-secondary institutions dedicated to distance learning were established in Canada, including Athabasca University in Alberta (1972), Télé-université in Québec (1972), and the Open Learning Institute in British Columbia (1978). At the same time, educational television networks were instituted, including the Knowledge Network in British Columbia, Access Alberta, TV Ontario, and, somewhat later, the Manitoba Satellite Network and the Saskatchewan Communications Network, which uses a cable system and interactive training. Today, these television services broadcast programs that are part of institutional course offerings as well as educational programs intended for a general audience whose members are not enrolled in accredited learning.

Modern telecommunications have pushed the possibilities of distance education much further since 1975. With satellite technology, we have witnessed the emergence of audio-teleconferencing, interactive television, and video teleconferencing. Audio-teleconferencing is telephone-based and allows many participants at multiple sites. Participants at each site are connected through a bridge, which enables everyone to speak, hear, and interact. Video teleconferencing or interactive television, which is still very costly, allows the transmission of video images between broadcast sites (two-way) or from one central site to satellites (one-way). One-way broadcasting, combined with audio-teleconferencing, enables many participants to interact from different locations. Audiographics technology (known as telewriters or electronic blackboards) has become popular for sharing images (such as drawings and illustrations) between sites.

In Canada today, in addition to the universities and colleges dedicated exclusively to distance education, there are many conventional universities and colleges using distance delivery in small remote communities. However, Bates (1993, 8) points out that spanning long distances is not the primary rationale for using distance education in Canada: "These days remote students are in fact a small minority of those who make use of distance education. The vast majority of distance education students live within one hour's travel time of a post-secondary institution. More than half live in urban areas. There are clearly other reasons than distance that drive most students to take distance education courses."

Distance education users in Canada often choose this delivery mode because it is more flexible or fits better with their everyday life (Bates 1993, 8). The average user of distance education services in Canada is between the ages of twenty-five and forty, with family and job responsibilities, and is studying part-time. Increasingly, professional development opportunities are being offered by distance education to those in the workforce (e.g., teachers and nurses) (Canada 1989, 6).

Although most distance education in Canada today is still primarily print and audio-cassette based, distance education practitioners locate their work on the brink of the technological revolution, with the introduction of digital technology, fibre optics, and expanded satellite services. In the field research for this study, practitioners emphasized repeatedly that distance education will be transformed in the next few years. The new technologies allow multimedia integration, with video, sound, graphics, and data to be combined at a single work station. Bates (1993, 11) suggests that the integrated services digital network (ISDN) will bring multimedia integration into the majority of Canadian homes within ten years. In some parts of the country it is already widely accessible. Other technological developments will improve the friendliness of interfaces and increase portability. Posed at this point of change, distance education technology will transform the options for delivery in substantial ways. Berg and Ohler (1991) have produced a comprehensive review of how the new technologies can revolutionize Native education in the United States. For Aboriginal distance education in Canada, the possibilities for the future may be expanded dramatically by technological breakthroughs that increase the means through which students can learn. But, as argued later, whether this technological revolution contributes to a higher quality of education for Aboriginal people will depend on how distance education meets the cultural challenges of Aboriginal education.

Summary of the Aboriginal Distance Education Literature

In 1984, the Association of Canadian Universities for Northern Studies produced an annotated bibliography entitled *Distance Education in the Canadian North*. This twenty-eight-page publication provides a clear snapshot of the evolution of distance education through the 1970s and into the 1980s. Many telecommunication specialists, educators, and communities saw the potential for using distance education to overcome geographical barriers. The new technologies (computers and satellites) had opened up the doors to experimentation, and there was an explosion of small pilot projects testing the possibilities of distance education delivery.

Looking back on that era, it is possible to see that some projects and technologies appeared only to disappear into history. At the same time, foundations were laid for distance education as it has emerged in the 1990s. Satellite communications and telephones represent a threshold that educators crossed, enabling an interactivity that has become commonplace in distance education delivery.

Most of the contemporary literature has been produced by institutions involved in distance delivery or by instructors or administrators reflecting on their experiences. As in the past, the case study is a popular form of reporting. In 1988, Confederation College (Thunder Bay, Ontario) produced an annotated bibliography entitled *The Native Learner and Distance Education*. Apart from references from the general literature on Aboriginal education, the section pertaining to technology-based distance education contains seventeen entries, five of which relate to computer-assisted learning experiences. The literature since then has been equally sparse. The richest sources continue to be produced not in academic journals, but in institutional reports. This assessment was shared by Baker and Oike (1993), who also found few references in academic databases. Aboriginal distance education has not yet established a strong research base that performs critical comparative analysis across methodologies and community experiences.

One might expect that the contemporary Aboriginal distance education literature would deal with topics familiar to those who work in Aboriginal post-secondary education: quality of curriculum, student support services, access and retention, appropriate teachers, learning styles and pedagogies, finances, and community control. While variations on these topics appear to a certain extent, the literature also focuses on issues unique to working in a distance milieu. There are few comparative studies that systematically evaluate specific variables. The following summary of the literature mentions themes that recur frequently in Aboriginal education.

Quality of Curriculum and Accreditation

The development of Aboriginal-specific curriculum in distance formats is still at an embryonic stage. Many of the courses being delivered in communities are pre-packaged accredited courses that have not been adapted for Aboriginal learners. They may have been prepared for correspondence or home-study and are now being used with more interactive technologies. If colleges or universities do not have their own distance education curriculum design capability, then they are likely to purchase the package from elsewhere.

The project profiles prepared for this chapter, together with the project inventory provided later, indicate that there have been some important efforts to design specialized curricula for distance delivery. Language courses (e.g., AVC-Lesser Slave Lake in Cree, Wahsa in Oji-Cree and Ojibwa) have been developed for different levels of fluency. There are also examples of specialized curricula for distance delivery. Examples from the project inventory include the First Nations Fisheries Technician Program at Malaspina College; the Aboriginal Resource Management Technician Program at Sault College (Ontario); and a human resources management course by Atii Training Incorporated for Inuit and Innu managers. The Open Learning Agency has developed a Native issues in social work course; a partnership of organizations has created the Native Community Care Curriculum for human services workers in Ontario; and a community-based process including Elders resulted in Laurentian University's bachelor of social work program. In Alberta, the Yellowhead Tribal Council, in partnership with Athabasca University, has produced a number of courses in the health development administration certificate program. Despite these important achievements, much pre-packaged course material remains in use, without being adapted to the specific life circumstances and values of Aboriginal learners.

For many years, Aboriginal communities have insisted that education and training services should be accredited. This accounts for the widespread use of pre-packaged accredited courses in distance education. However, the adaptation of packages for the specific needs of Aboriginal communities can be fraught with difficulty. Institutional faculty and/or course developers may feel resistant to changes in the course that they feel jeopardize their "standards," since new materials or activities may challenge course perspectives or Western theories that are reflected in the course. There are sometimes tensions in getting academics who may be responsible for marking students to recognize Aboriginal knowledge as being as valid as Western knowledge (Barnhardt 1986). On the other hand, Haughey (1992, 33) argues that distance education is becoming increasingly flexible, multimodal, and interactive, and suggests that education is becoming less content-focused and more dialogical. This opens up space to accommodate more styles of learning and ways of knowing.

In the literature and the projects contained in the inventory below, all the programs described are accredited courses developed and/or delivered in partnership with educational institutions. The one exception is the Atii Pilot Project, a non-accredited course in management studies, which will be discussed later in this report as a case study.

Pedagogies
Across different studies, there is substantial agreement that first-generation distance education programs – correspondence courses – have not been very successful with Aboriginal learners. The most frequent distance education design combines delivery by radio or television signal together with packaged curriculum, audio-teleconferencing with the instructor and other students, audiographic technologies, tutoring on-site or by hotline, and some personal contact (either by an itinerant instructor or by occasionally bringing students together at one site). There are different permutations.

The Secwepemc (Shuswap) Cultural Education Society/Simon Fraser University (SCES/SFU) Project has reported growing success with distance education delivery since the summer of 1993. The project has adopted a policy stating that only students in good academic standing can enrol. Of thirty-five initial enrolments, thirty-two have completed their programs with passing marks. The most successful venture has been a first-year course in the spring of 1994, delivered by video-conferencing, using fibre optics technology. Students were able to interact with the instructor using voice and screen. Audiographics and audiovisual materials were also used. These technologies were embraced by the students, and all five completed the program (SCES and SFU 1994).

Appropriate Instructors
The literature documents the recurring theme of the difficulty in finding Aboriginal instructors whose qualifications are acceptable to institutions (Oddson and Ross 1991, 13; Sault College in CADE 1993; SIIT 1990, 140). This is a familiar tension in Aboriginal education, one that often results in non-Aboriginal instructors being hired to teach at the secondary school, college, and university levels. As will be noted later, the use of non-Aboriginal instructors may account for the absence of course teaching in Aboriginal languages, even where the Aboriginal language is the community's first language.

Attrition, Retention, and Completion Rates

In correspondence courses, there have been very high attrition rates and low completion rates (Baker and Oike 1993, 19; Sharpe 1992, 80). The Saskatchewan Indian Institute of Technology's (SIIT) report notes that, in Canada, group-oriented distance education has higher rates of success than has individual-oriented distance education and that peer support and teamwork contribute to higher retention rates (SIIT 1990, 136).

Completion rates at the Open Learning Agency's community learning centres are around 70 percent. Bates (1993) and Oddson and Ross (1991, 19) note a rising completion rate in the Yellowhead Tribal Council's courses with Athabasca University: from 53 percent in 1987-8 to 62 percent in 1990-1. In the SCES/Simon Fraser University Program in Kamloops, courses taught on-site have a completion rate of 70 percent to 80 percent (SCES/SFU 1994). These last two examples, however, involve on-site delivery.

Student Characteristics

Patterns of enrolment in distance education courses as well as for courses delivered face-to-face in communities tend to follow the general pattern for Aboriginal post-secondary education: there are more female students than male (King 1993). In Memorial University's Native and Northern Education Program, most students are female, between twenty-five and thirty-five years of age, and married with children (Sharpe 1992, 78). In Wahsa's distance education high school, there are more females than males. The "typical" SCES/SFU student is a single mother in her mid- to late thirties (SCES/SFU in CADE 1993). Staff in continuing education at Brandon University have observed that the majority of adult students in northern Aboriginal communities are female, and in the courses offered by continuing education, about 80 percent of the learners have been female (Kathleen Matheos, Brandon University, personal communication, 1993).

Spronk and Radtke (1988, 226) explored some of the implications of this gender pattern for learning and study skills. They noted that family and community obligations are an important dimension of the students' lives and may be quite time-consuming. While these obligations bring many positive rewards, they may also interfere with studies. The authors comment that their students looked to their family and community networks for support in dealing with the problems they may face in their environment.

Community Ownership of Program

Since the National Indian Brotherhood issued its policy paper *Indian Control of Indian Education* in 1972, Aboriginal people have sent an unequivocal message that education must be under community control. Yet the determination of the education by institutions and agencies outside communities continues to be a recurrent theme in projects and often has devastating results.

McGreal (1992) reported on an initiative in secondary school education in the James Bay Area of northeastern Ontario. Begun in 1989, the SCAN (Students Can Achieve Now) project was based in Moosonee and used audiographic teleconferencing to deliver courses to four other coastal communities. But, McGreal reports, "the community had never accepted responsibility for the success of the project" (304).

In the SIIT report on Aboriginal literacy (1990, 144), the Distance Education Working Group members emphasized the importance of community control. These seasoned distance educators stressed that, based on their experience, large-scale projects are destined to fail. They concluded that the really successful programs are community-based and grassroots. With relatively small amounts of additional funding to small organizations, significant work can be accomplished.

Facilities
The community learning centre (CLC) is the most prominent facility in use in distance education. This is an adult learning centre that serves as the hub for adult learning in a community. In northern Alberta, this model was established with community vocational centres in the early 1970s and has grown to a network of community campuses. In 1987, Contact North also adopted this model as part of its network of learning centres in northern Ontario communities (Treftlin 1986). In British Columbia, the Open Learning Agency has promoted this model, and North Island College has been working with local learning centres since the mid-1970s. In the Yukon, CLCs were established in 1980, and they are now called community campuses.

Support Services
Most distance education project descriptions document ways in which student supports are built into their programs (e.g., telephone hotlines for academic support or counselling services, on-site tutors or facilitators, visits from itinerant teachers or specialists). Examples of these will be given in the case studies discussed later.

One of the most detailed discussions of learning and study skills is provided by Spronk and Radtke (1988, 218-22). They describe the failure of Athabasca University's standard study skills workshop with Aboriginal students and the subsequent development of a course customized to the unique needs of Aboriginal learners. Their redesign of the study skills workshop incorporated the following modifications: making extensive use of small groups; slowing down the pace of the workshop, particularly since

English was a second language; reworking the time management section of the course to better reflect Aboriginal understandings of time; providing more information on how much time is needed to complete full-time study work; increasing attention to anxiety and internal distractions to studying; and discussing the rules of the game, including teachers' expectations, in academic work.

Finances
It is impossible to discuss Aboriginal education without noting the chronic lack of adequate funding at all levels. Distance education is no exception. The SIIT report's first recommendation (1990, 142) is to make available appropriate funding for program development; resources (buildings, technology, network); operating costs; training of staff; and the development, purchase, or adaptation of resource materials.

Anderson (1992, 92) noted that a key element in enticing the cooperation of post-secondary institutions with Contact North's distance delivery infrastructure was the establishment of the Northern Distance Education Fund, which was used for course development or purchase of courses. Since these funds were allocated to projects that were collaborative and northern-focused, institutions were encouraged to enter into partnerships that they might not have considered otherwise.

Anderson's observations are repeated by King (1993), who has noted that post-secondary institutions are more likely to initiate Aboriginal programming and services when there are external funds available.

Institutional Constraints
Distance education creates tensions within institutions, where it is still perceived as low status relative to on-campus instruction and scholarship, despite Canada's stature in the field internationally (Bates 1993, 3; Black 1992). This tension can be illustrated in resistance to adapting course content and assignment structures (Oddson and Ross 1991) and in problems with getting professional expertise recognized by the university reward system (Barnhardt 1986). According to Anderson (1992, 92), "distance education challenges the role of teachers, physical facilities (notably libraries, bookstores), admission policies and practices, examination and assessment practices, and student services."

Inventory of Distance Education Programs and Projects
The following inventory of projects (see Figure 1) was compiled using a number of sources. First, there is the excellent paper by Baker and Oike (1993), which discusses the status of open learning in British Columbia. Second, the Canadian Association of Distance Education took the initiative to prepare a submission of projects to the Royal Commission on

Figure 1

Inventory of distance education programs and projects

	Location	Type of program	Program notes
Open Learning Agency	British Columbia	Literacy, adult basic, university transfer courses	Twelve community learning centres throughout British Columbia; on-site tutor or facilitator; materials with audio and visual cassettes; telephone line; some teleconferencing. Open Learning Agency has First Nations coordinator and advisory committee.
North Island College	British Columbia	Developmental courses; academic; career, technical, and trades	Sixteen small centres in small communities in northern Vancouver Island and central coast; on-site generalist instructor; content specialist by phone; courses delivered on site or through distance course packages; centres have video playback units and computers. Affiliated with Open Learning Agency.
Secwepemc (Shuswap) Cultural Education Society/Simon Fraser University (SCES/SFU)	British Columbia	University	Special initiative with largely on-site delivery in Kamloops. Experiment with video-conferencing.
University of Victoria	British Columbia	Post-graduate	Administration of Aboriginal Governments Certificate Program; teleconference in addition to three one-week sessions on campus per semester.
Malaspina College	British Columbia	First Nations fisheries technician program	Ten courses, sixty credit curriculum; teleconferencing, multi-use bulletin board, and field school.
Dene Training Network	Northern British Columbia	Diverse education and training	Consortia of Aboriginal partners and institutions; recommend setting up multi-use learning centres.

Alberta Vocational Centre, Lesser Slave Lake	Alberta	High school; university transfer courses	Community campuses; Distance Education High School; community learning centres; on-site facilitator; course packages; itinerant specialized instructors; various audio-visual materials; teleconferencing. Choice of group instruction, independent learning, correspondence. Community education committees make local decisions. (See case study.)
Saskatchewan Indian Federated College	Saskatchewan	Ojibwa language training	Satellite course via Saskatchewan Communications Network to students in six reserve communities (Yorkton Tribal Council).
Inter-Universities North (U of Man., Brandon U, U of Winnipeg)	Manitoba	1st-year university	Accredited courses show increasing Aboriginal enrolments.
Brandon University	Manitoba	University	Teleconferencing is introduced on limited basis in first year and then expanded in subsequent years. Cree language courses have been delivered successfully.
Swampy Cree Tribal Council with Brandon U, Inter-Universities North, and Keewatin College	Manitoba	University	Northern Business Management Training Program, leading to BA in business administration. On-site delivery with six communities, one linked in part by audio-conferencing.
Wahsa	Northwestern Ontario	High school	Wahsa Distance Education High School; radio teleconferencing across twenty-three Oji-Cree communities; run by Northern Nishnawbe Education Council using facilities of Wawatay Communications; community learning centres; three semesters, each with two terms – continual intake. (See case study.)

▼ *Figure 1*

Inventory of distance education programs and projects

	Location	Type of program	Program notes
Contact North	Northwestern Ontario	High school; post-secondary special courses	150 sites, thirty-five of them Anishnabe; community learning centres provided by community; hardware (fax machine, teleconferencing equipment, telewriter) provided by Contact North. Native liaison coordinator and advisory committee; non-accredited education programs (e.g., art tours, guest speakers on Aboriginal issues).
Sault College-Ministry of Natural Resources	Ontario	College	Two-year Aboriginal Resource Management Technician program; three days a week (nine hrs.) teleconferencing; two days on the job; Aboriginal curriculum in courses.
Laurentian University	Ontario	University	Native Human Services Program leading to four-year degree formatted for correspondence delivery with telephone and fax support and faculty consultants in their third and fourth year.
Union of Ontario Indians, Mohawk College, Cambrian College, Association of Iroquois and Allied Indians	Ontario	Native Community Care Program	Two-year program to train community health workers; ten weeks on campus per year; teleconferences every two weeks.
Wabnode Institute (Cambrian College)	Ontario	Land management	Four-semester program in 1993.

Cree School Board, Heritage College	Quebec	Effective writing skills; preparing for college success	Two courses delivered in three communities with plans to expand program in 1994; AGS audiographics technology.
University of New Brunswick	New Brunswick	University nursing program	Aboriginal nurses participate in this baccalaureate program for RNs.
Memorial University	Newfoundland	University	Bachelor of education in Native and northern education. Some distance education in upper years for courses with small enrolments.
Arctic College	Northwest Territories	Different levels of courses	Debra Pilot Project to test AGS-MX equipment, using a community antenna that will eliminate on-line phone costs; field test in trades upgrading courses in Fort Liard.
Atii Pilot Project	Northwest Territories, northern Quebec, Labrador	Non-accredited management courses	Pilot project in delivery of management education; two courses in English, one in Inuktitut; crossed four time zones; television broadcast and audioconferencing. (See case study.)
Yukon College	Yukon	Different levels of courses	Use of Television Northern Canada in delivery of some of its course materials; print-based self-instructional materials with help from telephone tutor.

Aboriginal Peoples (CADE 1993). And third, contact was made with various organizations and institutions across the country.

This inventory makes no claims to comprehensiveness. However, practitioners in this study indicated the importance of exchanging information about what kinds of projects are going on elsewhere, and I hope to contribute to that dialogue. Both long-standing and emerging initiatives are cited. The projects are listed by province or territory.

To help illuminate the dynamic aspects of distance education delivery and issues in the various centres and institutions, case studies were developed describing AVC-Lesser Slave Lake, the Atii Pilot Project, Wahsa, and the Yellowknife Tribal Council. They are described below.

AVC-Lesser Slave Lake

Alberta Vocational College-Lesser Slave Lake (AVC-LSL) is a provincial institution, located in north-central Alberta with offices at Grouard and Slave Lake. It serves a network of two major campuses, four medium-sized campuses, and a varying number of small satellite campuses (approximately sixteen). The institution offers upgrading programs, training and college programs, and some university transfer programs. In 1989, the AVC-LSL established a Distance Education and Program Development Unit in order to spearhead its distance education delivery (Athabasca University 1986; Vandermeulen in RCAP 1997).

From its beginnings with sixty students in 1989-90, it grew to a total of 550 students by 1992-3, at least 70 percent of them Métis and First Nations people. Most students are completing provincially accredited high school credits, using standardized curriculum packages that have been adapted for distance education but not for an Aboriginal context. Students can choose whether they wish to undertake their studies using a group approach, independent learning, or correspondence. The group approach has a strong teleconferencing component.

The major efforts of the Distance Education Unit in its first four years have been devoted to establishing the Distance Learning High School, and, in 1993, the first DLHS principal was appointed. Today, the electronic classroom can pull together two students in one community and three students at another site hundreds of miles away to form a learning group, and any course offered in one community can be offered just as easily across the network. Courses are offered during the day, which is an expensive commitment to students. At night, costs are considerably reduced when the government of Alberta opens its province-wide telephone network for distance education services, without charge.

More than sixty high school credit courses were offered in 1992-3 (AVC-LSL calendar 1993-4). Cree language courses represented the AVC's major thrust to prepare Aboriginal-specific materials, with the offering of Cree language at different levels of fluency. As yet, there are no courses in Métis history, Aboriginal studies and law, international Indigenous peoples, or other Aboriginal themes that have appeared in high school programs that are under Aboriginal control at the community level. The language of instruction is English, except in the Cree language courses.

Most of the AVC-LSL instructors are non-Aboriginal. In the Distance Education Unit, three of the nine instructors are Aboriginal: not surprisingly, these are the Cree language instructors. Many of the AVC-LSL counsellors are Aboriginal. Each community campus has a site coordinator, who works full- or part-time, depending upon enrolments in the local program. Sometimes a site coordinator is also a specialist instructor, who may broadcast a course to other campuses.

A standard equipment package goes into each community, including a teleconferencing bridge, a telewriter, fax machine, printer, and video playback equipment. Some community campuses have small libraries. Otherwise, students enrolled in the high school program request library resources from the two centres at Grouard and Slave Lake. These library catalogues are on-line at each of the community campuses. If the community has suitable existing space for an adult learning center, then the province leases the space. In communities where no reasonable lease space is available, the provincial government, through its department of public works, provides facilities for the community campus.

In each community, there is a community education committee made up of local people. Every month, one representative from each community meets on the Council of Community Education Committees, providing advice on programs and services overall. In 1993-4, each community campus was allocated 640 hours of discretionary staff time, which the local community education committee might decide to use for a support person, and/or literacy worker, and/or distance education support.

Distance Education Unit staff report that students tend to respond warmly to the teleconferencing technology. There is a lot of teasing, socializing, and even romancing long-distance. Some instructors believe that students are less inhibited in teleconferencing than in face-to-face classrooms, where the group dynamics are different. The interactive audio-graphics technology (telewriter) has been very popular, since students can use drawing and graphic skills to communicate. Course instructors will often travel, originating their broadcast from different communities so that students and teacher will have some personal contact. In the future, the AVC plans to use electronic bulletin boards to facilitate more interaction among the students. Apparently, a strong sense of community can be built across different campuses, and AVC staff suggest that there is a growing "college" identity emerging among the students. As an increasing number of community members take one or more courses at a distance, there is a base of community expertise, which members pass on to those who are new to a distance education course.

AVC-LSL built its community campuses on an existing network of community learning centres that originally formed in the early 1970s to address needs for literacy training in remote communities (Burkholder 1986). From there, it has expanded into high school education. With this history of repositioning itself to meet community needs, the institution is poised to play a leading role in the future as the demand for post-secondary education expands rapidly in Aboriginal communities.

Wahsa Distance Education High School

The Wahsa Project, established in 1989 by the twenty-three First Nations of Sioux Lookout District, represents a pragmatic response to the long-standing dilemma of how to give students a high school education without sending them out of the community (Fiddler 1992). Wahsa is a program of the Northern Nishnawbe Education Council (NNEC), the mandated area education authority of the First Nations of Sioux Lookout district, serving an area of about 200,000 square kilometres in northwestern Ontario. The Cree and Oji-Cree communities are small and isolated; most have only fly-in access.

NNEC provides off-reserve elementary, secondary, and post-secondary student services (NNEC brochure). Wahsa is a registered private school, offering high school courses (Grades 9 to 13) by FM radio or correspondence. Students enrolled in radio courses attend classes at a community learning centre in their home community. During the week, students work through a ten-hour lesson package for each course in which they are enrolled. Depending on the course, the teacher broadcasts once, twice, or three times a week, sometimes using the one-way data-casting system (telewriter) that Wahsa developed with Wawatay (the radio and television broadcasters of the Nishnawbe Aski Nation) and TV Ontario. Sometimes the radio broadcast originates in Sioux Lookout; at other times, since the teachers travel to different communities, teachers deliver the lesson from the community learning centre they are visiting. Students interact with the teacher on-air, using the telephone convener, and submit assignments for marking on a weekly basis (using local airlines). At no cost to the student, learners have access to fax services and a telephone hot-line for tutoring. Wahsa also funds an on-site tutor, who is available four to eight hours per week to help students with problems. At least once a term, a teacher from Sioux Lookout visits each community to support the students in their work. Each community learning centre has a locally hired and supervised distance education coordinator who serves as the on-site facilitator and maintains a continuing presence in the community.

Wahsa operates on a trimester system, and each semester is divided into two seven-week terms, with one study week per term. Each one-term course in the Wahsa system is worth a half-credit. Remarkably, Wahsa is equipped to do student intake every term (six intakes a year). This provides a highly flexible system, which allows students to receive credit for work completed without losing a whole year if they choose to take time out to participate in seasonal hunting and trapping activities, family responsibilities, or community cultural events. If students start their term in an urban centre and then return home part-way through, they can resume their studies immediately. Students normally take one, two, or three courses at a time.

Wahsa courses are accredited by the Ontario Ministry of Education, and any new courses must be reviewed by the ministry. To meet the ministry guidelines, each course has sixty hours of learning content, with a minimum of ten hours of work per weekly package, including reading material, back-up correspondence type materials, texts and reference materials, radio sessions, videotapes, research, and assignments. At present, Oji-Cree courses are offered at different levels of fluency, but the language of instruction in most courses is English. A student cooperative learning program has been instituted recently to link high school learning with the workplace. In addition to the usual core of humanities and science courses, there are Aboriginal studies courses, environmental science, Aboriginal law, outdoor education, and peer helping/communications. The school calendar is presented imaginatively, with inviting descriptions. A few examples serve to illustrate:

ENG 3G2 Focus on Drama. Move over, Graham Greene; here comes Theater Wahsa! Enjoy and appreciate a dramatic experience while involving yourself personally in script writing. Create your own production using radio or video camera. Get the whole gang together to register. Have fun, and earn credit as well.

BAI 3G1: BAI 3G2 Introductory Accounting. The Band Office and the Community store need people to keep the books, control cash flow and take care of banking. You can be that someone by learning accounting principles and how to put them to work. Your personal finance handling will benefit too. Bank on Wahsa to help you attain this useful knowledge.

The students also have an opportunity to interact with each other. There is one scheduled time every week for student club, where students from different communities are invited to participate in various activities over the radio with other students. There is also a student newsletter. At present, both activities are still facilitated by Wahsa staff, but they have the potential to be student-initiated and student-run.

Wahsa has known many successes, as more and more students graduate. Yet the organization has had its share of challenges. Finding qualified Aboriginal secondary school teachers has been a problem. Funding for adequate community facilities and for curriculum development has been difficult to find. Some of the problems are technical: there are four different types of telephone systems (satellite, microwave, terrestrial, radio-phone) in Wahsa-served communities, which affects the quality of teleconferencing services.

In evaluating this initiative, it is important to remember that Wahsa was founded on two existing strengths of the tribal region: the Northern Nishnawbe Education Council, which had a solid political and management infrastructure in place, and the Wawatay Native Communications Network, which had already established a broadcasting tradition in the communities. Wahsa's initiation came from the bottom up – from communities that wanted to try this approach to education.

Atii Pilot Project

Atii Training is an incorporated coordinating group founded in 1987 by Inuit organizations to organize and deliver training in preparation for the implementation of self-government in Nunavut. The job of training Inuit managers is being approached with urgency, yet because of the geographical challenges of the North, education and training are very costly. In 1992, Atii joined with a number of partners to launch a pilot project using interactive televised instruction (ITI) (Atii Training Inc. 1993a; 1993b).

The pilot project included three non-credit courses intended to upgrade the skills of existing managers: Phase 1 – Management Basics; Phase 2 – Developing Management Skills with People (English version); and Phase 3 – Developing Management Skills with People (Inuktitut version). About 160 people were trained in the three phases delivered between May 1993 and October 1993. In 1994, this project was awarded the Telesat Educational Telecommunications Award for innovation.

The pilot project was funded by a variety of donors, the largest being the National Aboriginal Management Board of Pathways. The sponsors, who made financial and in-kind contributions to the project, were Atii, Arctic College, Labrador College, Kativik School Board and Kativik Regional Government, Television Northern Canada and its members, Nunavut Tunngavik Inc., the Inuit Broadcasting Corporation, and NorthwesTel. In addition, the government of the Northwest Territories, the Uannarmiut Management Board for North Baffin, the Keewatin Management Board, the Kitikmeot Aboriginal Management Board, and the Kagita Mikam Management Board of Eastern Ontario all made financial contributions to see the pilot project through to completion. Inuit Communications Systems Ltd. was contracted by Atii to do the television productions, working with Inuit

Broadcasting Corporation TV studios and staff to produce the live seg-ments. Because of the importance of the pilot project in testing the effec-tiveness and possibilities of distance education delivery for self-government education, the sponsors built an evaluation component into all phases of implementation.

The courses were broadcast live from Iqaluit over Television North Canada (TVNC), which reaches an audience of 110,000 across the Arctic as well as viewers in southern Canada who receive satellite services. The students lived in communities across four time zones, from Nunavut to northern Quebec to Labrador (Innu in Sheshatshiu and Nain). The in-structors delivered presentations live on-air, interspersed with group exer-cises among the students off-air and interaction with the instructor using phone-ins on-air.

In each community, students met in a local learning centre with an on-site facilitator who was responsible for managing the site, stimulating student participation in group exercises, and keeping the learning process on track. The students received a comprehensive package of course mate-rials, including readings, exercises, and feedback sheets. Since this was non-credit learning, there were no individual assignments for grading, but the curriculum included group exercises and quizzes, some of which were to be faxed to the instructors.

Feedback on the delivery of the first course suggested that more cultural content and interactivity were needed. For the second course, considerable effort was made to adapt the curriculum to the Inuit context using north-ern examples, videotaped role plays, and guest speakers. The finished cur-riculum also incorporated questions that encouraged students to probe their own experiences and to question Western management concepts if they did not seem to fit with Inuit and Innu ways of doing things. The curriculum included such topics as the importance of informal networks, cross-cultural dynamics, and cultural norms. To assist in exploring these themes, guests were invited to participate; for example, an Elder came to answer students' questions about how Inuit traditionally give feedback to others about their behaviour. In addition, high profile Inuit managers were invited as guest speakers and they shared their experiences as managers.

Phases 2 and 3 of the Atii Pilot Project were rated positively by students in the courses. This one pilot project, carefully documented and evaluated in process, produced a wealth of resources and many insights into success-ful distance education in an Aboriginal context: the acceptability of this style of distance education among students; the multiple educational, financial, and technical partners required to stage such a complex project; the feasibility of offering post-secondary education in an Aboriginal lan-guage; the importance of making visible the value base of the curriculum materials being offered in courses; the cost-effectiveness of this kind of education over vast geographical distances; and the importance of inter-activity through TV/teleconferencing arrangements, small group discus-sions, and exercises in the learning process. The Atii Pilot Project courses were all videotaped and remain a training resource for future use. In addi-tion, group facilitators for each community centre were trained in a facili-tators' training program using distance education, and these tapes are also available as training resources.

We must also note that this was the only instance, in all of the projects reviewed in this study, in which the learning was non-accredited and in which an Aboriginal language was used to teach in a course other than one whose subject matter was language learning. One can speculate that the non-accreditation of the course offered a flexibility for delivery that may be much rarer where outside bodies control the terms of accreditation.

Yellowhead Tribal Council

The Yellowhead Tribal Council (YTC) provides a counterpoint to the geo-graphically distant circumstances that we have described across northern Canada. In contrast to circumstances in the vast territorial expanses in the North, the members of the Yellowhead Tribal Council are located just outside of Edmonton, an easy drive from major educational institutions. They have established their own post-secondary education institution, which brokers accredited college and university courses from the Univer-sity of Alberta, the University of Calgary, Athabasca University, and Grant McEwen College.

In 1992-3, YTC had 268 students on its own campus, and 172 graduated from their programs. Most of these programs were from institutions that had entered into agreements to deliver their programs at the YTC campus. The 1993 graduation ceremony brochure records an impressive slate of graduates: 20 with a bachelor of social work (University of Calgary); 28 with a social work diploma (Grant McEwen Community College); 20 with business management studies certificates (Athabasca University); 54 university and college entrance preparation program graduates; 24 in health development administration (Athabasca University); 84 graduates of the university transfer program between 1990 and 1993; and 42 graduates who had been students at other post-secondary institutions. This kind of completion track record is sufficient to attract attention across the country.

The availability of funding from the Department of Indian Affairs and other agencies, once in the hands of the Yellowhead Tribal Council, has allowed YTC some leverage in negotiating its needs with post-secondary institutions. For example, Athabasca University, which is a dedicated dis-tance education institution, worked with YTC to develop a community-based health development administration program that it delivered on-site. By having some control over resources, YTC has been able to enter into institutional partnerships that result in culturally sensitive components in its programs.

YTC also offers its own support services to students, regardless of the program they are undertaking. These services include collective learning and mutual support for the completion of assignments, peer counselling, tutoring, an orientation week, financial support (including crisis funding), and a library collection. Having access to funding to develop community-based support services, they have been able to provide a configuration of services that truly help their students succeed.

Aboriginally controlled institutions, like that operated by the YTC, respond to pressing post-secondary education needs of community members, occupying the centre of the circle, rather than serving as satellites on the margins of large externally controlled post-secondary institutions. As Aboriginally controlled institutions grow in scale and complexity, they function as tribal colleges, although to date they have not received the recognition and support that tribal colleges have been granted in the United States. Key to their success has been their capacity to gain access to funding that gives them some leverage in their relationship with mainstream post-secondary institutions.

What We Have Learned from
Distance Education in Aboriginal Communities

For over thirty years, efforts to use distance technologies in Aboriginal education have been yielding important insights that can guide future development. While there are few comparative studies in this field, it is possible to observe common patterns and issues that recur and inform practice.

(1) Culture and Assimilative Forces

Much of the curriculum being delivered by distance education consists of pre-packaged accredited materials that do not integrate Aboriginal perspectives or context. The greatest strides in the development of culturally and community-based curricula have been made by Aboriginally controlled programs and institutions. As in other areas of Aboriginal education, there is a constant struggle to get Aboriginal curriculum accredited and recognized by mainstream educational institutions. With the exception of Aboriginal language courses, almost all education delivered in Aboriginal communities is in the English or French language, even where the Aboriginal language is the first language of students. Because accrediting institutions insist upon having instructors with particular formal qualifications, Aboriginal people who speak their language are often excluded from the pool of potential instructors. Marie Battiste (Battiste and Barman 1995, viii) has used the term "cognitive imperialism" to refer to the way a dominant society saturates the whole way of thinking of a minority group by imposing its language and systems of meaning. This concept seems quite useful for further analysis of distance education, which has the potential to promote the continued use of Aboriginal languages rather than their erosion.

(2) Features of Best Practice

Much has been learned about the factors that contribute to successful distance education. Delivery modes with higher levels of interactivity (such as two-way audio- and TV-conferencing) create the conditions for forming a "virtual community" that supports learning. The community learning centre has emerged as the model of choice in a number of examples in defining a home base for distance delivery. It allows students to come together either to engage in collective learning or to provide mutual support. In many documented cases, the local site coordinator is seen to play a key role in creating a positive learning environment and providing immediate support so that students continue their studies. Academic and counselling support are crucial, as are adequate finances with which to support students during their studies.

Wahsa has implemented an innovative credit system that has considerable merit in Aboriginal education overall. Through its trisemester, two-term-per-semester system, it is able to move students through accredited learning with a minimum of disruption.

(3) Partnerships

One of the most salient features of distance education delivery is the high level of cooperation and partnership required to create a program that works. Quite apart from the organization that initiates or spearheads the distance education program, several elements have to come together. At the community level, there has to be a sense of ownership and responsibility for the program. Within educational institutions, there must be a spirit of cooperation that opens the doors to students who have known disempowerment in the education system. To make the venture work technically, the program needs sponsors with specialized services (e.g., broadcasting or telecommunications delivery). At the point of delivery, there are instructors and tutors whose skills and understanding of student needs must be fine-tuned to the community. And, finally, students need adequate resources and a positive learning environment that sends out "can-do" messages. Each of these elements has made the difference between the success and failure of a distance education program.

The role of funding agencies is also critical to successful distance education at all levels: resources to develop culturally based curriculum; funding so that students and their families can meet their daily needs during studies; and operational funds for programs. Strategically, this funding needs to be in the hands of Aboriginal organizations and institutions so that it can be used as a lever to negotiate with external educational institutions for customized programs that are appropriate to the needs of Aboriginal learners.

Increasingly, distance education enables the crossing of provincial and national jurisdictional boundaries so that courses can be offered to geographically dispersed populations. This can work for Aboriginal people if they are able to find institutional partners who are willing to develop high quality, culturally based programs. It loosens the grip of local post-secondary institutions that may have a poor track record with regard to responding to Aboriginal priorities.

Looking towards the Future
There is no doubt that distance education is now established as one viable delivery option in Aboriginal adult and youth education. The field of distance education in Canada is changing rapidly with digital technology and fibre optics, and the range of distance education possibilities will be expanding. As universities establish professional level accredited programs using advanced telecommunications systems, the image of distance education is becoming more prestigious.

Will Aboriginal communities in more remote areas have access to the new technologies as telecommunications companies reach out to larger, lucrative urban markets? Aboriginal organizations and communities will need to make their needs and presence felt as new institutional alliances emerge around distance education and tele-learning. Bates (1993, 6) has pointed out that the globalization of education will bring many educational channels into communities by television. Given the global reach of the new technologies and the search for economies of scale, educational services are on the verge of crossing traditional jurisdictional boundaries. While this may increase the range of programming available for Aboriginal communities, it remains to be seen how globalization will affect the availability of resources to undertake localized, specialized programming. Aboriginal communities should therefore press for access to telecommunications technologies that are the new trails into global networks.

Aboriginal distance education has grown within the overall expansion of distance education in Canada. No doubt, it will continue to be transformed with the advent of new technologies. At the time of this study, Internet connectivity was just emerging, and no projects were identified in which extensive use was being made of the Internet. This is changing rapidly, and today no study of this kind would omit such an important development. The Internet opens up many new possibilities for learners of all ages.

Despite the current preoccupation with finding the most successful configuration of technologies and support services, the most demanding challenge will be to find ways to infuse educational programs with Aboriginal values and perspectives. Enabled by advanced telecommunications, networking approaches can bring students together with Elders, teachers, and resource people from many nations. Current initiatives highlight the importance of Aboriginal control for the design and delivery of distance education programs. If distance education is to fulfill its promise, then it will need to evolve in ways that enable Aboriginal communities to define their own educational priorities and to determine the values and perspectives that pervade the educational experience.

Acknowledgments
This chapter is based upon Lynne Davis, "Electronic Classrooms, Electronic Highways: A Review of Aboriginal Distance Education in Canada," Royal Commission on Aboriginal Peoples (Ottawa, 1994).

This study relied on the assistance of many practitioners and scholars who are committed to improving the access of Aboriginal learners to education programs. I extend my heartfelt thanks to those who contributed to the research by sharing their knowledge and experiences: Bob Annis (Brandon University), Doug Baker (University of British Columbia), Ray Barnhardt (University of Alaska Fairbanks), Tony Bates (Open Learning Agency), Brian Beaton (Wahsa Distance Education Project), Doug Brown (Dene Training Network, Carrier Sekani Tribal Council), James Brule (Yellowhead Tribal Council), Harvey Burkholder (AVC-Lesser Slave Lake), Archie Cunningham (AVC-Lesser Slave Lake), Penny Erickson (University of New Brunswick, CAUSN), Jim Evans (Arctic College), Boyd Fradsham (Memorial University), Don Frenelle (Malaspina College), Steve Gruber (Concordia University, Universalia Consultants), Lorna Hanuse (Open Learning Agency), Margaret Haughey (University of Alberta, CADE), Pat Larson and Staff (Alberta Vocational College-Lesser Slave Lake), Kathleen Matheos (Brandon University), John Rowlandson (Wordshares Consulting), Marion Roze (North Island College), Esther Sanderson (Saskatchewan Indian Federated College), Deborah Schnitzer (University of Winnipeg), Charles Shobe (Inter-Universities North, Manitoba), Bernard Simand (Cree School Board), Rob Sutherland (Yukon College), Lorraine Thomas (Atii Training Inc./Inuit Broadcasting), and Glenn Treftlin (Contact North). In addition, there was a community interview at the Yellowhead Tribal Council in Spruce Grove, Alberta with elder Nancy Potts and graduates of the Bachelor of Social Work Program (Gina Alexis, Sandra Potts, Leslie Bearhead, and Verna Kootenhayoo).

References
Anderson, Terry. 1992. "Distance Education Delivery Networks Role in Community and Institutional Development." In *Distance Education and Sustainable Community Development*, ed. D. Wall and M. Owen, 87-103. Edmonton: Canadian Circumpolar Institute with Athabasca University Press.
Assembly of First Nations. 1988. *Tradition and Education: Towards a Vision of Our Future.* Ottawa: Assembly of First Nations.
Association of Canadian Universities for Northern Studies. 1984. *Distance Education in the Canadian North: An Annotated Bibliography.* Ottawa: Association of Canadian Universities for Northern Studies.
Athabasca University, Community Vocational Centres, Alberta Vocational Center Grouard. 1986. *Organizing Distance Education Alternatives: Final Report.*
Atii Training Inc. 1993a. *Developing Management Skills with People: Participant's Study Guide and Facilitator's Manual.* Joint Project with Arctic College, Kativik School Board, and Labrador College. Distance Education Pilot Project.

–. 1993b. *Evaluation Report to Atii Training Inc. on the Pilot Project: Introduction to Management.* Prepared by Brystra Consultants. Waterloo, Ontario.

Baker, Doug, and Nancy Oike. 1993. "First Nations and Open Learning Services Provided by British Columbia's Post-secondary Education System." Paper submitted to University of British Columbia, Higher Education 513 (course).

Barnhardt, R. 1986. "Domestication of the Ivory Tower: Institutional Adaptation to Cultural Distance." Paper presented at the American Anthropological Association Meeting, 5 December 1985, University of Alaska, Fairbanks.

Bates, A.W. 1993. "The Future of Distance Education in Canada: Opportunities and Challenges." Unpublished manuscript.

Battiste, Marie, and Jean Barman. 1995. *First Nations Education in Canada: The Circle Unfolds.* Vancouver: UBC Press.

Berg, Paul, and Jason Ohler. 1991. "Strategic Plans for Use of Modern Technology in the Education of American Indian and Alaska Native Students." Indian Nations At Risk Task Force Commissioned Papers. ERIC #ED343765.

Black, J. 1992. "Faculty Support for University Distance Education." *Journal of Distance Education* 7 (2): 5-30.

Burkholder, Harvey. 1986. "The Evolution and Development of the Community Vocational Centres Program: 1960-1985." MEd thesis, University of Alberta.

Canada. Secretary of State with the Open Learning Agency of BC. 1989. *Open Learning and Distance Education in Canada: Canadian Studies Resource Guide.* Ottawa: Ministry of Supply and Services.

Canadian Association of Distance Education (CADE). 1993. Submission prepared by Dr. Margaret Haughey for the Royal Commission on Aboriginal Peoples.

Confederation College and Contact North. 1988. *The Native Learner and Distance Education: An Annotated Bibliography.* Thunder Bay: Confederation College.

Davis, Lynne. 1997. "Electronic Classrooms, Electronic Highways: A Review of Aboriginal Distance Education in Canada." In *For Seven Generations: An Information Legacy of the Royal Commission on Aboriginal Peoples.* CD-ROM. Ottawa: Libraxus.

Fiddler, M. 1992. "Developing and Implementing a Distance Education Secondary School Program for Isolated First Nation Communities in Northwestern Ontario." In *Distance Education and Sustainable Community Development*, ed. D. Wall, and M. Owen, 105-18. Edmonton: Canadian Circumpolar Institute with Athabasca University Press.

Haughey, M. 1992. "Trends and Issues in Distance Education with Implications for Northern Development." In *Distance Education and Sustainable Community Development*, ed. D. Wall and M. Owen, 29-37. Edmonton: Canadian Circumpolar Institute with Athabasca University Press.

King, Cecil. 1997. "The State of Aboriginal Education: Southern Canada." In *For Seven Generations: An Information Legacy of the Royal Commission on Aboriginal Peoples.* CD-ROM. Ottawa: Libraxus.

Kirkness, V., and S. Bowman. 1992. *First Nations and Schools: Triumphs and Struggles.* Toronto: Canadian Education Association.

McGreal, R. 1992. "The SCAN Programme: Bringing Distance Education to Isolated Native Communities on the James Bay Coast, 1989-1991." *Distance Education* 13 (2): 300-8.

National Indian Brotherhood. 1972. *Indian Control of Indian Education.* Ottawa: National Indian Brotherhood.

Nielsen Task Force Report. 1985. *Improved Program Delivery: Indians and Natives.* Ottawa: Government of Canada.

Oddson, Lori, and Lynda Ross. 1991. *Athabasca University's Role in Native Education Programmes.* Athabasca: Athabasca University.

Royal Commission on Aboriginal Peoples. "Testimony at Public Hearings: Dan Vandermeulen, AVC Slave Lake/Grouard, at Slave Lake, Alberta, 27 October 1992." In *For Seven Generations: An Information Legacy of the Royal Commission on Aboriginal Peoples.* CD-ROM. Ottawa: Libraxus.

Saskatchewan Indian Institute of Technologies (SIIT). 1990. *Aboriginal Literacy Action Plan: A Literacy Practitioners' Guide to Action*. Saskatoon: SIIT.

Secwepemc Cultural Education Society (SCES) and Simon Fraser University (SFU). 1994. *The Fifth Report: A Great Leap Forward*. Bi-Annual Report of the SCES/SFU Program. Fall 1992 to Spring 1994.

Sharpe, D. 1992. "Successfully Implementing a Native Teacher Education Program through Distance Education in Labrador." In *Distance Education and Sustainable Community Development*, ed. D. Wall and M. Owen, 75-85. Edmonton: Canadian Circumpolar Institute with Athabasca University Press.

Spronk, B., and D. Radtke. 1988. "Problems and Possibilities: Canadian Native Women in Distance Education." In *Toward New Horizons for Women in Distance Education: International Perspectives*, ed. K. Faith, New York: Routledge.

Treftlin, Glenn. 1986. "Adult Education on Indian Reserves in the Fort Frances District." PhD diss., Ontario Institute for Studies in Education, University of Toronto.

Conclusion:
Fulfilling the Promise

Marlene Brant Castellano, Lynne Davis,
and Louise Lahache

This collection of case studies and research papers presents a snapshot of
the complex landscape in which Aboriginal education is taking place – a
landscape in which hope and possibility live side by side with constraint
and frustration. Hope is kindled in the insistence of communities, families, and educators that a foundation of Aboriginal values and knowledge
is the best way to ensure the well-being of children and youth, and to
guide them in taking up their responsibilities as Aboriginal citizens. Constraint and frustration lie in trying to realize the goals of Aboriginal education in an environment in which state authority and popular culture
challenge Aboriginal efforts politically, ideologically, and economically.

Aboriginal education has always been practised on a terrain of intense
political negotiations. The negotiations go on at the micro level in day-to-
day interactions in the classroom, around the content of lessons, in racist
encounters, and in communications between the school and parents.
Power relations are also played out at the macro level in the larger arena of
school-state relations. We note, for example, that many of the articles
make reference to the shortage of funding for developing and delivering
Aboriginal curricula. Where such funding is made available, it tends to be
short-lived, and there are difficulties in moving from a small-scale pilot
project to a lasting secure implementation arrangement. In fact, although
governments have, from time to time, funded significant culture-based
initiatives in Aboriginal education, they are slow to sanction the products
of Aboriginal curriculum development as provincially approved curriculum. The Akwesasne Science and Math Pilot Project is an important exception. This aggressive gate-keeping of "standards" has repeatedly challenged
the legitimacy of Aboriginal knowledge and values, imposing an assimilative cultural agenda that is both pervasive and coercive.

Watt-Cloutier picks up this theme in her discussion of the impact of
provincial curricula at the elementary and secondary levels in the Kativik
school programs. Hampton makes similar observations with regard to

post-secondary education. Both authors point to the way in which conventional curricula give legitimacy to particular versions of history, ways of knowing, and sets of ideas. As worldviews that govern the thinking of society, they remain unquestioned by the majority: and they resist questioning. Valaskakis emphasizes that, like school curricula, media also construct worldviews by circulating stories and images that serve to shape identities, actively determining what viewers and readers come to consider acceptable and true. Within this dominant conceptual world, Aboriginal values and thought present a different set of understandings and truths, carving out spaces where Aboriginal students can engage with traditional perspectives. The case studies presented in this volume tell about the remarkable efforts of Aboriginal educators to create these spaces in the provincially approved curricula of community-controlled institutions and in the nooks and crannies of provincial education systems.

Provincial decision making has a powerful practical impact upon the possibilities in Aboriginal education. In recent years, provincial government funding cutbacks and changes in thinking about curriculum have had a profound effect upon the programming options of students in provincial school systems, including access to Aboriginal studies and other Aboriginal content. The Vancouver case study illustrates that the struggle to preserve hard-won gains in Aboriginal curriculum must continue into the future.

Nowhere are the hopes for Aboriginal education higher than in the area of language revitalization. Schooling has been seen as the salvation of dying languages, yet there is little evidence to suggest that it can fulfill such a mandate. On the contrary, Norton and Fettes see the school as one partner in an intergenerational effort on the part of families and communities to restore language fluency. Even within a single language group, the school system's contribution to language fluency has usually been less than has been desired by communities. In urban settings, where students of many Aboriginal backgrounds and languages mix, the technical challenges for attaining fluency through schools are enormously difficult. In light of the systematic destruction of Aboriginal languages through assimilative schooling, the inability of schools to repair what has been broken represents perhaps the greatest betrayal in the education of Aboriginal people.

In schools controlled by Aboriginal people, language and cultural activities have become prominent features of programming. A frequent debate in communities is the relative balance of culture-based and provincially prescribed curriculum. Parents may disagree on how to give satisfactory weight to each. The dilemma of navigating two conflicting worlds is poignantly captured in the experience of a Métis man who presented testimony to the Royal Commission:

> When I was going to school people would say: "It's written right here in
> the books." And I'd say: "Well, that's not what my father told me" or
> "My grandfather didn't say that's right and I'm going by word of mouth."
> And then my father would tell me to just believe what they said at
> school. He wanted me to finish school so I had to go by what they
> were saying. (RCAP 1996, 1:618)

Like their parents and grandparents, today's parents want their children
to succeed in school. But to succeed should not mean that children have
to forsake the truth taught to them in the home. Aboriginal control of
Aboriginal education has sought to reverse the experience of cultural
denial that has been lived by generations of Aboriginal people in assimilative educational institutions. What the case studies illustrate so well is the
determination of Aboriginal people to question the educational experience
and to challenge the unthinking continuance of an assimilative agenda.

Such questioning exists not only at the classroom level, where individual teachers may prepare stimulating culture-based lessons. It is also happening among Aboriginal scholars and researchers who are rethinking
what Aboriginal education means. In the work contained in this volume
(and in other Aboriginal education publications such as *The Circle Unfolds*)
there is much evidence of the fertility of the present historical moment.
Attempts to create Aboriginally defined paradigms, models, and processes
of education have shifted attention away from earlier research themes,
such as the learning-styles focus reviewed by Hodgson-Smith; instead, we
have experimentation that takes Aboriginal values and philosophy as the
central design principle and a sustained conversation among Aboriginal
educators who are motivated to break new ground in theory and practice.

Throughout this book, we have seen that Aboriginal education comes
into being in this milieu of hope and constraint, possibility and frustration. It is appropriate to ask what difference recommendations by the
Royal Commission on Aboriginal Peoples (RCAP) can make to opening up
new possibilities, loosening the stranglehold of entrenched constraints,
turning frustration into understanding, and transforming hope into trust.
Experiences and analyses documented in these pages give a fuller context
to particular RCAP recommendations (see Appendix). In what way will
the quality of education improve for Aboriginal people as a result of these
recommendations?

While there is no easy answer to this question, it is important to analyze
the present moment in a broader historical context. We observe that
Aboriginal education issues are not at the forefront of the federal or
provincial government policy agenda. The federal government's 1998
response to the RCAP report focused on the destructive legacy of residential schools and the need for healing, relegating to the background many

other important areas addressed by the commission. However, the RCAP report has contributed to the momentum for treaty negotiations and self-government agreements. The terms of engagement for education will be shaped within this framework. It is premature to assess whether such agreements will result in the financial and other essential supports needed to transform the practice of education in schools (Castellano 1999, 109).

To understand the potential impact of the RCAP recommendations on education in an environment in which there appears to be little move-ment on the political front, it is helpful to think about the RCAP recom-mendations as another chapter in the long conversation that Aboriginal peoples and Canadian governments have engaged in since early contact on the subject of education. Abele, Dittburner, and Graham review the history of such conversations through the discourse contained in official education reports and studies issued by governments and Aboriginal orga-nizations since 1966. Their study indicates that the public discourse has shifted markedly over time and is increasingly leaning towards viewing education within the framework of self-government, with Aboriginal peo-ple as full partners in determining what will happen.

The RCAP recommendations take up many of the themes addressed in previous education evaluations and reports, but, in addition, the recom-mendations are embedded within a framework that assumes Aboriginal self-government as an existing right. This means that Aboriginal authori-ties already have the authority to implement whatever kind of education they desire. Practically, of course, the state has controlled the flow of finances and has established "approved standards." These pressure points serve as a powerful control mechanism with regard to what school boards actually do. One way to view public discourse is to see it as introducing a set of ideas, a way of thinking and talking that pushes against existing boundaries, enlarging the space for new possibilities. The new possibilities, in turn, become the ground on which further discourse is generated. In this way, for example, it is possible to trace progressively how talk of "local control" became "self-government," which, in turn, became "the inherent right to self-government." As the public discourse changes, so does the space for renegotiating power relations.

In the same way, the RCAP report has articulated education concerns and recommended policy changes as part of a holistic policy framework whose centrepieces are recognition, respect, sharing, and responsibility between Aboriginal and non-Aboriginal people in Canada. Education is recognized as a core area of Aboriginal jurisdiction, tied to the wide-ranging relationship between Aboriginal and Canadian society as a whole. While the specifics of Aboriginal education may be receiving little atten-tion from present governments, we have noted that education is impli-cated in the larger negotiations that are taking place in self-government agreements and treaty processes. The RCAP recommendations become tools that can be used by Aboriginal communities and organizations in negotiating education structures as well as funding. They can also serve as a guide for local action.

This book has recorded the opportunities for, and difficulties of, negotiating the terms of Aboriginal education in the final decades of the twentieth century. What have we learned about the potential for fulfilling the promise in the twenty-first century?

In these decades the seeds of the future have been planted. Increasingly, Aboriginal control of education has expanded the opportunities for innovation and creativity. At the same time, explosive changes in worldwide communications and the increasing interdependence of regional economies have created intense, homogenizing pressures on small societies and their capacity to maintain distinctive constructions of reality.

Political gains in the area of Aboriginal self-government can provide breathing space while the spirit of Aboriginal people provides the impetus for cultural survival. In addition to opportunity and will, survival will require strategy, seizing the possibilities that now exist for sharing wisdom within and between Aboriginal nations and with the world at large. Traditional ecological knowledge (TEK) is just one area in which the wisdom of Aboriginal peoples is gaining recognition around the globe.

The promise of education is that it will enable Aboriginal people to sustain well-being while meeting their responsibilities in the circle of life. Those responsibilities are seen to reach further today than in any previous generation. Fulfilling the promise will require preparing successive generations to participate fully in their own communities and to assume their place as Aboriginal citizens and peoples in global society. Achieving a balance between these goals is the challenge confronting educators, leaders, and policy makers in the twenty-first century.

References

Castellano, Marlene Brant. 1999. "Renewing the Relationship: A Perspective on the Impact of the Royal Commission on Aboriginal Peoples." In *Aboriginal Self-Government in Canada*, ed. John H. Hylton, 92-111. Second edition. Saskatoon: Purich.

Royal Commission on Aboriginal Peoples. 1996. *Report of the Royal Commission on Aboriginal Peoples*. Volume 1: *Looking Forward, Looking Back*. Ottawa: Canada Communications Group.

Appendix: Recommendations of the Royal Commission on Aboriginal Peoples Regarding Education

Chapter 5 Education
The Commission recommends that

Education
and Self-
Government

3.5.1
Federal, provincial and territorial governments act promptly to acknowledge that education is a core area for the exercise of Aboriginal self-government.

Transitional
Control of
Education

3.5.2
Federal, provincial and territorial governments collaborate with Aboriginal governments, organizations or education authorities, as appropriate, to support the development of Aboriginally controlled education systems by
(a) introducing, adapting or ensuring the flexible application of legislation to facilitate self-starting initiatives by Aboriginal nations and their communities in the field of education;
(b) mandating voluntary organizations that are endorsed by substantial numbers of Aboriginal people to act in the field of education in urban and non-reserve areas where numbers warrant until such time as Aboriginal governments are established; and
(c) providing funding commensurate with the responsibilities assumed by Aboriginal nations and their communities, or voluntary organizations, given the requirements of institutional and program development, costs of serving small or dispersed communities, and special needs accruing from past failures of education services.

Early Childhood
Education
Support

3.5.3
Federal, provincial, and territorial governments co-operate to support an integrated early childhood education funding strategy that
(a) extends early childhood education services to all Aboriginal children regardless of residence;
(b) encourages programs that foster the physical, social, intellectual and spiritual development of children, reducing distinctions between child care, prevention and education;
(c) maximizes Aboriginal control over service design and administration;
(d) offers one-stop accessible funding; and
(e) promotes parental involvement and choice in early childhood education options.

Transfer Between Education Systems

3.5.4

Aboriginal, provincial and territorial governments act promptly to reach agreements for mutual recognition of programs provided by their respective educational institutions so as to facilitate the transfer of students between educational systems while protecting the integrity of cultural dimensions of Aboriginal education.

Curriculum Development

3.5.5

Federal, provincial and territorial governments collaborate with Aboriginal governments, organizations and educators to develop or continue developing innovative curricula that reflect Aboriginal cultures and community realities, for delivery

(a) at all grade levels of elementary and secondary schools;

(b) in schools operating under Aboriginal control; and

(c) in schools under provincial or territorial jurisdiction.

Priority of Aboriginal Language Education

3.5.6

Aboriginal language education be assigned priority in Aboriginal, provincial and territorial education systems to complement and support language preservation efforts in local communities through

(a) first- or second-language instruction or immersion programs where parents desire it and numbers warrant;

(b) recognition of Aboriginal language competence for second-language academic credit whether competence is acquired through classroom or out-of-school instruction;

(c) involving elders and fluent Aboriginal speakers in programs to enhance Aboriginal language acquisition and fluency;

(d) developing instructional materials; and

(e) encouraging and rewarding language teaching as a career path and language research in lexical elaboration, structural analysis and cultural contexts as professional and academic specializations.

Involvement in Decision Making

3.5.7

Where Aboriginal children attend provincial and territorial schools, provincial and territorial governments take immediate steps to ensure that Aboriginal people are involved fully in the decision-making processes that affect the education of their children. Aboriginal control of education and parental involvement should be implemented through a variety of actions:

(a) legislation to guarantee Aboriginal representation on school boards where population numbers warrant;

(b) recognition of Aboriginally controlled schools under the jurisdiction of Aboriginal community of interest governments;

(c) establishment of Aboriginally governed schools affiliated with school districts, if requested by Aboriginal people; and

(d) creation of Aboriginal advisory committees to school boards.

Involvement in School Activities

3.5.8

All schools serving Aboriginal children adopt policies that welcome the involvement of Aboriginal parents, elders and families in the life of the school, for example, by establishing advisory or parents committees, introducing teaching by elders in the classroom, and involving parents in school activities.

Required School
Board Strategy

3.5.9

Provincial and territorial ministries require school boards serving Ab-original students to implement a comprehensive Aboriginal education strategy, developed with Aboriginal parents, elders and educators, including

(a) goals and objectives to be accomplished during the International Decade of Indigenous Peoples;

(b) hiring of Aboriginal teachers at the elementary and secondary school level, with negotiated target levels, to teach in all areas of school programs, not just Aboriginal programs;

(c) hiring of Aboriginal people in administrative and leadership positions;

(d) hiring of Aboriginal support workers, such as counsellors, community liaison workers, psychologists and speech therapists;

(e) curriculum, in all subject areas, that includes the perspectives, traditions, beliefs and world view of Aboriginal peoples;

(f) involvement of Aboriginal elders in teaching Aboriginal and non-Aboriginal students;

(g) language classes in Aboriginal languages, as determined by the Aboriginal community;

(h) family and community involvement mechanisms;

(i) education programs that combat stereotypes, racism, prejudice and biases;

(j) accountability indicators tied to board or district funding; and

(k) public reports of results by the end of the International Decade of Indigenous Peoples in the year 2004.

Youth
Empowerment

3.5.10

Aboriginally controlled, provincial, and territorial schools serving Aboriginal youth develop and implement comprehensive Aboriginal youth empowerment strategies with elements elaborated in collaboration with youth, including

(a) cultural education in classroom and informal settings;

(b) acknowledgement of spiritual, ethical and intuitive dimensions of learning;

(c) education to support critical analysis of Aboriginal experience;

(d) learning as a means of healing from the effects of trauma, abuse and racism;

(e) academic skills development and support;

(f) sports and outdoor education;

(g) leadership development; and

(h) youth exchanges between Aboriginal nations, across Canada and internationally.

Community
High School
Programs

3.5.11

High school programs be extended to communities, using cost-effective options agreed upon by parents and families, including

(a) complete school facilities for local high school delivery;

(b) regional high schools in Aboriginal communities;

(c) culturally appropriate, interactive distance education; and

(d) seasonal institutes.

Secondary
Study Re-entry

3.5.12

Aboriginal authorities and all provincial and territorial ministries of education fund programs for Aboriginal youth who have left secondary school before graduation to enable them to resume their studies with appropriate curriculum, scheduling, academic and social support.

Co-op Education **3.5.13**
Federal, provincial and territorial governments encourage co-op initiatives by offering funding inducements to secondary schools that develop active co-op education programs for Aboriginal young people.

Expanded **3.5.14**
Teacher Educa- Federal, provincial and territorial governments expand financial support
tion Programs to post-secondary institutions for existing and new Aboriginal teacher education programs, contingent on
(a) evidence of Aboriginal support for the program;
(b) Aboriginal participation in the governance of the program;
(c) the incorporation of Aboriginal content and pedagogy into the program; and
(d) periodic evaluations that indicate that the quality of teacher education conforms to standards of excellence expected by Aboriginal people.

Aboriginal Sec- **3.5.15**
ondary School Canadian governments, Aboriginal education authorities, post-secondary
Teachers institutions and teacher education programs adopt multiple strategies to increase substantially the number of Aboriginal secondary school teachers, including
(a) promoting secondary school teaching careers for Aboriginal people;
(b) increasing access to professional training in secondary education, for example, community-based delivery of courses and concurrent programs; and
(c) offering financial incentives to students.

Teacher Educa- **3.5.16**
tion Accessible in Federal, provincial and territorial governments provide support to in-
Communities crease the number of Aboriginal people trained as teachers by
(a) expanding the number of teacher education programs delivered directly in communities; and
(b) ensuring that students in each province and territory have access to such programs.

Career Paths **3.5.17**
Teacher education programs, in collaboration with Aboriginal organizations and government agencies that sponsor professional and para-professional training, adopt a comprehensive approach to educator training, developing career paths from para-professional training to professional certification in education careers that
(a) prepare Aboriginal students for the variety of roles required to operate Aboriginal education systems; and
(b) open opportunities for careers in provincial education systems.

Aboriginal **3.5.18**
Components in Provinces and territories require that teacher education programs
All Teacher Edu- (a) in pre-service training leading to certification include at least one com-
cation Programs ponent on teaching Aboriginal subject matter to all students, both Aboriginal and non-Aboriginal;
(b) develop options for pre-service training and professional development of teachers, focused on teaching Aboriginal students and addressing Aboriginal education issues; and
(c) collaborate with Aboriginal organizations or community representatives in developing Aboriginal-specific components of their programs.

Aboriginal Delivery of Integrated Adult Training

3.5.19

Federal, provincial and territorial governments collaborate with Aboriginal governments and organizations to facilitate integrated delivery of adult literacy, basic education, academic upgrading and job training under the control of Aboriginal people through

(a) delegating responsibility for delivery of training under current jurisdictions by concluding agreements with Aboriginal governments, their mandated education authorities, or voluntary organizations representing Aboriginal communities of interest;

(b) supporting adaptation of program design, admission criteria, language of instruction, and internal allocation of funds by Aboriginal delivery agents, to accommodate Aboriginal culture and community needs;

(c) acting promptly to conclude agreements for multi-year block funding agreements to enable Aboriginal nation governments, during the transition to self-government, to assume primary responsibility for allocating funds to meet training needs through programs of Aboriginal design.

Treaty Promise of Education

3.5.20

The government of Canada recognize and fulfil its obligation to treaty nations by supporting a full range of education services, including post-secondary education, for members of treaty nations where a promise of education appears in treaty texts, related documents or oral histories of the parties involved.

Federal Support of Post-Secondary Students

3.5.21

The federal government continue to support the costs of post-secondary education for First Nations and Inuit post-secondary students and make additional resources available

(a) to mitigate the impact of increased costs as post-secondary institutions shift to a new policy environment in post-secondary education; and

(b) to meet the anticipated higher level of demand for post-secondary education services.

Métis and Aboriginal Scholarship Fund

3.5.22

A scholarship fund be established for Métis and other Aboriginal students who do not have access to financial support for post-secondary education under present policies, with

(a) lead financial support provided by federal and provincial governments and additional contributions from corporate and individual donors;

(b) a planning committee to be established immediately,

    (i) composed of Métis and other Aboriginal representatives, students, and federal and provincial representatives in balanced numbers;

    (ii) given a maximum two-year mandate; and

    (iii) charged with determining the appropriate vehicle, level of capitalization, program criteria and administrative structure for initiation and administration of the fund; and

(c) provisions for evaluating demand on the fund, its adequacy and its impact on participation and completion rates of Métis and other Aboriginal students in post-secondary studies.

Aboriginal Languages Equivalent to Modern Languages

3.5.23
Canada's post-secondary institutions recognize Aboriginal languages on a basis equal to other modern languages, for the purpose of granting credits for entrance requirements, fulfilment of second language requirements, and general course credits.

Mainstream Post-Secondary Initiatives

3.5.24
Public post-secondary institutions in the provinces and territories undertake new initiatives or extend current ones to increase the participation, retention and graduation of Aboriginal students by introducing, encouraging or enhancing

(a) a welcoming environment for Aboriginal students;
(b) Aboriginal content and perspectives in course offerings across disciplines;
(c) Aboriginal studies and programs as part of the institution's regular program offerings and included in the institution's core budget;
(d) Aboriginal appointments to boards of governors;
(e) Aboriginal councils to advise the president of the institution;
(f) active recruitment of Aboriginal students;
(g) admission policies that encourage access by Aboriginal applicants;
(h) meeting spaces for Aboriginal students;
(i) Aboriginal student unions;
(j) recruitment of Aboriginal faculty members;
(k) support services with Aboriginal counsellors for academic and personal counselling; and
(l) cross-cultural sensitivity training for faculty and staff.

Residential University Colleges

3.5.25
Where there is Aboriginal support for an Aboriginal college within a university, and where numbers warrant, universities act to establish an Aboriginal college to serve as the focal point for the academic, residential, social and cultural lives of Aboriginal students on campus, and to promote Aboriginal scholarship.

Fund Aboriginal Post-Secondary Institutions

3.5.26
Federal, provincial and territorial governments collaborate with Aboriginal governments and organizations to establish and support post-secondary educational institutions controlled by Aboriginal people, with negotiated allocation of responsibility for

(a) core and program funding commensurate with the services they are expected to provide and comparable to the funding provided to provincial or territorial institutions delivering similar services;
(b) planning, capital and start-up costs of new colleges and institutes;
(c) improvement of facilities for community learning centres as required for new functions and development of new facilities where numbers warrant and the community establishes this as a priority; and
(d) fulfilment of obligations pursuant to treaties and modern agreements with respect to education.

Regional and National Aboriginal Boards

3.5.27
Aboriginally controlled post-secondary educational institutions collaborate to create regional boards and/or a Canada-wide board to

(a) establish standards for accrediting programs provided by Aboriginal post-secondary institutions;

(b) negotiate mutual recognition of course credits and credentials to facilitate student transfer between Aboriginal institutions and provincial and territorial post-secondary institutions;

(c) establish co-operative working relationships with mainstream accreditation bodies such as the Association of Universities and Colleges of Canada and professional associations such as the Canadian Association of University Teachers; and

(d) pursue other objectives related to the common interests of Aboriginal institutions.

Elders' Role in Education

3.5.28

Elders be reinstated to an active role in the education of Aboriginal children and youth in educational systems under Aboriginal control and in provincial and territorial schools.

Elders' Compensation

3.5.29

Elders be treated as professionals and compensated for their education contribution at a rate and in a manner that shows respect for their expertise, unique knowledge and skills.

Recognize Aboriginal Knowledge

3.5.30

Provincial and territorial education ministries, boards of education and educators recognize the value of elders' knowledge to all peoples' understanding of the universe by

(a) giving academic credits for traditional Aboriginal arts and knowledge whether acquired in the classroom or through non-formal means in cultural activities, camps and apprenticeships; and

(b) collaborating with elders to determine how traditional Aboriginal knowledge can be made accessible in the education of all students, whether Aboriginal or non-Aboriginal, in institutions under Aboriginal, provincial, or territorial control.

Exchanges Among Elders and with Academics

3.5.31

Educational institutions facilitate opportunities for elders to exchange traditional knowledge with one another and to share traditional knowledge with students and scholars, both Aboriginal and non-Aboriginal, in university settings.

Establish Aboriginal Peoples' International University

3.5.32

A university under Aboriginal control, which could be called the Aboriginal Peoples' International University, and with the capacity to function in all provinces and territories, be established to promote traditional knowledge, to pursue applied research in support of Aboriginal self-government, and to disseminate information essential to achieving broad Aboriginal development goals.

Steering Group to Plan APIU

3.5.33

First Nations, Inuit and Métis leaders in collaboration with the federal government establish a steering group funded by the federal government, with a three-year mandate

(a) to explore options, conduct consultations and prepare a plan to implement an Aboriginal Peoples' International University by the year 2000; and

(b) to collaborate with other working groups in determining the appropriate location of a documentation centre and archive, an electronic information clearinghouse, and statistical data bases.

Electronic Clearinghouse	**3.5.34** An electronic clearinghouse be established to facilitate the free flow of information among Aboriginal communities, education and self-government workers and individuals, the planning and development of this clearinghouse to be carried forward by a working group (a) established in collaboration with First Nations, Inuit and Métis leaders; (b) funded by the federal government and given a two-year mandate; and (c) attentive to the need for Canada-wide and international communication as well as exchange in Aboriginal languages within linguistic communities.
Working Group for Statistical Clearinghouse	**3.5.35** First Nations, Inuit and Métis leaders establish a working group, funded by the federal government, with a two-year mandate to plan a statistical clearinghouse controlled by Aboriginal people to (a) work in collaboration with Aboriginal governments and organizations to establish and update statistical data bases; and (b) promote common strategies across nations and communities for collecting and analyzing data relevant to Aboriginal development goals.
Documentation Centre on Residential Schools and Relocations	**3.5.36** The federal government fund the establishment of a national documentation centre to research, collect, preserve and disseminate information related to residential schools, relocations and other aspects of Aboriginal historical experience, the planning and development of the centre to be carried forward by a working group (a) established in collaboration with First Nations, Inuit and Métis leaders; and (b) having a two-year mandate.
Education for Self-Government Funding	**3.5.37** Federal, provincial and territorial governments establish funding programs to support education for self-government, to be available to (a) public post-secondary institutions that have entered into partnerships with Aboriginal people to initiate or expand training and education in areas identified as priorities by Aboriginal governments, organizations and communities for the implementation of self-government; and (b) Aboriginally controlled post-secondary institutions for program innovation to enhance capacity for self-government.
Youth Careers Campaign	**3.5.38** Aboriginal governments and organizations collaborate to launch a Canada-wide campaign to make youth aware of the opportunities to serve their nations that will open up with the advent of self-government and of the tangible and intangible rewards that accompany public service.
Student Incentives for Self-Government Studies	**3.5.39** The federal government make funds available to First Nation and Inuit governments and organizations to support incentives to encourage students to complete bachelor's and master's level studies and professional training in areas of priority to self-government, including such measures as (a) employee release time for concurrent work and study; (b) paid leave to pursue full-time study; (c) scholarships in studies related to self-government; (d) top-up of educational assistance for family needs, including exceptional housing costs; and

(e) student loans that are forgivable on completion of a period of employment in the service of self-government.

Co-op Place-
ments in
Business and
Government

3.5.40
Canada's corporations, small businesses and governments become active
partners in Aboriginal self-government education by identifying co-op
placement and internship opportunities in their organizations, in consultation with Aboriginal people.

Executive
Interchange

3.5.41
Canada's corporations and governments at all levels establish executive
interchange opportunities in partnership with Aboriginal governments.

Professional
Associations Sup-
port Aboriginal
Training

3.5.42
Professional associations and self-governing bodies in the professions
actively support the professional training of Aboriginal people by
(a) entering into dialogue on such issues as credentials, recruitment,
mentoring, career paths linking para-professional and professional
training, education based on Aboriginal culture, systemic discrimination and racism;
(b) establishing scholarships for Aboriginal people;
(c) encouraging their members to gain an understanding of Aboriginal
perspectives;
(d) spearheading initiatives to introduce Aboriginal cultural perspectives
into professional training programs; and
(e) providing leadership by encouraging implementation of the recommendations in this report that are relevant to their areas of expertise.

Support of Dis-
tance Education
Models

3.5.43
The federal government, media corporations, provincial and territorial
governments and private donors provide funding and/or gifts in kind (for
example, access to facilities and technology) to establish a distance education model of professional training suitable for Aboriginal people who
wish to pursue post-secondary studies from their communities.

Canada-Wide
Aboriginal
Human Resources
Inventory

3.5.44
The federal government provide funding for national Aboriginal organizations to co-ordinate establishment of a Canada-wide Aboriginal human
resources inventory that is amenable to regular updating.

Chapter 6 Arts and Heritage
The Commission recommends that

Determining Lan-
guage Status a
Core Power of
Self-Government

3.6.8
Federal, provincial and territorial governments recognize promptly that
determining Aboriginal language status and use is a core power in Aboriginal self-government, and that these governments affirm and support
Aboriginal nations and their communities in using and promoting their
languages and declaring them official languages within their nations, territories and communities where they choose to do so.

Nations
Implement a
Multi-Faceted
Language
Strategy

3.6.9
Each Aboriginal nation in the various stages of nation building, capacity
building, negotiating and implementing self-government consult with its
constituent communities to establish priorities and policies with respect
to Aboriginal language conservation, revitalization and documentation,
including

(a) assessing the current state of Aboriginal language use and vitality;
(b) determining priorities of communities for language conservation, revitalization and documentation;
(c) consulting on the most effective means of implementing priorities;
(d) facilitating initiatives to support Aboriginal language use in families and the broader community;
(e) incorporating their Aboriginal language in education policies and programs;
(f) enhancing co-operation among nations and communities of the same language group to promote research, curriculum development and language elaboration;
(g) using their Aboriginal language in public forums and Aboriginal government business; and
(h) declaring their Aboriginal language an official language on nation territory.

Endowed Aboriginal Languages Foundation

3.6.10

The federal government make a commitment to endow an Aboriginal Languages Foundation for the purpose of supporting Aboriginal initiatives in the conservation, revitalization and documentation of Aboriginal languages, the foundation to be
(a) capitalized by an annual federal grant of $10 million for five years, beginning in 1997;
(b) eligible to receive charitable contributions, to be matched by the federal government in a ratio of two dollars for each dollar contributed;
(c) established to support language initiatives undertaken or endorsed by Aboriginal nations and their communities;
(d) developed by a federally funded planning body, with a majority of First Nations, Inuit and Métis representatives and a two-year mandate; and
(e) directed in its operation by a board with a majority of First Nations, Inuit and Métis members.

Special Status of Aboriginal-Language Broadcasting

3.6.11

The government of Canada recognize the special status of Aboriginal-language broadcasting explicitly in federal legislation.

CRTC Require Representation of Aboriginal Programming

3.6.12

The Canadian Radio-Television and Telecommunications Commission include in licence conditions for public and commercial broadcasters, in regions with significant Aboriginal population concentrations, requirements for fair representation and distribution of Aboriginal programming, including Aboriginal language requirements.

Access to Aboriginal Media Products

3.6.13

Public and private media outlets, in particular the Canadian Broadcasting Corporation, provide access to Aboriginal media products for Aboriginal and non-Aboriginal Canadians by
(a) purchasing and broadcasting Aboriginal programming from independent Aboriginal producers; and
(b) producing English and French versions of original Aboriginal programs for regional and national redistribution.

Employment Equity in Public and Private Media

3.6.14

Public and private media outlets address the need for training and better representation of Aboriginal people in public communications by developing and implementing employment equity plans.

Freedom of Expression for Aboriginal Media	**3.6.15** Governments, including Aboriginal governments, recognize the critical role that independent Aboriginal print and broadcast media have in the pursuit of Aboriginal self-determination and self-government, and that they support freedom of expression through (a) policies on open access to information; and (b) dedicated funding at arm's length from political bodies.
Aboriginal Access to Media Training	**3.6.16** Colleges and universities with programs in communications, journalism and film co-operate to support access for Aboriginal students by providing transition courses, scholarships and counselling services.
Fees and Joint Ventures to Finance Aboriginal Media Products	**3.6.17** The Canadian Radio-Television and Telecommunications Commission be mandated to establish fee structures and provisions for joint ventures as part of licensing conditions to ensure a stable financial base for the production and distribution of Aboriginal broadcast media products, particularly in southern Canada.
Core Funding and Incentives for Private Support	**3.6.18** Federal, provincial, territorial and Aboriginal governments provide core funding for Aboriginal media that (a) is accessible to all Aboriginal nations and communities; (b) builds upon existing government programs and Aboriginal media organizations; (c) results in long-term funding agreements that realistically reflect Aboriginal media requirements and promote self-financing; and (d) encourages private and corporate support through tax incentives.

Source: Royal Commission on Aboriginal Peoples, Volume 3, *Gathering Strength, Recommendations of the Royal Commission on Aboriginal Peoples Regarding Education* (Ottawa: Canadian Government Publishing, 1997).

Contributors

Frances Abele is director of the School of Public Administration at Carleton University in Ottawa. She holds a PhD in political science. Dr. Abele has been working and learning in northern Canada for over twenty years, publishing books and articles on Canadian public policy, public management, northern political and economic development, and issues affecting Indigenous peoples. She was co-investigator for the major study *Public Policy and Aboriginal Peoples, 1965-1992* for the Royal Commission on Aboriginal Peoples, and co-author of Volume 1 of the subsequent report: *Soliloquy and Dialogue* (Canada Communications Group 1996).

Marie Battiste, a member of the Mi'kmaq Nation, is a professor at the University of Saskatchewan in the Indian and Northern Education Program. She received her doctorate from Stanford University and has worked as teacher, principal, education director, and curriculum developer with Mi'kmaq Nation band-operated schools. She co-edited, with Jean Barman, the influential volume *First Nations Education in Canada: The Circle Unfolds* (UBC Press 1995). She is editor of *Reclaiming Indigenous Voice and Vision* (UBC Press 2000).

Marlene Brant Castellano (volume editor), a Mohawk from Tyendinaga, was co-director of research for the Royal Commission on Aboriginal Peoples. She is professor emerita and former chair of the Department of Native Studies at Trent University, where she was on faculty from 1973 to 1996. Her contributions to Aboriginal education and development have been recognized through honorary LLD degrees from Queen's University and St. Thomas University, respectively. She was a recipient of the Order of Ontario in 1994 and a National Aboriginal Achievement Award in 1996.

Lynne Davis (volume editor) is a consultant and researcher who has worked and taught in Aboriginal community development since 1975. She holds a PhD from the Ontario Institute for Studies in Education, University of Toronto. Lynne contributed to the work of the Royal Commission on Aboriginal Peoples as researcher, project manager, policy analyst, and writer for the education chapter of the final report. She teaches in the Department of Native Studies at Trent University and the Faculty of Social Work, University of Toronto.

Carolyn Dittburner is a graduate of the MPA program at Carleton University and is currently working in the area of community-based First Nations Government with Ian B. Cowie and Associates Inc. She has written on First Nation governance and fiscal relations, and collaborated with Katherine Graham and Frances Abele in writing *Soliloquy and Dialogue: Overview of Major Trends in Public Policy Relating to Aboriginal Peoples* for the Royal Commission on Aboriginal Peoples. She served as a research assistant to the project, which produced a four-volume report: *Public Policy and Aboriginal Peoples, 1965-1992.*

John Dorion is a Métis from Cumberland House, Saskatchewan. He has a degree in education from the University of Saskatchewan and has a background in Aboriginal rights and cross-cultural education. John worked for the Gabriel Dumont Institute as director of CORE operations, and he was responsible for curriculum and program development, research, and Métis self-government planning. He is currently a consultant with Aboriginal organizations.

Mark Fettes, a New Zealander, came to the field of Aboriginal language policy from work in the international Esperanto movement. He has served as a consultant to the Assembly of First Nations and other organizations. His PhD dissertation, at the Ontario Institute for Studies in Education, develops a critical realist theory of language and explores its connections with the theory and practice of Aboriginal education.

Ethel B. Gardner, of Sto:lo heritage, is the program manager of education for the Sto:lo Nation in British Columbia. She is former associate director of the First Nations House of Learning at UBC. She holds two master's degrees: one from the Ts' 'kel Graduate Program at UBC and a second from Harvard Graduate School of Education. She is currently enrolled in doctoral studies at Simon Fraser University, conducting research on Sto:lo Halq'emeylem Language Renewal. She has published creative writing and work on First Nations education and Aboriginal Languages.

Katherine A. Graham is professor and associate dean of the Faculty of Public Affairs and Management at Carleton University. She has been active as a researcher and policy analyst on Aboriginal issues since the mid-1970s.

She was principal investigator for the project that produced the four-volume study *Public Policy and Aboriginal Peoples* (Canada Communications Group, 1993, 1994, 1996) for the Royal Commission on Aboriginal Peoples, and she was co-author of Volume 1 of the report *Soliloquy and Dialogue.*

Eber Hampton, a member of the Chickasaw Nation, is president of the Saskatchewan Indian Federated College in Regina. He holds an EdD from Harvard University, has directed the American Indian Program at the Harvard Graduate School of Education, and has been associate dean of the College of Rural Education at the University of Alaska, Fairbanks. His writing on the philosophy of First Nations education is highly regarded and widely quoted.

Yvonne Hébert is a professor at the University of Calgary in Alberta. She co-edited *Indian Education in Canada,* Volume 1, *The Legacy,* and Volume 2, *The Challenge.* She is currently working in the area of literacy and minority language education, identity formation, immigration, and citizenship education. She is active in national educational organizations, serves as leader of the Education Domain with the Prairie Centre of Excellence for Research on Immigration and Integration, and coordinates the newly formed Citizenship Education Research Network.

Kathy L. Hodgson-Smith is a Métis teacher, lecturer, researcher, and writer from MacDowall, Saskatchewan. She has earned a master's degree in education from the University of Saskatchewan, Department of Educational Foundations. She is currently on leave from her faculty position at the Saskatchewan Urban Native Teacher Education Program and is employed by the Métis Nation of Saskatchewan as researcher. She has published previously in *First Nations Education: The Circle Unfolds* and *For Seven Generations: An Information Legacy of the Royal Commission on Aboriginal Peoples* (CD-ROM). She co-authored *Making the Spirit Dance Within, Joe Duquette High School and an Aboriginal Community* (Lorimer 1997).

Brenda Tsioniaon LaFrance is a Mohawk consultant in the fields of management, education, and environmental restoration (from an Aboriginal cultural perspective). She holds a bachelor's degree in biology and chemistry as well as two master's degrees from Clarkson University – one in business administration and one in computerized information systems. She lives in Akwesasne and is a former member of the St. Regis Mohawk Tribal Council.

Louise Lahache (volume editor) is a Mohawk from Kahnawake, Quebec. She has a master's degree in Native and Northern Studies from Carleton

University and serves as director of language education with the Assembly of First Nations. Louise has taught at both high school and college levels and has developed curriculum from junior kindergarten to college levels. She was principal for seven years at Amo Ososwan, an Algonquin band-operated school in Winneway, Quebec, that offers education from kindergarten to Grade 12. She served as social/cultural research associate with the Royal Commission on Aboriginal Peoples.

Ruth Norton is principal of Sagkeeng Anicinabe High School in Manitoba, where Anicinabe philosophy and the Ojibwa language form the foundation for teaching and learning. She has taught at the elementary level and provided guidance and counselling at high school, college, and university levels, assisting with the establishment of Brandon University Native Teacher Education Program (BUNTEP) and other education projects in Manitoba. She was the founding director for the Manitoba Association for Native Languages, national director of education, and director of Aboriginal languages and literacy with the Assembly of First Nations.

Gail Guthrie Valaskakis comes from the Lac du Flambeau Band of Lake Superior Chippewa. She grew up on the Lac du Flambeau reservation in Wisconsin. She is the former dean of arts and science at Concordia University in Montreal and continues as university research professor and special advisor to the rector for Aboriginal affairs. She is a founding board member of the Native Friendship Centre of Montreal, Manitou College, and Waseskun Native Half-Way House. A northern Native communications scholar, she has also written on issues of Native representation, experience, and cultural appropriation. She is currently the director of research for the Aboriginal Healing Foundation.

Sheila Watt-Cloutier, from the Inuit community of Kuujjuaq in northern Quebec, is the vice-president for Canada of the Inuit Circumpolar Conference. Previously, she has worked on a review of the education system in Nunavik (Northern Quebec 1991-5) and contributed to a published report *Silatunirmut: The Pathway to Wisdom*. Ms. Watt-Cloutier also held the elected position of corporate secretary for Makivik Corporation from 1995 to 1998. She is a strong advocate of education issues and has extensive experience dealing with human development issues.

Lorna Williams is a Lil'wat from Mount Currie, British Columbia. She is currently on leave from Vancouver School District No. 39 while being a doctoral candidate at the University of Tennessee at Knoxville. Her innovative work with Feuerstein's mediated learning is documented in the video *The Mind of a Child* (NFB 1995). Lorna was co-director and writer for the educational video series *First Nations: The Circle Unbroken* and has recently published "Aboriginal Children: Educating Canada's Throw-Aways" in *Educating the Throw-Away Children* (Joyce Taylor, ed., Jossey-Bass 1997).

Kwan R. Yang worked with the Gabriel Dumont Institute (GDI) when he prepared the research report on GDI for the Royal Commission on Aboriginal Peoples. No information on his current activities is available.

Index